Seven Myths of the Russian Revolution

by Jonathan Daly and Leonid Trofimov

Series Editors
Alfred J. Andrea and Andrew Holt

Hackett Publishing Company, Inc.
Indianapolis/Cambridge

Seven Myths of the
Russian Revolution

CONTENTS

For my UIC colleagues, J. D.

For my wife Julia, L. T.

SERIES EDITORS' FOREWORD

In 1939, Winston Churchill famously described Russia as "a riddle, wrapped in a mystery, inside an enigma." The same can be said of the long-fermenting Russian Revolution of 1917, which ended Russia's participation in the world war, resulted in the establishment of a one-party dictatorship, and ushered in the Soviet Union (1922–1991). This multi-stage sequence of events—beginning in late February/early March, continuing through an anarchic summer, the seizure of power by the Bolsheviks in late October/early November, and ending only with the Bolshevik triumph in 1920 in the Russian Civil War—was so complex in origin, execution, and consequences that it immediately became the focal point of numerous fantasies, false reports, fabrications, and fallacious interpretations. And, as Jonathan Daly and Leonid Trofimov, the authors of this splendid little book, argue, those erroneous notions have continued down to the present, with differing degrees of consequence.

Some of the myths, such as the putative survival of Grand Duchess Anastasia Nikolaevna and the dichotomous reputation of Grigorii Rasputin, became and remain significant cultural phenomena, as numerous books and every imaginable form of performance art bear witness. Factions within the Russian Orthodox Church have even unofficially canonized Anastasia and Rasputin and captured their idealized images on holy icons.

Other myths were poisonous in origin and have continued their baleful impact into the twenty-first century. Falling within this category are the "Judeo-Bolshevik" myth and the myth of the United States' attempt to murder the revolution in its infancy and colonize Russia by means of an intervention in Siberia. The former myth contributed significantly to an antisemitism that produced the Nazi-generated Holocaust, Soviet persecution of its Jewish minority, and antisemitic rhetoric that has had not only disturbing but deadly consequences in the United States and Europe. The latter myth has dangerously infected relations between the United States and the Soviet Union and its successor, the Russian Federation, right down to today.

Other myths, such as the notion that Tsar Nicholas II was the victim of treasonous conspiracy, that Vladimir Lenin and the Bolsheviks were active and obedient secret agents of imperial Germany, and that the Bolshevik victory was inevitable, might seem to many to be obscure issues debated by even more obscure historians. But that is not so. Not only do they live on in popular histories and even textbooks, but they obscure the past, feed the paranoid fears of authoritarian rulers, and muddy our understanding of one of the most significant series of events in world history.

If we are to profit from our investigation of this revolution, it is our duty to seek to know it as fully and honestly as our discipline allows. The study of history never renders a complete and flawless picture of the past, but careful investigation of the available evidence does allow us to look beyond the clichés, illusions, half-truths, and untruths and to understand that past in a manner that has valid meaning.

As editors of this series, we point with pride to the fact that our colleagues Jonathan Daly and Leonid Trofimov have succeeded in their effort to strip away fable and fantasy from the Russian Revolution and guide us toward a more nuanced and deeper understanding of it.

Alfred J. Andrea
Andrew Holt

PREFACE

We wrote this book for history students in the broadest possible sense. We hope it will prove helpful in university-level courses, both those that focus specifically on Russia and those that cast Russia in such twentieth-century historical contexts as World War I, American foreign relations, Nazi Germany, and antisemitism. We also expect it to interest the well-read general public and our peers. Our goal is to offer new ways of thinking about, studying, and teaching the Russian Revolution in an age when distinguishing between mythical and true realities is more important than ever.

The book is organized both topically and chronologically. Some myths preceded and superseded one another, and others emerged concurrently; some were utter falsehoods, others contained kernels of truth atrociously exaggerated and blown out of proportion. All had a long shelf life, traceable in some instances to the present.

We sought to avoid reviving any of these myths or strengthening them at all costs. Recent cognitive findings have challenged earlier assumptions about how well humans can distinguish between truths and falsehoods, especially with the passage of time. It is a function of our memory to remember best not what is most accurate, but quite often what is most colorful or graphic. Our nightmare scenario would be to discover ten years from now that some readers of our book had come to believe that the Bolsheviks' coming to power in Russia in 1917 really was part of a Jewish plot for world domination, that American military forces intervening in civil-war Russia in 1918 really aimed at dismembering the country, or that Princess Anastasia really survived the murder of her entire family in summer 1918 and then traveled in a peasant cart from the Ural Mountains to Romania.

We deliberately chose to present the facts first, examine them in detail, and only then introduce readers to the hopes, fears, rumors, and myths surrounding them. Our expectation is that readers will not only take note of how powerful these myths were but also how ridiculous, or at least implausible, when compared to the historical record.

Yet the historical record is never complete, and this book is not meant to provide final answers to scholarly questions about the Russian Revolution. Indeed, we have intended to stimulate the posing of such questions as: Why did the Russian Revolution generate powerful myths? Why were these myths pervasive and persistent? What can they add to our understanding of one of the most transformative events in modern history? We hope such questions will spark new and lively conversations about the Russian Revolution in classrooms, conferences, and coffee shops.

We are grateful to many colleagues and institutions for their generous support and encouragement. Our editor Rick Todhunter kindly encouraged us to pursue this study; he and his efficient and unflagging team supported us throughout the process.

ix

Sung-Eun Choi, Cliff Putney, Annette Wong, Kristen Richards, and librarians at Bentley University, the University of Illinois at Chicago, and the Slavic Reference Service at the University of Illinois, Urbana-Champaign, helped us to access historical resources that, amid the pandemic, had to be scanned, copied, purchased, and shipped against all odds. Generous support from the University of Illinois at Chicago, Bentley University, and Queen's University made it possible to commission maps and secure copyright permissions. Special thanks to Peter Bull, who once again worked his cartographical magic. For helpful research assistance, we are grateful to Nolan Eyre and Viviana Urbano. For suggestions and scholarly advice, we thank Rex Wade, Michael Melancon, Tsuyoshi Hasegawa, Cyrus Veeser, Gregory Freeze, and the two anonymous outside readers whose expert knowledge in our field has guided and inspired us. We are especially thankful to the series editors, Alfred J. Andrea and Andrew Holt, whose wisdom, diligence, kindness, and competence made this book far better than it could have been. For any remaining mistakes and other inadequacies, we alone bear responsibility.

Technical Matters

All dates before January 1, 1918, follow the older Julian calendar (O.S.), which was in use in Russia until that date. It lagged thirteen days behind the Gregorian calendar (N.S.) used in all Western countries. Dates indicated thus: July 24/August 6, 1914, should be read as July 24 (O.S.)/August 6 (N.S.), 1914. We follow the Library of Congress transliteration system, minus the diacritical marks, except for widely accepted Latinizations of names, such as Nicholas (not Nikolai) and Trotsky (not Trotskii). Throughout the book, ellipses without spaces (...) are from the original. Unless otherwise specified, all translations are by the authors.

LIST OF MAPS AND ILLUSTRATIONS

Maps

Illustrations

Alekseev, Mikhail: Nicholas II's chief of staff at military headquarters

Aleksei Nikolaevich: Heir to the Russian throne

Alexander III: Nicholas II's father

Alexandra Feodorovna: Empress of Russia

Anastasia Nikolaevna: Grand duchess

Anderson, Anna: Born Franziska Schanzkowska, claimed to be Anastasia Nikolaevna

Armand, Inessa: Friend and possibly lover of Vladimir Lenin

Beliaev, Mikhail: War minister

Bochkareva (pronounced Bochkaryova), Maria: Organizer of women's battalion in World War I

Botkin, Gleb: Son of Nicholas II's doctor, advocate of Anna Anderson

Brusilov, Aleksei: Russian military commander; organized major offensive in summer 1916

Buxhoeveden, Baroness Sophie: Lady-in-waiting to Alexandra Feodorovna

Chicherin, Georgii: Soviet commissar of foreign affairs

Denikin, Anton: Anti-Bolshevik military leader

Diterikhs, Mikhail (alternate spelling: Dietrichs): Anti-Bolshevik military commander

Dzhunkovskii, Vladimir: Deputy minister of internal affairs

Fräulein Unbekannt: *See* Anderson, Anna

Frederiks, V. B. Count: Minister of imperial court

Gajda, Rudolf: Commander of Czechoslovak Legion

Ganetsky (or Hanecki), Yakov: Born Jakub Fürstenberg, close associate of Vladimir Lenin

Gilliard, Pierre: Romanov children's French teacher

Goldman, Emma: American anarchist who visited Vladimir Korolenko

Golitsyn, Nikolai: Briefly Russian prime minister in early 1917

Goloshchekin, Filipp: Military commissar of the Ural region

Gorky, Maxim: Russian writer, close to Bolsheviks

Key Figures

Graves, William S.: Commander of the American Expeditionary Force in Siberia

Guchkov, Aleksandr: Octobrist Party leader

Hermogenes: Russian Orthodox cleric, onetime supporter of Rasputin

Iliodor (Sergei Trufanov): Lapsed religious figure, onetime supporter of Rasputin

Ivanov, Nikolai: Briefly commander of Petrograd military district

Kalmykov, Ivan: Ataman of Ussuri Cossacks

Kerensky, Alexander: War minister, then prime minister of Provisional Government

Khabalov, Sergei: Commander of Petrograd military district during February Revolution

Khvostov, Aleksei: Minister of interior and Rasputin supporter

Kokovtsov, Vladimir: Prewar imperial prime minister

Kolchak, Aleksandr: Anti-Bolshevik military leader in Siberia

Kollontai, Alexandra: Prominent Bolshevik activist

Kornilov, Lavr: Military commander; sought to restore order in Petrograd

Korolenko, Vladimir: Writer and human rights activist

Krupskaia, Nadezhda: Wife of Vladimir Lenin

Kuhn, Bela: Communist leader of Hungarian Soviet Republic in 1919

Lenin, Vladimir: Bolshevik leader

Lokhtina, Olga: Follower of Rasputin

Lunacharskii, Anatolii: Bolshevik commissar of culture and education

L'vov, Georgii, Prince: Public activist, first post-imperial prime minister of Russia

Makarov, Alexander: Minister of interior, 1911–1912

Maria Feodorovna: Nicholas II's mother

Markov, Nikolai: Right-wing Duma deputy

Michael, Grand Duke: Nicholas II's brother

Miliukov, Pavel: Constitutional Democratic Party leader

Nikolai Nikolaevich, Grand Duke (Nikolasha): Nicholas II's cousin, military commander

Olga, Grand Duchess: Nicholas II's sister

Pankhurst, Emmeline: British fighter for women's voting rights

Parvus (Alexander Helphand), Aleksandr: Revolutionary activist and financier

Platten, Fritz: Swiss ally of Lenin

Plekhanov, Grigorii: Founder of Russian Marxism

Protopopov, Aleskandr: Octobrist Duma deputy and minister of interior

Purishkevich, Vladimir: Monarchist co-assassin of Rasputin

Rakovskii, Khristian: Head of Bolshevik Ukrainian government

Rasputin, Grigorii: Siberian peasant, influential with imperial couple

Rodzianko, Mikhail: Chairman of State Duma

Rosenberg, Alfred: Baltic German promoter of "Judeo-Bolshevik" myth

Ruzsky, Nikolai: Commander of Northern Army Group

Semenov, Grigorii: Ataman of Trans-Baikal Cossacks

Smith, Eugenia: Claimed to be Anastasia

Sokolov, Nikolai: Investigated murder of Romanov family

Spiridovich Aleksandr: Chief of imperial court security

Stalin, Joseph: Bolshevik, successor to Vladimir Lenin

Stolypin, Piotr: Russian prime minister, assassinated in 1911

Sverdlov, Iakov: Bolshevik leader

Theophanes, Bishop: One-time supporter of Rasputin

Trotsky, Leon: Bolshevik leader

Upovalov, Ivan: Menshevik Party activist

Vishniakova, Maria: Confidante of Empress Alexandra

von Kühlmann, Richard: German foreign minister

Vyrubova, Anna: Lady-in-waiting to Empress Alexandra

William II, Kaiser: Ruler of Germany

Witte, Count Sergei: Russian statesman

Yusupov, Prince Felix: Wealthy nobleman, co-assassin of Rasputin

Zahle, Herluf: Danish envoy in Berlin

Zinoviev, Grigorii: Bolshevik leader

Glossary of Terms

Allied: *See* Entente

American Expeditionary Force (AEF): U.S. military unit operating in Siberia in 1918–1919

"Anastasia": False claimant to identity of Anastasia, daughter of Tsar Nicholas II

April Theses: Speech by Vladimir Lenin advocating socialist revolution

ataman: Cossack leader

Babi Yar: Place where Jews were massacred in 1941 near Kyiv

Bloody Sunday: January 9, 1905, when Russian troops fired on peaceful demonstrators

Bolshevik Party: Founding and ruling party of the Soviet Union (Bolsheviks, formerly called Bolsheviki)

Central Powers: Germany, Austria-Hungary, and their allies in World War I

Cheka: Bolshevik secret police (1917–1922)

commissar: Bolshevik high state official

Constituent Assembly: Democratically elected political body shut down by Bolsheviks

Cossacks: Peoples of various ethnic backgrounds on Russia's frontiers who provided loyal troops sometimes used for the suppression of popular unrest and who were known for participating in violence against Jewish settlements

Council of People's Commissars: Bolshevik government, executive branch

Czechoslovak Legion: Military force formed in Russia to fight Central Powers

Decree on Peace: Demand by Bolsheviks to end world war

dictatorship of the proletariat: Regime Bolsheviks claimed to establish

dowager empress: Widowed mother of reigning monarch

Duma: Lower chamber of imperial Russian parliament

Eastern Front: Military theater on western border of Russia

Entente powers: France, Russia, Great Britain, and their allies in World War I, also known as Triple Entente

Freemasons (or Masons): Members of fraternal organizations, often secretive

Fundamental Laws: Russian constitution granted by Nicholas II in 1906

General Headquarters: Decision-making center of military, south of Petrograd

holy fool (*iurodivyi*): Person with disabilities seen as spiritually authoritative

Ipatiev House: Where Romanov family was murdered in 1918

July Days: Mass rebellion in Petrograd in summer 1917

***Khlyst*:** Member of secretive religious sect, deemed heretical

Kremlin: Fortress in Moscow, seat of Soviet government from March 1918

Kronstadt naval base: Place of frequent rebellion off the coast from Petrograd

Marxism: Political theory opposed to private property and free markets

***Mein Kampf*:** Book written by Hitler while in prison in 1923–1924

Menshevik Party: Marxist organization that split from Bolsheviks

New Economic Policy: Temporary relaxation of anti-market policies (1921–1928)

October Manifesto: 1905 promise by Tsar Nicholas II to grant parliament and civil rights

Octobrist Party: Political organization founded to support October Manifesto

Omsk Directory: Anti-Bolshevik government in Siberia

"Our Friend": Nickname Nicholas and Alexandra called Rasputin

Pale of Settlement: Russian Empire's western provinces where Jews were allowed to reside

Pavlovsky Guards: Military unit in Petrograd that joined protesters in February 1917

People's Will (Narodnaia volia): Terrorist group that assassinated Alexander II in 1881

Petrograd: Name of Saint Petersburg from 1914 until 1924

***Pravda*:** Flagship newspaper of Bolshevik (later Communist) Party

proletarian: Industrial worker

***Protocols of the Elders of Zion*:** Fake plan for alleged Jewish world domination

Provisional Government: Russian government from February to October 1917

Red Army: Bolshevik military force

red partisans: Irregular pro-Bolshevik fighters

Second International: Organization of socialist and labor parties, 1889–1916

Social Democratic Party: Russian Marxist organization (including Bolsheviks and Mensheviks)

socialism: Ideology emphasizing social justice and common ownership of property

Socialist Revolutionary Party: Peasant-oriented political organization in Russia

soviet: Council, institution of local self-government gradually co-opted by Bolsheviks

***startsy*:** traveling religious elders

Taurida Palace: Meeting house of Duma and, later, Constituent Assembly in Petrograd

Trans-Siberian Railway: Rail lines running from Moscow to Vladivostok

Treaty of Brest-Litovsk: Ended war between Russia and Central Powers in 1918

tsar: Monarch of Russia

Tsarskoe Selo ("Tsar's Village"): Suburb outside Petrograd where Nicholas II and his family usually resided

Western Front: Military theater on western border of Germany

Whites: Anti-Bolshevik forces in Russian Civil War

Women's Death Battalion: All-female combat unit authorized by Provisional Government

KEY DATES

All dates Old Style (Julian Calendar), unless dual dates given

1881

1 March: People's Will assassinates Tsar Alexander II

1905

9 January: Troops fire at demonstrators in Saint Petersburg (Bloody Sunday)

5 September: Russo-Japanese War ends with Russia's defeat

17 October: Tsar's Manifesto promises civil liberties and parliament

1 November: Nicholas and Alexandra first meet Rasputin

1906

27 April: Duma opens

1914

June–July: Mass strikes in Saint Petersburg

15/28 July: Austria-Hungary declares war on Serbia

17/30 July: Russian order for general mobilization

19 July/1 August: German declaration of war on Russia

1915

Military supply crisis (insufficiency of shells and equipment)

March: France and Britain promise Russia control over Constantinople after war

26 August: Nicholas assumes supreme military command against advice of ministers

1916

Gradual disorganization of railroads; fuel and food shortages; massive inflation

21 February: Battle of Verdun begins

22 May/4 June: Brusilov Offensive begins, dealing powerful blow to Austria-Hungary

1 November: Miliukov's "Stupidity or Treason" speech in Duma

17 December: Rasputin murdered

1917

22 February: Nicholas II leaves Tsarskoe Selo for General Headquarters

23 February: Demonstrations in Petrograd protesting bread shortage

25 February: Most factories closed in Petrograd

26 February: Nicholas II orders troops to restore order in Petrograd

27 February: Troops mutiny in Petrograd; mob frees inmates from prisons; Temporary Committee of State Duma formed; Petrograd Soviet formed

28 February: Mutinies spread; dozens of officers and NCOs murdered in Kronstadt

March: Soviets form in cities, factories, military units, and countryside

1 March: Nicholas II arrives in Pskov

2 March: Provisional Government formed; Nicholas abdicates

27 March/9 April: Lenin and other socialists depart from Zurich

4 April: Lenin's "April Theses" call for deepening of revolution

18 June–14 July: Failed Russian offensive against Germans; troops mutiny

16–20 July/3–7 August: July Days revolt in Petrograd

25–31 August: Alleged mutiny by General Kornilov

16 October: Petrograd Soviet votes to create Military Revolutionary Committee

25–26 October (night): Bolsheviks seize power, pass decrees on peace and land

Late October–November: Soviet power spreads across country and through military units

12 November: Elections to Constituent Assembly begin

17 November: Nationalization of private enterprise

7 December: Cheka (political police) set up

9 December: Brest-Litovsk peace talks begin between Russia and Central Powers

14 December: Nationalization of banks

1918

2 January: Decrees on "laborers' rights" and universal labor obligation

5–6 January: Constituent Assembly opens, later shut down at gunpoint

25 January: The Ukrainian People's Republic proclaims independence

27 January: Ukraine signs peace treaty with Central Powers

1/14 February: Gregorian calendar instituted

18 February: Germany and Austria abrogate truce and begin offensive against Russia

3 March: Treaty of Brest-Litovsk signed between Russia and Central Powers

8 March: Bolshevik party renamed Russian Communist Party

10–12 March: Government moves to Moscow

5 April: Allied military intervention begins

22 April: Foreign trade nationalized; establishment of universal military training

13 May: Beginning of "War Communism"

14 May: Czechoslovak regiment clashes with Hungarian POWs

25–26 May: Czechoslovak Legion refuses Bolshevik order to disarm

28 May: Martial law instituted across country

29 May: Universal military draft

8 June: Czechoslovaks occupy Samara

28 June: Nationalization of all heavy industry, railroads, and steam plants

July–August: Peasant revolts

16–17 July: Execution of imperial family in Ekaterinburg

25 July–August: Czechoslovaks take Ekaterinburg, Simbirsk, Ufa, Kazan, Irkutsk, and Chita

August: American Expeditionary Force (AEF) lands in Vladivostok

2 August: Allies occupy Archangelsk

8 August–12 November: Worker uprising in Izhevsk and Votkinsk

30 August: Socialist-Revolutionary terrorist wounds Lenin

2 September: Decree declaring Red Terror

29 October: Sailors revolt in Wilhelmshaven, Germany

3 November: Sailors revolt in Kiel, Germany

11 November: Armistice ends World War I

1919

5–12 January: Spartacist League uprising in Berlin

18 January: Paris Peace Conference opens in Versailles

2–6 March: First Congress of Communist International (Comintern)

21 March–1 August: Hungarian Soviet Republic

April: Red Scare begins in United States.

6 April–3 May: Bavarian Soviet Republic

18 November: Omsk Directory overthrown, Admiral Kolchak seizes power in Siberia

19 November: General offensive of Red Army begins in south and southeast

1920

4 February: Massive anti-Bolshevik peasant uprising breaks out in Volga region

27 February: Fräulein Unbekannt attempts suicide in Berlin

29 March–5 April: Party Congress votes to abolish private property and militarize economy

April: American Expeditionary Force leaves Siberia

July–September: Peasant uprising in Saratov province

21 July–6 August: Second Congress of Comintern imposes 21 conditions of admission

1921

28 February–11 March: Strikes in Petrograd

28 February–18 March: Kronstadt sailors rebel "for soviets without Communists"

8–16 March: Tenth Party Congress proclaims New Economic Policy

Summer: Famine begins in Volga region and southern Ukraine (1.5–2 million die)

1922

30 December: Formation of USSR

INTRODUCTION

The great political and economic progress imperial Russia made in the decades prior to 1914 had alleviated but not eliminated its many problems, including underdevelopment, alienation of educated elites, land-hunger of peasants, poor living conditions of urban workers, pervasive disrespect for the law, arbitrariness of government officials, and inefficient bureaucracy. As a result, even without the world war, which dramatically exacerbated social tensions, Russia was, to some extent, ripe for revolution. Three grueling years of war, which left millions homeless, wounded, maimed, and killed, combined with shortages of bread and fuel in Petrograd in early 1917, made massive popular protest all but inevitable. The incompetence and unpopularity of Tsar Nicholas II and his senior officials allowed unrest to escalate to revolution and the collapse of the monarchy in February 1917 amid a massive rebellion of soldiers and industrial workers in Petrograd. But Russia's woes were far from over.

The three-hundred-year-old Romanov dynasty had given way in early 1917 to competing liberal and socialist contenders for political power. The idealistic abolition of police forces by the liberal Provisional Government contributed to a massive outbreak of violence and criminality. Its failure to end the war, institute land reform, conduct democratic elections, and offer opportunities for self-determination to the dozens of non-Russian peoples within the Russian Empire enabled popular discontent to fester and intensify during the summer and fall. No wonder many ordinary people, both Russians and non-Russians, were drawn to the revolutionary parties. Because they claimed they could end the chaos and create a truly fair, prosperous, technologically advanced, and just society, and a shining path to the entire world, the Bolsheviks enjoyed increasing popularity.

In late 1917, in part because of the near-total breakdown of public order, the Bolsheviks seized power and established the world's first communist dictatorship. In subsequent decades, "the world's first socialist society" inspired communist revolutionary movements and the creation of socialist polities around the world. Positive visions of the Russian Revolution captivated the hearts and minds of hundreds of millions of people, while fears of communist threats to civilization contributed to the rise and spread of fascism, National Socialism (Nazism), virulent racism, and institutionalized xenophobia.

Yet despite its enduring global impact, the Russian Revolution has often been poorly understood. Both friends and enemies of the Russian Revolution saw in it what their ideological proclivities predisposed them to see. Passionate attachment to—or rejection of—revolutionary ideas and values coupled with a lack of knowledge of the specific historical circumstances of the Russian Revolution led to the development of potent myths that colored, shaped, and distorted the perception of this crucial historical event for many decades and, in some respects, to this day.

This book aims to discuss and dispel seven of these persistent myths—falsehoods, distortions, misconceptions, half-truths, and oversimplifications—surrounding key developments of the Russian Revolution, to trace their origins and explain their remarkable resilience.

Myth 1—Grigorii Rasputin: A Man of Many Myths

Few people in Russian history generated more myths, rumors, and speculation than Grigorii Rasputin. For Tsar Nicholas and his wife Alexandra, this semiliterate Siberian peasant was a holy man and "a Friend." At the same time, revolutionary, liberal, and even conservative critics of the imperial regime attributed vast, nearly demonic power to him. He was rumored to be a German agent, Alexandra's lover, a master puppeteer behind the throne (as reflected in the cover image), a member of an esoteric religious sect, and so forth. This chapter focuses on Rasputin's true role and influence (and their limits), examines the mechanics of the Rasputin myth, and discusses the real dysfunctionalities of the Russian monarchy in the final years of its existence.

Myth 2—The Myth of Treasonous Conspiracy Causing the Russian Monarchy's Fall

The collapse of the Russian monarchy in February 1917 took many by surprise. Key supporters of the last tsar refused to recognize the severity of the regime's military, socio-economic, and political crises, turning instead to conspiracy theories that presented Nicholas II as an innocent victim of a sinister plot. Conspiracy theorists blamed revolutionaries, liberals, Jews, Freemasons, Germans, and even senior Russian military officers, in various combinations. This chapter traces the origins of some such conspiracy theories and their impact on both historical and politicized writing about the Russian Revolution and analyzes them in comparison with the real revolutionary dynamics of February 1917.

Myth 3—The Myth of Lenin and the Bolsheviks as Secret German Agents

When the Russian monarchy collapsed, the Bolshevik presence in the imperial capital of Petrograd was modest, and the first soviets (revolutionary representative councils) were often dominated by members of other revolutionary parties, most prominently Socialist-Revolutionaries and Mensheviks. Yet, in the course of 1917, the Bolshevik ranks swelled, and by the end of the year, the Bolshevik Party, led by Vladimir Lenin, seized power and established a new government in Russia. A host of anti-Bolshevik critics, including members of the liberal- and socialist-dominated Provisional Government, came to view the Bolsheviks as agents of a hostile military power—imperial Germany. For decades, even as the appeal of this myth began to wane, many opponents of the Bolsheviks continued to believe and argue that they were a force alien to Russia and Russian society. This chapter discusses the evidence of German support for the Bolsheviks and examines both why their opponents used this evidence to misrepresent the Bolsheviks and how such mischaracterizations influenced the course of Russian history.

Myth 4—The Myth that Princess Anastasia Survived the Assassination of the Imperial Family

The horrific details of the assassination of the Romanov family began to circulate shortly after their execution took place in the summer of 1918. Some were not fully accurate; others were too graphic and cruel to believe. Many supporters of the imperial family in Russia and abroad continued to hope that at least some of the imperial family members survived the massacre. Several individuals in the 1920s claimed to be surviving members of the imperial family, including, most famously, "Princess Anastasia." This chapter surveys the events of the assassination, places them in the broader context of Bolshevik civil war policies, analyzes numerous inconsistencies in the Anastasia "survivor accounts," and contemplates the reasons for these accounts' persisting appeal.

Myth 5—The "Judeo-Bolshevik" Myth

Tsarist Russia was a traditional, hierarchical society in which government officials and propertied elites enjoyed high status, while most people—peasants, industrial workers, soldiers, petty clerks, and even lower-ranked state employees—barely made ends meet and faced constant mistreatment and disrespect. On top of this came ethnic and religious oppression against the empire's many minorities, including Jews, who faced rampant and stultifying discrimination, driving many to join revolutionary parties, including the Bolsheviks. Traditionally, Russian elites had mistrusted the empire's minorities, especially the Jews. Moreover, many people supposed that only people alien to Russian culture could wish to topple the tsar and overthrow the Russian political and economic structures. Thus, traditional prejudice combined with conspiracy theories about Jews allegedly seeking global control, added to the prominence of some Jews within the Bolshevik leadership, led conspiratorially minded observers to imagine Bolsheviks and Jews joining forces to take over Russia and spread an alien ideology across its boundaries and into the wider world. This chapter looks at the origins, spread, and deadly consequences of what perhaps was the most dangerous and destructive myth of the Russian revolution.

Myth 6—The Myth of a U.S. Crusade in Siberia to Overthrow the Bolsheviks and Colonize Russia, 1918–1920

Even before seizing power, Lenin and other Bolsheviks believed that coercion and violence would be necessary to hold on to power and "build socialism." Having seized power in October 1917, the Bolshevik leadership promoted an ideological framework built around the concept of "hostile capitalist encirclement" to justify this violence. Pointing to U.S. involvement in a 1918–1920 foreign intervention into Russian terri- tory, Soviet and contemporary Russian propaganda have portrayed the United States as an existential threat to Russia then and now. This chapter examines the real motives and activities of the American Expeditionary Force in Siberia. It argues that U.S. actions in Russia lacked the purpose, organization, and cohesiveness attributed to them within the "capitalist encirclement" framework and shows how their mythical misrepresentations continue to poison U.S.-Russian relations to this day.

Myth 7—The Myth of an Inevitable Bolshevik Victory

The Bolsheviks enjoyed spectacular success in establishing a one-party communist dictatorship that dominated nearly all the territory of the former Russian Empire and, after World War II, most of eastern Europe as well. It is hardly surprising that for many decades the public and scholars focused the bulk of their attention on "the party of Lenin and Stalin." The historical record was unequivocal: the Bolsheviks won, and historians have argued about the reasons and factors that made their victory possible. Some cited Marxist "laws of history"; others stressed Bolshevik brutality, Lenin's polit- ical genius, or growing popular support. Implicit (and sometimes explicit) in these arguments was the assumption that the Bolshevik victory was inevitable, or at least highly likely. This assumption is not unique to the Russian Revolution, as we often tend to think about the past in oversimplified linear terms. Unlike all previous chap- ters, this chapter does not categorically refute such linear thinking but encourages a less simplified, multilinear approach to the past. It draws readers' attention to a wealth of goals, ideals, projects, and visions born out of the Russian Revolution and formu- lated and fought for by the widest imaginable range of activists: peasants and workers, socialists and liberals, anarchists and nationalists, religious believers and atheists—all hoping for a better world. By focusing on this human diversity—personified by a woman military organizer, an industrial worker socialist activist, and a liberal human rights defender—the chapter makes readers more aware of the many paths and visions of transformation that temporarily opened up in revolutionary Russia.

1. Grigorii Rasputin: A Man of Many Myths

Hearken unto our Friend, believe Him, he has yr. interest & Russia's at heart—it is not for nothing God sent Him to us—only we must pay more attention to what He says.[1]
—*Alexandra to Nicholas II, June 10, 1915*

I realized now who Rasputin really was. It was the reincarnation of Satan himself who held me in his clutches and would never let me go till my dying day.[2]
—*Prince Felix Yusupov, Rasputin's assassin*

By the end of 1916, Grigorii Rasputin was probably the best-known person in the Russian Empire, apart from Nicholas II (r. 1894–1917). His closeness to the tsar and his wife, Alexandra, was notorious. Dozens of rumors circulated about Rasputin. Some concerning his religious status, his relationship with Empress Alexandra, his political influence, and his sexual prowess persist today.[3] Such myths fall into two overarching groups. The first is "Rasputin the Holy Man." The second and perhaps most pervasive is "Rasputin the Holy Demon."

A small but devout group of admirers believed that Rasputin was a man of God, a prophet-like figure endowed with divine wisdom and healing powers. Some went so far as to believe that anything from Rasputin was holy. Olga Lokhtina, the wife of a senior government official, considered him a reincarnation of Christ. The imperial family was also counted among Rasputin's ardent admirers. Figure 1.1

Figure 1.1: Alexandra Feodorovna with her children, the governess Maria Ivanovna Vishniakova (bottom row right), and Rasputin, 1908.

---

1. Joseph T. Fuhrmann, ed., *The Complete Wartime Correspondence of Tsar Nicholas II and the Empress Alexandra, April 1914–March 1917* (Westport, CT: Greenwood Press, 1999), 135.

2. Prince Felix Youssoupoff, *Lost Splendor: The Amazing Memoirs of the Man Who Killed Rasputin*, trans. Ann Green and Nicholas Katkoff (New York: Helen Marx Books, 2003), 250.

3. An authoritative recent study is Douglas Smith, *Rasputin: Faith, Power, and the Twilight of the Romanovs* (New York: Farrar, Straus, and Giroux, 2016).

depicts Rasputin as a member of the Romanov family. It is also reminiscent of Eastern Orthodox icons depicting Christ surrounded by his apostles.

Figure 1.2: "The Ruling Russian House," 1916.

"Rasputin the Holy Demon" was the title of an influential anti-Rasputin book whose author, former Rasputin supporter Hieromonk Iliodor, also known as Sergei Trufanov (1880–1952), portrayed Rasputin as a sinister force, a sexually depraved liar, and an all-powerful manipulator.[4] Such beliefs were widespread. Like all powerful myths, it contained elements of truth but remained a gross distortion of reality. Some who believed in the "Holy Demon" fantasy thought Rasputin's powers were supernatural and demonic. Figure 1.2 expresses the conviction that the imperial couple were helpless pawns in the hands of a monstrous creature.

Why did Rasputin generate such intense reactions among those who met him and those who never did? Who was the actual person behind the myths? What does his story tell us about society and politics in late imperial Russia, a country on the threshold of revolution?

Rasputin is mentioned in countless memoirs and autobiographies, but historians need to view such recollections skeptically since those who wrote them tended to be either supporters or enemies of Rasputin. To begin separating reality from fiction, one needs to start with some basic facts.

From Siberian Village to Saint Petersburg Palaces

Rasputin was a peasant. Born in the village of Pokrovskoe in western Siberia, he spent his early years as a rowdy youth, drinking and chasing women. At the age of twenty,

---

4. Byvsh. Ier. Iliodor (Sergei Trufanov), *Sviatoi chort (Zapiski o Rasputine)*, pref. S. P. Mel'gunov (Moscow: Izd. zhurnala "Golos minuvshago," 1917).

he married and settled down, but not for long. He journeyed to a nearby monastery, then to other holy places, including Mount Athos in Greece, a vibrant hub of Eastern Orthodox monasticism. During his travels, Rasputin claimed to have had visionary experiences that set him on a path toward God. Common beliefs to the contrary, however, he became neither a priest nor a monk.

This way of life was not altogether unique. Pilgrims and traveling elders (*startsy*; singular: *starets*) belonged to a peculiar substratum of Russian society.[5] Most were of peasant background, but instead of working the land, they lived by praying and preaching in exchange for alms. Their lifestyle was tough, adventurous, and financially unpredictable, but it could also be exciting and spiritually and psychologically rewarding. Many ordinary people sought spiritual guidance from such "godly ones" (*Bozhie liudi*). A few even attracted the notice of elites seeking otherworldly experiences or sources of divine wisdom. Church leaders were uncertain whether to view the traveling elders as allies or competitors.

Rasputin's demeanor was eye-catching. Critics and devotees alike thought he exuded magnetism. Lady-in-waiting Anna Vyrubova, Empress Alexandra's confidante, described him as "an elderly peasant, thin, with a pale face, long hair, an uncared-for beard, and the most extraordinary eyes, large, light, brilliant, and apparently capable of seeing into the very mind and soul of the person with whom he held converse."[6] Prince Felix Yusupov, a wealthy nobleman, married to the tsar's niece, described "a healing" session:

> Rasputin had tremendous hypnotic power. I felt as if some active energy was pouring heat, like a warm current, into my whole being. I fell into a torpor, and my body grew numb; I tried to speak but my tongue no longer obeyed me, and I gradually slipped into a drowsy state, as though a powerful narcotic had been administered to me. All I could see was Rasputin's glittering eyes; two phosphorescent beams of light melting into a great luminous ring which at times drew nearer and then moved farther away.
>
> I heard the voice of the *starets* but could not understand what he said.
>
> I remained in this state, without being able to cry out or to move. My mind alone was free, and I fully realized that I was gradually falling into the power of this evil man.[7]

Many people were impressed by Rasputin's folksy sayings. Some concerned the difficult path of religious faith. "It is hard to obtain salvation in the world," he proclaimed, "especially these days. Everybody is watching those who are looking for

---

5. On the *startsy* tradition, see John Binns, *The T&T Clark History of Monasticism: The Eastern Tradition* (London: T&T Clark, 2020), 207–11.

6. Anna Vyrubova, *Memories of the Russian Court* (London: Macmillan and Co., 1923), 153.

7. Youssoupoff, *Lost Splendor*, 228.

salvation as if he is some kind of a bandit and everybody is trying to mock him." Others emphasized the true simplicity of the Orthodox Christian soul: "How happy we are, Orthodox Christians! . . . Others have craft—they even trade in sacred things, but one can see they have no joy."[8] He also admitted that the peasant's life was full of travails: "Even the Tsar Autocrat lives by the peasant, feeds off his laboring hands, and all the birds use the peasant and even the mouse feeds off him."[9] Yet what mattered most was not what Rasputin said, but how he said it. His persona radiated mystery.

Background to Rasputin's Rise to Power

Calling Rasputin "Grigorii, a man of God from Tobolsk province," Nicholas noted in his diary that he and Alexandra first met him on November 1, 1905, in the company of Princesses Milica and Anastasia of Montenegro, who had married two of the tsar's cousins and were occult enthusiasts.[10] Russia was plunged in crisis. Japan had just defeated Russia—the first major victory of an Asian power over a major European power. Government troops firing on peacefully demonstrating protesters in Saint Petersburg on Bloody Sunday (January 9) had sparked mass unrest.[11] Peasants attacked gentry estates, workers struck, soldiers and sailors mutinied, and elites denounced government corruption, police brutality, the arbitrary power of officials, the death penalty, religious and ethnic discrimination, and the lack of civil rights, and demanded political freedom and representative government. Nicholas held fast to the unlimited authority of the Russian tsars, a model that had grown obsolete as Russia became more urban, more literate (some 41 percent of the Russian population by 1914),[12] and, at least as far as the educated classes were concerned, more aware of the "inalienable rights" that citizens enjoyed in most European countries. By fall 1905, Russia was engulfed in revolution.

Count Sergei Witte, a senior government official who had recently negotiated peace with Japan, convinced Nicholas to offer political concessions to split the opposition and then crush the radicals with military force.[13] Nicholas reluctantly agreed.

---

8. Grigorii Rasputin, *Moi mysli i razmyshleniia. Zhitiie opytnogo strannika: Pis'ma* (Moscow: Vagrius, 2001), 28, 72, 74.

9. Rasputin, *Moi mysli*, 33.

10. Nicholas, Emperor of Russia, *Dnevniki imperatora Nikolaia II (1894–1918)*, 2 vols., ed. S. V. Mironenko (Moscow: ROSSPEN, 2011, 2013), 1:1042.

11. For these and allied events, see Abraham Ascher, *The Revolution of 1905: A Short History* (Stanford, CA: Stanford University Press, 2004).

12. Ben Eklof, "Russian Literacy Campaigns, 1861–1939," in *National Literacy Campaigns: Historical and Comparative Perspectives*, ed. Robert F. Arnove and Harvey J. Graff (New York: Plenum Press, 1987), 123–72 (here: 129).

13. On Witte, see Francis W. Wcislo, *Tales of Imperial Russia: The Life and Times of Sergei Witte, 1849–1915* (Oxford: Oxford University Press, 2011).

On October 17, 1905, he signed a declaration promising basic civil rights—freedom of speech, press, and assembly—and the creation of a parliament. In spring 1906, Nicholas made good on these promises. Most important, he established a bicameral legislature with an elected lower chamber, the State Duma, without whose consent no bill could become law.[14] Russia thus became a constitutional or at least a semi-constitutional monarchy. Although Nicholas remained the supreme ruler of Russia, in command of its armed forces, with the right to appoint and dismiss ministers, the October Manifesto launched an era of open, participatory politics and convinced at least moderate political activists that change could now be pursued through legal means. Conservative and liberal political parties formed, such as the Union of October 17 (the Octobrists) and the Constitutional-Democratic Party (the Kadets). Socialists were also elected to the Duma.[15]

Yet many liberals and radicals demanded further change—for example, making the government answerable to the parliament or even abolishing the monarchy. Moreover, Nicholas's concessions embittered him as well. He had promised his father, Alexander III, to uphold the principle of unlimited monarchy. Nicholas quickly lost trust in Witte, considering him duplicitous and power-hungry, and replaced him as prime minister with Piotr Stolypin, an effective, forceful, and talented administrator.[16]

Throughout 1906, Nicholas felt distressed as unrest continued, and the State Duma proved unruly. Alexandra shared his distress. Unlike the optimistic Russian liberals, the Russian tsarina, born Princess Alix of Hesse-Darmstadt in Germany and raised in part at the court of her grandmother, Queen Victoria, had an even greater disdain for constitutional rule and an even more ardent religious devotion than Nicholas.

Our Friend, Grigorii

The first meeting between the imperial couple and Rasputin lasted for three hours. Four days later, Rasputin wrote to Nicholas: "You, as our Master, and we, as your subjects, must do our best; we tremble and pray to God to keep you safe from all evil, to protect you from wounds, now and in the future, so that your life will forever flow like a life-giving spring."[17]

Rasputin made an enormous impression on Nicholas and Alexandra when they met again in July and October 1906. The reason for the July meeting is unclear,

---

14. On the October Manifesto and the Fundamental Laws of 1906, see Stephen F. Williams, *The Reformer: How One Liberal Fought to Preempt the Russian Revolution* (New York: Encounter Books, 2017), 87–122.

15. Peter Enticott, *The Russian Liberals and the Revolution of 1905* (Abingdon, UK: Routledge, 2016).

16. On Stolypin, see Abraham Ascher, *P. A. Stolypin: The Search for Stability in Late Imperial Russia* (Stanford, CA: Stanford University Press, 2001).

17. Smith, *Rasputin*, 69.

but the October meeting resulted from Rasputin's request to present Nicholas with a gift—a religious painting (an icon of Saint Simeon of Verkhoturie, the Miracle Worker). He claimed it would protect Nicholas throughout his life and assist him for the benefit of his loyal subjects. Nicholas noted that Rasputin "made a remarkably strong impression both on Her Majesty and on myself, so that instead of five minutes our conversation went on for more than an hour."[18] As the revolution raged and then subsided, Rasputin seemed to them to be a messenger sent from God. He usually found words of spiritual consolation that the royal couple desperately needed. They now trusted him.

Rasputin also met their social needs. In a society that valued social connections, Nicholas and Alexandra were often lonely and isolated. Few prominent people had warm feelings toward them. Liberally minded educated elites considered Nicholas too rigid, while conservatives thought him weak and inexperienced, especially compared to his father, the domineering Alexander III (r. 1881–1894). Alexandra fared even worse. She spoke Russian with an accent and felt ill at ease in grand social gatherings, suffering from an anxiety disorder that made her face break out in red blotches.[19]

Rasputin, by contrast, accepted the royal couple as they were and, at least at first, did not appear to seek any favors from them. In their personal correspondence, they referred to him as "Our Friend," and quite often, he seemed to be their only friend. As for Rasputin, he developed a vast network of acquaintances and connections in Saint Petersburg, and his sociability eased the sense of imperial isolation. He also presented a window onto the world of simple peasant life and what appeared to be ordinary people's piety. But the closer the imperial couple drew to Rasputin, the greater was their alienation from aristocratic society and even from other members of the extended royal family.

Efforts to Drive Rasputin Away

Bishop Theophanes, an imperial confessor, spiritual advisor, and devout monarchist, had introduced Rasputin to the Montenegrin princesses. Subsequently, Theophanes confronted Rasputin about rumors that he sometimes visited bathhouses in the company of women. Rasputin confirmed the rumors but insisted there was nothing impure involved. In summer 1909, Theophanes, who in February had been appointed rector of the Saint Petersburg Theological Academy and a bishop of the Saint Petersburg diocese—perhaps thanks to support from Rasputin—traveled to Rasputin's home village and did not like what he saw. He was told that Rasputin avoided religious observances and lived luxuriously.[20]

---

18. Richard S. Wortman, *Scenarios of Power: Myth and Ceremony in Russian Monarchy from Peter the Great to the Abdication of Nicholas II* (Princeton, NJ: Princeton University Press, 2006), 371.

19. A. F. Koni, *Sobranie sochinenii v vos'mi tomakh*, vol. 2, *Vospominaniia o dele Very Zasulich* (Moscow: Izd. Iuridicheskaia literatura, 1966–1969), 386–87.

20. Edvard Radzinskii, *Imperator i muzhik* (Moscow: AST, 2014), 141–42.

Upon returning to the capital, Theophanes confronted Rasputin again, accusing him of succumbing to worldly temptations. He later claimed that Rasputin admitted his guilt and promised to depart but did not.[21] Theophanes then brought the issue directly to Alexandra. He did not question Rasputin's ability to prophesy and heal. To him, as to Alexandra, these were real divine gifts. But, he argued, a person who cannot resist worldly temptation is in danger of succumbing to the devil. Alexandra called these accusations "lies and slander." Theophanes then wrote to Nicholas, accusing Rasputin of seductive acts. Nicholas and Alexandra did not believe Theophanes. Had he not supported and praised Rasputin and enjoyed his patronage? Theophanes was soon transferred to a bishopric in the Crimea.

In spring 1910, the Montenegrin princesses, who had become estranged from the imperial couple, in part because they had also grown hostile toward Rasputin, warned Alexandra that he was a threat to the dynasty. Alexandra was not convinced. Far more serious, Maria Vishniakova, nanny to the royal couple's only son, Aleksei, claimed to have been sexually assaulted by Rasputin in Pokrovskoe in 1909. Her complaint to Alexandra fell on deaf ears, however. "Everything that Rasputin does is holy," she defiantly said.[22]

In early 1911, Prime Minister Stolypin met with Rasputin upon Nicholas's urging. Stolypin later stated that he had felt a strong hypnotic influence but resisted. He yelled at Rasputin and threatened him with exile.[23] By that time, Stolypin had fallen from the emperor's grace. In September, the prime minister was assassinated in the presence of Nicholas, generating rumors of the tsar's complicity.[24]

There is no evidence to substantiate such rumors. Yet Stolypin's death—and Nicholas's miraculous escape—may have confirmed the imperial couple's faith in the saving power of God's grace, as delivered through Rasputin. The assassin, because of his Jewish origin, said he had deliberately spared Nicholas to avoid antisemitic vengeance.[25] (Rasputin himself favored equality for Jews.[26]) But to Nicholas and Alexandra, everything in this world happens by God's will. Alexandra later remarked that perhaps God willed Stolypin's death to make way for his successor, Vladimir Kokovtsev, whom she trusted more.[27]

In sum, neither religious preaching nor the fears of ladies-in-waiting nor the prime minister's warnings could convince the imperial couple to part with Rasputin, whom they considered a man of God.

21. Radzinskii, *Imperator*, 143.

22. Radzinskii, *Imperator*, 151.

23. Mikhail Rodzianko, *Krushenie imperii* (Moscow and Berlin: Direct Media, 2016), 40–43.

24. Charles Ruud and Sergei Stepanov, *Fontanka 16: The Tsars' Secret Police* (Montreal: McGill University Press, 1999), 197.

25. Ruud and Stepanov, *Fontanka 16*, 180.

26. Richard Pipes, *The Russian Revolution* (New York: Alfred A. Knopf, 1990), 249.

27. Vladimir Kokovtsev, *Iz moego proshlago: Vospominaniia 1903–1919 gg.*, 2 vols. (Paris: Izd. zhurnala Illustrirovannaia Rossiia, 1933), 2:8.

Fear of Publicity

Yet one factor led them to create, however reluctantly, some room between themselves and their beloved Friend: fear of publicity. As mentioned above, public opinion toward the royal couple was lukewarm.

Things became worse when the governmental breakdown in 1905 and a new law in 1906 eased censorship, creating a scandal-mongering press.[28] To be sure, it remained illegal to disparage the imperial family publicly. But Russian literary culture had a long tradition of using hints to convey what could not be stated openly. Government authorities had to decide whether, for example, a poetic rebuke of tyrannical Egyptian pharaohs subtly targeted the tsar. Furthermore, friends of the imperial family enjoyed no such legal protection.

Nicholas and Alexandra had always taken steps to keep their personal affairs private. Rasputin himself was anything but discreet. He enjoyed the company of women and liked to brag about his closeness to the royal family. He proudly wore shirts sewn by Alexandra and called her "Mommy." He even showed off letters he received from Alexandra and her daughters.

In December 1911, a former friend, the hieromonk[29] Iliodor invited Rasputin to visit Bishop Hermogenes in Saint Petersburg. According to Iliodor, Hermogenes started beating Rasputin with a cross, accusing him of lechery and undermining the sacred tsarist autocracy.[30] Hermogenes had brought to Saint Petersburg Mitya Kozelsky, an epileptic, deaf, half-blind paraplegic. Mitya's physical and mental disabilities made him a holy fool (*iurodivyi*) in Russian eyes, a status that gained him access to the imperial couple, along with many other "charlatans, 'holy fools,' and miracle workers," in the words of one historian.[31] Clearly, he was Rasputin's intended replacement. To cap it off, Iliodor and his associates forced Rasputin to swear never to return to the imperial entourage. He agreed, then rushed to Anna Vyrubova to accuse them of attempted murder.

Nicholas's response was predictable: he ordered Bishop Hermogenes and Iliodor, not Rasputin, to leave the capital. They disobeyed, however, and publicly attacked Rasputin. Iliodor also supplied Duma deputies with a copy of an affectionate letter from Alexandra to Rasputin. This disclosure provoked a major scandal in both the Duma and the press.

---

28. Charles A. Ruud, *Fighting Words: Imperial Censorship and the Russian Press, 1804–1906* (Toronto: University of Toronto Press, 2009), 219–24. On rising literacy, see Jeffrey Brooks, *When Russia Learned to Read: Literacy and Popular Literature, 1861–1917* (Evanston, IL: Northwestern University Press, 2003).

29. In Eastern Orthodox Churches, a hieromonk combines the roles of both monk and priest.

30. Iliodor, *Rasputin: Muzhik v tsarskom dome* (Moscow: Algoritm, 2014), 173.

31. Robert D. Warth, "Before Rasputin: Piety and the Occult at the Court of Nicholas II," *Historian* 47, no. 3 (May 1985): 323–37 (quotation: 323).

The copy of Alexandra's letter to Rasputin, which was circulated in the Duma, read as follows:

> My beloved and unforgettable teacher, savior, and mentor. How tiring it is for me without you. I am calm in spirit, feel at rest only when you, my teacher, are seated next to me, and I kiss your hands and lay my head on your blessed shoulder. Oh, how easy things are for me then. Then I wish for only one thing—to fall asleep, fall asleep forever on your shoulder, in your embrace. Oh, what happiness it is merely to feel your presence near me. Where are you? Whither have you flown? Yet it is so difficult for me, there is such anguish in my heart . . . But you, my beloved mentor, do not tell Anya [Vyrubova] about my sufferings without you. Anya is good. She is kind. She loves me, but do not reveal to her my sorrow. Will you once again be near me soon? Come as soon as you can. I await you and am tormented without you. I request your sainted blessing and kiss your blessed hands.
>
> Loving you forever,
>
> Mama.[32]

The minister of interior, Alexander Makarov, retrieved the stolen letters and gave them to Nicholas. Perhaps he wished to compromise Alexandra or Rasputin or both in Nicholas's eyes. To no avail. Upon receiving the letters, Nicholas turned pale, confirmed their authenticity, and cast them into a drawer.

Nicholas could not ward off an avalanche of publicity about Rasputin. Since Rasputin was not a member of the imperial family, government efforts to stop unwanted press attention were futile. Nicholas and Alexandra grew disappointed with Stolypin and Stolypin's successor as prime minister, Vladimir Kokovtsov, in part because they could not rein in the press. Kokovstov suspected Alexandra believed this made him no longer the tsar's servant but the servant of those who invented fake stories about the tsar and his family.[33] Alexander Mosolov, chief of the Imperial Chancellery, remembered it being difficult to explain to Nicholas and Alexandra, given their beliefs about autocratic power, the lack of any legal basis on which to silence the press.[34] The imperial couple were thus at odds not only with the press, the Duma majority, and high society but also with many senior government officials. Even Nicholas's mother, Maria

32. As quoted from Andrei Amal'rik, *Rasputin: Dokumental'naia povest'* (Moscow: Slovo/Slovo, 1992), 103–4.

33. Kokovtsev, *Iz moego proshlago*, 2:356.

34. A. A. Mosolov, *Pri dvore poslednego Rossiskogo imperatora: Zapiski nachal'nika kantseliarii Ministerstva Imperatorskogo Dvora* (Moscow: Ankor, 1993), 244–45.

Feodorovna, warned Nicholas that rumors of Rasputin's bad behavior threatened the prestige of the dynasty.[35]

Member of a Secret Sect?

Many of Rasputin's critics considered him a *Khlyst*, a member of an illegal and secretive religious sect that the Orthodox Church deemed heretical. *Khlysty* typically led highly ascetic lifestyles, practicing mortification of the flesh, including self-flagellation; some also took part in ecstatic rituals, in which they danced in wild abandon.[36] Such ceremonies were rumored to culminate in sexual orgies. Rumors and allegations that Rasputin engaged in sexual debauchery and even sexual assault seemed to confirm his membership in the sect, even though such practices were unusual among *Khlysty*. His claim that, like certain Christian saints, he had no sexual desire, fit more properly with the general understanding of *Khlyst* ways. So did the fact that Rasputin became a cult-like figure among some female admirers.

Few went further than Olga Lokhtina, mentioned above, a noblewoman-turned-beggar, who followed Rasputin wherever she could, recorded his religious utterances, and considered him the Messiah. A publisher and banker, Aleksei Filippov, who cultivated ties with Rasputin, testified to the Extraordinary Investigating Commission of the Provisional Government in 1917 that he had visited Rasputin in 1911 and saw him beating up Lokhtina. "I rushed over to him. . . . 'What are you doing!' Filippov recalled shouting: 'You are beating a woman!' Rasputin answered, 'She won't let me alone, the skunk, and demands sin!'"[37]

Whatever the truth of this and other stories, no convincing evidence exists that Rasputin was a *Khlyst*. Unless such evidence comes to light, the rumor should be considered an unsubstantiated legend.

Rasputin, Healer

Nicholas and Alexandra believed God's grace manifested itself through Rasputin because of his apparent ability to comfort and heal their only son. Aleksei suffered from hemophilia, then a disease without any reliable means of treatment. This rare

---

35. Coryne Hall, *Little Mother of Russia: A Biography of the Empress Marie Feodorovna (1847–1928)* (New York: Holmes and Meier, 2001), 236–42.

36. On the *Khlysty*, see Laura Engelstein, *Castration and the Heavenly Kingdom: A Russian Folktale* (Ithaca, NY: Cornell University Press, 1999), 13–25; Leonid Heretz, *Russia on the Eve of Modernity: Popular Religion and Traditional Culture under the Last Tsars* (Cambridge: Cambridge University Press, 2008), 81–98.

37. Edvard Radzinsky, *The Rasputin File*, trans. Judson Rosengrant (New York: Anchor Books, 2000), 74.

inherited condition prevented his blood from clotting properly. Minor injuries, instead of resulting in bruises, often cause painful internal bleeding, putting the sufferer at constant risk of premature death. Alexandra's emotional distress was particularly agonizing since she knew that hemophilia ran in her family and that she had passed it on to her son. In this context, Rasputin brought her hope. He assured her that after a certain age, Aleksei would outgrow his disease. The challenge was to keep him safe in the meantime.

When Rasputin spent time with Aleksei, praying and chanting religious songs, Aleksei would feel better, his fevers subsiding. Grand Duchess Olga, Nicholas's younger sister and not an admirer of Rasputin, recalled that when Nicholas introduced her to Rasputin in 1907, she could tell that the children "were completely at ease with him." She also witnessed him relieving Aleksei's suffering from a swollen leg.[38] In 1912, when Aleksei suffered a particularly acute episode of internal bleeding, a high fever, and unbearably painful spasms, Rasputin was not in Saint Petersburg. He therefore cabled Alexandra: "God has perceived your tears and attends to your prayers . . . your son will live." To the doctors' surprise, Aleksei survived.[39] It is not difficult to guess Nicholas's and Alexandra's thoughts: God was with them, and Rasputin was God's messenger.

Attraction to Rasputin but also revulsion against him was doubtless heightened by the widespread public fascination with the supernatural and the demonic in the late nineteenth and early twentieth century, as evidenced in the music, literature, painting, and theater of the era, a period of extraordinary cultural efflorescence known as Russia's Silver Age.[40] By 1914, there were dozens of registered and unregistered occult associations in Saint Petersburg.[41] Across Europe and America, writers, musicians, and artists led people to view the world as a battlefield between good and evil and to ascribe supernatural qualities to both. No wonder many viewed Rasputin as either a holy man or the devil's tool.

Rasputin and the Great War

In summer 1914, the outbreak of World War I and Russia's participation dominated news coverage. As in the other belligerent countries, the Russian press, political establishment, and educated public initially rallied behind the war effort.[42] Crowds

---

38. Ian Vorres, *The Last Grand Duchess: Her Imperial Highness Grand Duchess Olga Alexandrovna* (New York: Scribner, 1965), 134–40.

39. Robert K. Massie, *Nicholas and Alexandra* (New York: Ballantine Books, 2000), 183–88.

40. John E. Bowlt, *Moscow & St. Petersburg 1900–1920: Art, Life, & Culture of the Russian Silver Age* (New York: Vendome Press, 2008).

41. Smith, *Rasputin*, 89–97.

42. Joshua Sanborn, *Imperial Apocalypse: The Great War and the Destruction of the Russian Empire* (New York: Oxford University Press, 2014).

spontaneously poured into Palace Square to greet Nicholas appearing with Alexandra on the balcony of the Winter Palace.[43]

On the eve of war, Rasputin was convalescing in Siberia, having been stabbed by a female follower of Illiodor. Alexandra sent Rasputin a series of increasingly desperate telegrams. In one of his responses, according to Vyrubova, Rasputin wrote: "Let Papa not plan for war, for war will mean the end of Russia and yourselves, and you will lose to the last man."[44] The authenticity of this wording cannot be confirmed, but a letter that Rasputin wrote to the royal family during these days survived. In it he warned that

> a menacing cloud is over Russia, lots of sorrow and grief, it's dark and there's not a ray of hope. A sea of tears, immeasurable, and as to blood? What can I say? There are no words, indescribable horror. I know they all want war from you, evidently not realizing this means ruin. . . . don't allow the madmen to triumph and destroy themselves and the people.[45]

Rasputin's words were prophetic. The war unleashed "a sea of blood," with Russia losing more lives than Germany and more than Britain and France combined. It also led to the collapse of the monarchy and the physical destruction of the royal family.

Nicholas vacillated but went against Rasputin's advice.

Rumors of Rasputin's reputed influence impelled favor-seekers to besiege him with requests. The complexity and inefficiency of Russian imperial bureaucracy had always driven petitioners to appeal to the monarch or people close to him. A belief that justice rested not with laws or institutions but with the benevolent autocratic ruler has been an intrinsic feature of Russian political culture, even to the present day.[46] Russia's rulers and those in their entourage received so many requests that, in 1767, Catherine II prohibited direct petitions from peasants to the monarch, while Nicholas I delegated the task of "wiping away people's tears" to his head of secret police in 1826.

The telephone in Rasputin's central Saint Petersburg apartment on Gorokhovaia Street rang incessantly. Gifts from petitioners made him a wealthy man. Perhaps because of his peasant background, Rasputin was usually willing to help. He typically responded with personal notes, which the petitioners could take to government officials. Requests for promotions were common, as were pleas for clemency, exemption from military service, and so on. Rasputin's notes were brief, cryptic, and sometimes barely legible. Some officials complied with Rasputin's notes, while others claimed to

---

43. A. S. Lukomskii, *Vospominaniia generala A. S. Lukomskogo*, 2 vols. (Berlin: Otto Kirchner, 1922), 1:53.

44. Bernard Pares, *The Fall of the Russian Monarchy* (New York: Vintage Books, 1961), 188.

45. Smith, *Rasputin*, 362–63.

46. The annual phone-in "Direct Lines with President Putin" on state TV always attracts a litany of complaints about failing infrastructure, local corruption, and economic inequality.

discard them. Regardless, it seems likely that satisfied petitioners spread word of their success and thus amplified the rumors of Rasputin's power.

Despite the increased tempo of Rasputin's unofficial involvement in official matters, his status declined in the war's first year. Nicholas disapproved of the flow of notes from Rasputin circulating through the bureaucracy. The dire challenges of the war made Nicholas more reliant on his first cousin once removed, Grand Duke Nikolai Nikolaevich, whom he appointed commander-in-chief of the Army. The husband of one of the Montenegrin princesses, he was Rasputin's bitter enemy. According to a widely circulated story, when Rasputin requested permission to visit the troops to bless them, the grand duke cabled back: "Come. Will hang you."[47]

But the war went badly for Russia. Already in August 1914, two Russian armies were nearly destroyed in Germany's region of East Prussia. Occasional Russian successes against Austria-Hungary were nullified by speedy German intervention. Unlike the stalemate on the Western Front, Russia suffered a gradual retreat under incessant German pressure. Just as defeat in the Russo-Japanese War helped trigger the Revolution of 1905, Russian losses in 1914–1916 portended similar dangers.

Why did Russia fare so badly? Who was to blame? Such questions were on many people's minds. Fury toward supposed culprits resulted in a major outbreak of violence in Moscow in May 1915. The primary targets of this violence were "Germans," real and imagined.[48] Shouts were heard blaming Rasputin, as well as Alexandra because of her German origin and relatives. Crowds approached the Mary and Martha Convent and Hospital, which Alexandra's sister, Grand Duchess Elizabeth, had founded in 1909, denouncing the tsarina and her sister as German spies.[49] (Grand Duchess Elizabeth and other Romanov family members were murdered by the Bolsheviks in July 1918; see Chapter 4.)

Around the same time, Vladimir Dzhunkovskii, the chief of the Gendarme Corps and deputy minister of Internal Affairs, made yet another attempt to neutralize Rasputin. On the night of March 26–27, Rasputin visited Yar, a Moscow restaurant. Rumors quickly circulated about alleged debauchery and lewd behavior.[50] The relevant Moscow security police report mentioned the restaurant visit but without details, noting only that earlier in the evening, Rasputin had become drunk, took part in a disturbance, and had attempted to seduce an underage girl.[51] Dzhunkovskii then

---

47. Georgii Shavelskii, *Vospominaniia poslednego protopresvitera russkoi armii i flota*, 2 vols. (Moscow: Krutitskoe Patriarshee Podvorie, 1996), 1:128.

48. Eric Lohr, *Nationalizing the Russian Empire: The Campaign against Enemy Aliens during World War I* (Cambridge, MA: Harvard University Press, 2003), chap. 2.

49. Greg King, *The Man Who Killed Rasputin: Prince Youssoupov and the Murder That Helped Bring Down the Russian Empire* (Secaucus, NJ: Carol Pub. Group, 1995), 119.

50. Maurice Paléologue, *An Ambassador's Memoirs*, trans. F. A. Holt, 2 vols. (New York: George H. Doran Company, 1923), 1:331–33.

51. Smith, *Rasputin*, 373–75.

requested that the chief of the Moscow security police, Aleksandr Martynov, produce a more thorough report; this report included details about lewd behavior at the restaurant. Smith speculates that Martynov understood Dzhunkovskii to be demanding a hatchet job.[52] Although Martynov admitted in his memoir that he had "an organic aversion to people like Rasputin,"[53] it is hard to believe that he would risk his career by providing false information that could be refuted by eyewitnesses, especially when the target was a powerful figure in court circles.

Dzhunkovskii reported the incident directly to Nicholas in June 1915.[54] Like many senior officials, Dzhunkovskii profoundly disliked Rasputin. But he was a military officer with an impeccable service record and apparently little appetite for political intrigue, something Nicholas must have appreciated. Nicholas seemed willing to put more distance between the imperial family and Rasputin for the war effort. Dzhunkovskii appeared to have achieved the impossible—to convince Nicholas that Rasputin's words and actions were doing more harm than good.

And yet, ultimately, Dzhunkovskii failed. He failed not because of Rasputin's power but because of someone far more powerful—Alexandra. In the first months of the war, Nicholas seemed to have distanced himself from the tsarina and Rasputin. By summer 1915, Alexandra sincerely thought that enemies surrounding her husband threatened the monarchy. She believed she had to act fast. Dzhunkovskii was an enemy to Alexandra because of his attempt to remove the holy man, but he was also, she believed, part of a greater conspiracy led by Grand Duke Nikolai Nikolaevich and his entourage: to depose Nicholas and become the emperor of Russia himself. No evidence of such a conspiracy exists, only rumors, although it seems that Nikolai Nikolaevich, while at General Headquarters, had used some unceremonious language not only about Rasputin but also about Alexandra. "She is leading us all to ruin," he apparently said. Those around him engaged in loose talk as well.[55]

Dzhunkovskii was fired in August. So was Grand Duke Nikolai Nikolaevich. To replace him, at the urging of Alexandra and with the blessing of Rasputin, Nicholas made one of the most fateful decisions of his reign: to become commander-in-chief of the Russian army, in order to lend his prestige to the war effort.[56]

---

52. Smith, *Rasputin*, 375–77.

53. Aleksandr P. Martynov, *Moia sluzhba v Otdel'nom korpuse zhandarmov: Vospominaniia*, ed. Richard Wraga (Stanford, CA: Stanford University Press, 1973), 284.

54. Pavel Schegolev, ed., *Padenie tsarskogo rezhima: Stenograficheskie otchety doprosov i pokazanii, dannykh v 1917 g. v Chrezvychainoi Sledstvennoi Komissii Vremennogo Pravitel'stva*, 7 vols. (Leningrad: Gosudarstvennoe izdatel'stvo, 1924–1927), 5:101–4.

55. Shavelskii, *Vospominaniia*, 2:316–17. See also Boris Kolonitskii, "Voin 'starogo vremeni': Obrazy velikogo kniazia Nikolaia Nikolaevicha v gody pervoi mirovoi voiny," *Studia Russica Helsingiensia et Tartuensia* 10, pt. 2 (2006): 297–326.

56. Richard G. Robbins Jr., *Overtaken by the Night: One Russian's Journey through Peace, War, Revolution, & Terror* (Pittsburgh, PA: University of Pittsburgh Press, 2017), 317–18.

With Nicholas attending to his duties as commander-in-chief, someone had to oversee domestic politics and policy. Alexandra eagerly took on this role, frequently turning to Rasputin for advice. Thus, a vicious circle was born: the more Alexandra sought Rasputin's opinion on candidates for top government positions, the more rumors and anger about his nefarious influence and power swelled, which only caused the imperial couple to close ranks and embrace Rasputin even more. At the heart of Rasputin's growing influence in these years was Alexandra's desire to protect him (and, by extension, the dynasty and Russia) and her bitter realization that she had few other people to rely on.

Yet even in the last year of Rasputin's life, when his influence at the court peaked, he was far from becoming the ruler of the Russian Empire. His main concern was not to rule Russia, but to protect his privileged standing with the imperial family. Over the years, Rasputin successfully cultivated ties with and secured promotions for hierarchs of the Russian Orthodox Church. Finding reliable friends in government circles was much harder. Without a good knowledge of the imperial bureaucracy, Rasputin turned to acquaintances who put him in touch with unscrupulous figures seeking power and career advancement. Showing a friendly attitude to Rasputin became a litmus test of the seeker's loyalty in Alexandra's eyes. Her letters to Nicholas, written in late 1915 and 1916, contain frequent references to the guidance of "Our Friend."[57] They leave the impression not of someone taking dictation from "a holy man" but rather of a forceful and energetic person relying on Rasputin to validate her own opinions and preferences.

Although several key ministerial positions were either proposed or endorsed by Rasputin in 1915–1916, he seems to have been out of his depth. In her letters to Nicholas, Alexandra lavished praise on Aleksei Khvostov, who became minister of interior with Rasputin's blessing in September 1915. Yet he schemed to assassinate Rasputin, whom he apparently considered no longer useful. The press got wind of the plot, which led to Khvostov's dismissal the following March.[58]

In late 1915 and early 1916, Rasputin played a key role in bringing about the appointment of an aged Boris Shtiurmer as a replacement for an even more aged Ivan Goremykin. Shtiurmer tried his best to present himself as Rasputin's faithful admirer, but he was deeply ineffective and unpopular. Nicholas fired him in November 1916, to Alexandra's and Rasputin's dismay.[59]

Rasputin's influence in the appointment of Aleksandr Protopopov, a former Octobrist Duma deputy and wealthy industrialist and landowner, as minister of interior is

---

57. Fuhrmann, *Wartime Correspondence*, 574, 577.

58. Sean McMeekin, *The Russian Revolution: A New History* (New York: Basic Books, 2017), 3.

59. Joseph T. Fuhrmann, *Rasputin: The Untold Story* (Hoboken, NJ: John Wiley and Sons, 2013), 162–63, 181.

well documented.[60] On September 7, Alexandra wrote to Nicholas at General Head-quarters: "Grigorii begs you earnestly to name Protopopov." Two days later, Nicholas wrote back to her that Protopopov was a good man but added: "I must think over that question as it takes me quite unexpectedly." Rasputin's ideas "about men," he added, "are sometimes queer, as you know." Although he worried that administration officials were being replaced too often, which he considered "not good for the interior of the country," the appointment went through.[61] Nicholas's response to Alexandra's request shows that he was not a blind follower of Rasputin's advice. Protopopov's eventual appointment is a testament to Alexandra's unswerving persistence, not Rasputin's cunning. On September 14, Alexandra gushed, "our Friend says you have done a very wise act in naming him."[62] Yet Protopopov alienated his former Duma colleagues, who considered him a traitor to the constitutionalist cause, and irked Nicholas with his inability to stay focused because of a neurological ailment. Nicholas decided to dismiss him, going so far as to ask Alexandra "not to get our Friend involved in this." Aleksandra convinced Nicholas to change his mind, but Protopopov proved a complete failure during the February Revolution.[63]

Although Rasputin typically lacked the capacity to navigate high politics, his understanding of ordinary people's experiences and needs was often sound. He feared Russia's entry into the Great War because of its inevitable impact on the mass of peasant soldiers. He also objected to the second round of military conscription in 1915 and fretted about disorganization in the transportation and food supply systems and the rising toll of the Brusilov Offensive, a massive yet ultimately unsuccessful operation against Austria-Hungary in summer 1916.[64] Rasputin also displayed little prejudice toward the persecuted ethnic minorities of the Russian Empire, helping some Jewish residents avoid deportation from Moscow for breaking residency requirements and even declaring his support for the abolition of such anti-Jewish restrictions altogether.[65]

Everyone's Enemy

Liberal critics of the monarchy charged that Rasputin was "a dark force" who ruled Russia with or without Nicholas and Alexandra's acquiescence. On November 1, 1916, from the rostrum of the Duma, the Constitutional Democratic Party leader, Pavel Miliukov, blamed military reversals, weak senior officials, and alleged German

60. Jonathan W. Daly, *The Watchful State: Security Police and Opposition in Russia, 1906–1917* (DeKalb, IL: Northern Illinois University Press. 2004), 189–92.

61. Fuhrmann, *Wartime Correspondence*, 574, 577.

62. Fuhrmann, *Wartime Correspondence*, 582.

63. Daly, *Watchful State*, 198–204.

64. Fuhrmann, *Wartime Correspondence*, 135, 272–73, 612.

65. Smith, *Rasputin*, 535–38.

influence on Nicholas's government. Miliukov punctuated his litany of disasters with the refrain: "Is it stupidity or treason?" and concluded that all of Russia's recent failures could not result from mere stupidity.[66] Two years after the revolution, Duma chairman Mikhail Rodzianko asserted that there had been an "inter-connection of the German Staff and Rasputin: there can be no doubt about it."[67] Monarchists believed that Nicholas's ultimate crime was undermining the prestige of the dynasty. Rumors about Rasputin's influence at the imperial court contributed to such negative opinions. Anxious members of the extended imperial family grew desperate.

On the day of Miliukov's "Stupidity or Treason" speech, Grand Duke Nicholai Mikhailovich, a well-regarded left-leaning historian, visited the tsar at General Headquarters. He warned that "dark forces" influenced both Alexandra and the tsar. In a letter he delivered to Nicholas, he wrote: "You find yourself on the eve of an era of new disturbances, and I will say even more: on the eve of an era of murder." In order to avoid this fate, Nicholas had to free himself from those "forces." Alexandra was deeply offended and outraged when she read the letter.[68] Other close family members also unsuccessfully sought to drive a wedge between Rasputin and the royal family.

Finally, Vladimir Purishkevich, an ultraconservative monarchist, attacked Rasputin from the rostrum of the Duma on November 19, declaring that he was governing Russia along with other "dark forces" (a hint at the political role of Alexandra). Purishkevich urged the cabinet ministers to rush to the tsar and warn him of Rasputin's abominable role. His main message was clear: confronting Rasputin was a matter of patriotic duty and a call to action—for himself and like-minded conservatives.

On the morning of December 17, Minister of Interior Protopopov received alarming news from the city governor of Petrograd. That night, having heard shots near the palace of Prince Felix Yusupov, a policeman rushed to the scene. Purishkevich told him that Rasputin had been killed but urged him to keep quiet for the sake of the motherland. The police launched an immediate investigation. Rasputin's body was found two days later, on the surface of the frozen Neva River, with several bullet wounds and signs of battery.

These basic details of the murder we learn from the police record.[69] Other facts can be culled from accounts written by the two assassins. Yusupov produced a dramatic tale: together with accomplices, the prince invited Rasputin to his palace, where, on the lower level, he fed him wine and pastry supposedly laced with poison. It had no effect. Then, Yusupov, telling Rasputin to pray before an ornate, sixteenth-century Italian crucifix, shot him. He "gave a wild scream and crumpled up" on the floor. One accomplice, Dr. Lazovert, came downstairs and pronounced Rasputin dead. After

---

66. Melissa Kirschke Stockdale, *Paul Miliukov and the Quest for a Liberal Russia, 1880–1918* (Ithaca, NY: Cornell University Press, 1996), 233–36.

67. George Katkov, *Russia 1917: The February Revolution* (New York: Harper & Row, 1967), 425.

68. Smith, *Rasputin*, 566.

69. "Ubiistvo Rasputina," *Byloe*, no. 1(23) (July 1917): 64–83.

some time, however, "with a sudden violent effort, Rasputin leapt to his feet, foaming at the mouth." Yusupov rushed upstairs to the others. Rasputin began crawling up the stairs "on hands and knees, gasping and roaring like a wounded animal." He then fled outside. Purishkevich rushed after him, firing four shots at him in the palace courtyard. Rasputin collapsed in the snow. Police officers came to the door and were sent away with a confession of murder and swearing to silence. Then two other participants in the crime, Grand Duke Dmitrii, Nicholas's cousin, and Lieutenant Sergei Sukhotin, an officer in the elite Preobrazhensky Guards Regiment, joined Dr. Lazovert and Purishkevich in disposing of the body. They "wrapped the corpse in a piece of heavy linen" and drove to the outskirts of the city, where they flung it into the Neva River.[70] Purishkevich's briefer account, written soon after the events, corroborates this basic story.[71]

The coroner found no evidence of poisoning, while according to his daughter Maria, Rasputin never ate sweets.[72] It is unclear whether the bullets that killed Rasputin were fired from a distance or at close range.

In virtually the entirety of public opinion, the assassins were hailed as patriots, heroes, and celebrities.[73] Nicholas, by contrast, was appalled. The police investigation was halted, and the culprits banished from the capital: Purishkevich and Grand Duke Dmitrii were sent to the battlefront; Prince Yusupov was to be confined to one of his numerous estates. Members of the extended royal family urged Nicholas to lighten Grand Duke Dmitrii's punishment. The tsar's response was firm: "I am ashamed before Russia, that the hands of my relations should be smeared with the blood of this peasant."[74] These words highlighted the rift between the imperial couple and both Russian society and members of the extended royal family, many of whom approved of the deed, even if most were not personally complicit.

In policy and administration, nothing changed, suggesting that Rasputin's influence had been grossly exaggerated.[75]

The Myths Live On

Even before his death, Rasputin's celebrity status had reached far beyond Russia. In 1914, after he suffered a knife attack in Pokrovskoe, the British newspaper *Standard*

---

70. Youssoupoff, *Lost Splendor*, 244–53.

71. V. M. Purishkevich and Michael E. Shaw, *The Murder of Rasputin* (Ann Arbor, MI: Ardis, 1985).

72. Nina Martyris, "Fact or Fiction? Even When It Comes to Food, It's Hard to Tell with Rasputin," The Salt, NPR, January 31, 2017, https://www.npr.org/sections/thesalt/2017/01/31/510802220/fact-or-fiction-even-when-it-comes-to-food-its-hard-to-tell-with-rasputin.

73. Smith, *Rasputin*, 635–37.

74. Pipes, *Russian Revolution*, 267.

75. Dominic Lieven, *Towards the Flame: Empire, War and the End of Tsarist Russia* (London: Allen Lane, 2015), 347.

asserted that Rasputin's power was "above the power of the Czar's Ministers who were over-ruled by him despite the protests by the Duma." The article did not elaborate on Rasputin's alleged sexual escapades, noting only that "his private life is said to have been very questionable."[76] The *New York Times* ran a front-page story in which Rasputin was referred to as a "notorious monk" and "the Richelieu[77] of Russia." "No question of importance," it stated, "is decided by the Czar or his Ministers without Rasputin's counsel."[78] Other Western newspapers sensationalized his role with head-lines like "Priest Who Might Have Averted War" and "Is Russia's Real Ruler Illiterate Siberian Monk Said to Be Power Behind the Throne in Czar's Realm."[79]

No one contributed more to bringing Rasputin to worldwide attention than Ilio-dor. Having fled Russia in summer 1914, he settled in the United States and launched a negative publicity campaign against Rasputin, a man he claimed to have wielded "more influence than any other man in all Russia."[80] More explosive in wartime was Iliodor's claim that Rasputin was a German agent.

Rasputin's allegedly pro-German stance gained frenzied attention in the interna-tional press. The *New York Times* asserted that he was "known for his pro-German sympathies."[81] The *New York Times Magazine* wrote that "Rasputin was believed to be the chief agent in the 'underground' that leads from Petrograd to Berlin."[82] Other newspapers were even more unequivocal: "No one doubts the existence at Petrograd of an influential element which favors and is strenuously promoting the negotiation of a separate peace. It includes the court and the bureaucracy and it had a powerful agent in the monk Rasputin. . . ."[83] These reports gave an international dimension to a consensus view in Russia. The court, in the words of the Russian periodical *Russkaia volia* (The Russian Will), was "a nest of German spies," an assertion quoted in the *New York Times*.[84]

---

76. "Rasputin Stabbed," *Standard*, July 14, 1914, 3.

77. Cardinal Armand Jean du Plessis, Duke of Richelieu (1585–1642), was King Louis XIII's chief advisor from 1624 until his death.

78. "Favorite of Czar Stabbed by Woman: Rasputin, Peasant Monk-Mystic, Said to Be at the Point of Death," *New York Times*, July 14, 1914, 1, 3.

79. "Priest Who Might Have Averted War," *Washington Post*, August 6, 1914, 6; "Is Russia's Real Ruler Illiterate Siberian Monk Said to Be Power Behind the Throne in Czar's Realm?," *Washington Post*, August 9, 1914, 4.

80. "'Mad Monk' Repeats Suppressed Story," *New York Times*, December 27, 1916, 6. Iliodor was first referred to in the Western press as "a mad monk," a label later attached to Rasputin.

81. "Hint That Nobles Killed Rasputin Stirs Petrograd: Gossip Alleges a Plot Involving a Prince Allied to the Czar by Marriage," *New York Times*, January 3, 1917, 1, 4.

82. Mary Austin, "Germany's Mexican Intrigue—What it Means," *New York Times Magazine*, March 11, 1917, 2–3.

83. "What Is Going on in Russia?" *Philadelphia Inquirer*, March 15, 1917, 10.

84. "Ex-Czar Joins Wife as Captive at Palace," *New York Times*, March 23, 1917, 3.

The *Washington Post* and the *New York Herald* sent a joint special correspondent to Russia to collect information about Rasputin's murder. Herman Bernstein met with Iosif Gessen, the editor of the liberal newspaper *Rech'* (Speech), and even with an unnamed participant in the assassination plot. The latter told Bernstein that the fateful soirée at Prince Yusupov's palace involved two women and that Grand Duke Nikolai Mikhailovich was the actual mastermind behind the plot. Rich with factual detail about the assassination (some corroborated by other accounts, some not), Bernstein's report still boosted the Rasputin myth by stating that the tsar was a slavish puppet in the hands of Rasputin who worked with Alexandra to achieve a separate peace with Germany.[85]

After the fall of the monarchy, the Provisional Government established a commission to investigate the crimes of the old regime.[86] Not surprisingly, Rasputin was a major focus. The commission interrogated dozens of highly placed individuals, generating a unique body of witness testimony, but found no evidence of Rasputin's ties to Germany or of a royal effort to conclude a separate peace.[87] Since the leaders of the Provisional Government would have delighted in finding such evidence, one should consider the pro-German allegations all but disproven.

The figure of Rasputin quickly made the transition to the world of popular culture. A silent film starring Iliodor as himself and depicting Rasputin as demonic and sexually licentious came out in 1917, though apparently, all copies of the movie are lost. In a 1932 MGM production, *Rasputin and the Empress*, Rasputin rapes a character named Princess Natasha, who resembles Princess Irina, Prince Yusupov's wife. Princess Irina successfully sued the movie studio, which settled for an apparently astronomical sum (allegedly $900,000, or some $15.5 million in 2020 dollars) and agreed to withdraw the film from circulation and purge the questionable scene. (The lawsuit resulted in the film-industry disclaimer: "The characters and events presented in this film are fictitious. Any resemblance to persons and events living or dead is purely coincidental."[88]) Prince Yusupov brought an unsuccessful suit against the producers of the 1932 German film *Rasputin, der Dämon der Frauen* (Rasputin, Demon with Women), again requesting the removal of a compromising sequence.[89] Yusupov probably did not like the British horror film *Rasputin, the Mad Monk* (1966). The emphasis

85. Herman Bernstein, "Rasputin Killed by Grand Dukes Who Saw Their Own Influences over Czar Destroyed," *Washington Post*, October 16, 1917, 2.

86. Daly, *Watchful State*, 209–12.

87. Boris Kolonitskii, "The Decentralization of the Monarchy: Rumors and Political Pornography during World War I," in *Language and Revolution: Making Modern Political Identities*, ed. Igal Halfin (London: Frank Cass, 2002), 38–68 (here: 49–51).

88. John T. Aquino, *Truth and Lives on Film: The Legal Problems of Depicting Real Persons and Events in a Fictional Medium* (Jefferson, NC: McFarland & Co., 2005), 14–19, 25.

89. John T. Soister, *Conrad Veidt on Screen: A Comprehensive Illustrated Filmography* (Jefferson, NC: McFarland & Co., 2002), 233–36.

in both films is on Rasputin's demonic charisma and willpower.[90] The following year, he got the film he wanted: a Franco-Italian production, *J'ai tué Raspoutine* (I Killed Rasputin), which is based on Yusupov's book, *Lost Splendor.*[91]

Rasputin's fame and myth spread across genres. In 1978, the Euro-Caribbean disco group Boney M. brought out a pop song, "Rasputin," which made it to the top of the pop charts in several European countries. The lyrics reiterated several common misconceptions and exaggerations about Rasputin ("hunger for power," "love machine," "lover of the Russian queen," "They put some poison into his wine. He drank it all and he said, 'I feel fine.'"). The chorus line, "Ra Ra Rasputin," even became the name of a band three decades later.[92] The character of Rasputin was apparently "the porn industry's golden boy throughout the 20th century," featured in such movies as the "hilarious" 1984 *Rasputin—Orgien am Zarenhof* (Rasputin: Orgies in the Tsar's Court).[93] *Rasputin*, an opera in two acts, premiered in 1988 at the New York State Theater (now the David H. Koch Theater) in New York City. The Siberian peasant, according to a theater critic, "through a combination of sexual prowess, power lust, and fundamentalist fervor, virtually assumes control over an empire in its death throes."[94] A rock opera, *Rasputin: Miracles Lie in the Eye of the Beholder* (1999), featuring the prominent British actor John Hurt, stresses the ambiguities of Rasputin's persona—man of God or manipulator?[95] In 2003, the Finnish composer Einojuhani Rautavaara brought out an opera in three acts, entitled *Rasputin*, at the Finnish National Opera.[96] Even Ozzy Osbourne, a founding heavy-metal rocker, was working on a rock opera about Rasputin in 2005. "Rasputin," he said, "was like the rock god of his time, the original goth guy."[97]

On the centennial of Rasputin's assassination, in 2016, *Time* magazine summarized and debunked fallacies about Rasputin's life and death, writing that "there is no evidence to suggest Rasputin was a sex-crazed maniac who had a secret affair with Russia's queen."[98]

---

90. David Huckvale, *Movie Magick: The Occult in Film* (Jefferson, NC: McFarland & Co., 2018), 86.

91. Peter Cowie, ed., *World Filmography, 1967* (London: Tantivy Press, 1967), 127.

92. Mark Jenkins, "Ra Ra Rasputin's 'Ra Ra Rasputin,'" *Washington Post*, December 10, 2010, https://www.washingtonpost.com/wp-dyn/content/article/2010/12/08/AR2010120806270.html.

93. Max Fram, *The Motherland of Elephants* (Morrisville, NC: LuLu Press, 2015), 225.

94. Donal Henahan, "Mad Monk Redux in City Opera's New 'Rasputin,'" *New York Times*, September 19, 1988, C17.

95. Thomas Bergmann, *Rasputin: Dämon, Heiler oder Magier?* (Wasungen, Germany: Twilight-Line Medien, 2010), 41.

96. Guy Rickards, "Einojuhani Rautavaara Obituary," *Guardian*, July 28, 2016, https://www.theguardian.com/music/2016/jul/28/einojuhani-rautavaara-obituary.

97. Marc Spitz, "Q & A: Ozzy Osborne," *Spin*, March 2005, 18.

98. Albinko Hasic, "5 Myths and Truths about Rasputin," *Time*, December 29, 2016, https://time.com/4606775/5-myths-rasputin/.

But the myth of Rasputin as a holy man is not dead even today, at least in Russia. In 2016, a group of Russian writers, historians, and members of the clergy formed "A People's Commission to Publicly Rehabilitate Grigorii Rasputin and Gather Evidence of His Miracles."[99]

The commission's interest in Rasputin's miracles seems to be driven by a desire to achieve Rasputin's canonization as a saint. These attempts date back to the 1990s when they were rejected by the Russian Orthodox Church, which reiterated its position in 2004: neither Ivan the Terrible nor Grigorii Rasputin could be canonized.[100]

Nevertheless, reports of myrrh streaming from icons of Rasputin and their healing powers continue to emerge. So do testimonies of Rasputin's appearances in dreams, responses to prayer, and ability to cause willows to briefly bloom near his burial place on the anniversary of his assassination.[101] Rasputin's closeness to the imperial family, alleged miracles, and violent "martyr-like" death are likely to continue to inspire sentiments of nostalgia and veneration.

In fact, it does not seem that the Rasputin "magic" will dissipate anytime soon. The journalist Amos Barshad recently appropriated the very name "Rasputin" to signify manipulators seeking to exercise power behind the scenes.[102]

Getting Real about Rasputin

Rasputin's role in the circumstances that brought down the Russian Empire was unique but not essential. Tensions between government and society were strong. The war strained Russia's institutions dramatically. Nicholas II was ill-equipped to manage Russia's social, geopolitical, and economic challenges and chronically unable to address popular discontent. But turning to supernatural guidance is as old as political power itself. Court astrologers were a regular feature of royal governance as late as the Scientific Revolution era when astronomers like Galileo filled that role. Examples can be found even in the contemporary world.

---

99. "Sozdana Narodnaia Komissiia po obshchestvennoi reabilitatsii Grigoriia Rasputina i sboru svidetel'stv o ego chudesakh," Russkii monarchist, March 3, 2017, http://www.ruskmir.ru/2017/03/sozdana-narodnaya-komissiya-po-obshhestvennoj-reabilitacii-grigoriya-rasputina-i-sboru-svidetelstv-o-ego-chudesax/.

100. "Prilozhenie # 2 k dokladu mitropolita Krutitskogo i Kolomenskogo Iuvenaliia, predsedatelia Sinodal'noi komissii po kanonizatsii sviatykh," Russkaia Pravoslavnaia Tserkov', June 7, 2008, http://www.patriarchia.ru/db/text/420877.

101. Igor Evsin, "O mirotochenii izobrazhenii Grigoriia Rasputina," Zyorna, December 10, 2014, https://zyorna.ru/news/publications/igor-evsin-o-mirotochenij-izobrazhenij-grigorija-rasputina-2160.html.

102. Amos Barshad, *No One Man Should Have All That Power: How Rasputins Manipulate the World* (New York: Abrams Press, 2019).

After President Ronald Reagan survived an assassination attempt in 1981, his wife Nancy reportedly contacted her astrologist seeking advice. While both Ronald and Nancy Reagan denied astrology played any role in presidential decision-making, the timing of some of Reagan's speeches, press conferences, and meetings, including summit meetings with the Soviet leader Mikhail Gorbachev and the signing of the Intermediate-Range Nuclear Forces (INF) Treaty in 1988, allegedly reflected astrological advice.[103]

Recent media reports suggest a growing interest among Russia's political and business elites in seeking spiritual guidance in deciding questions of personal and professional life. Clerical elder Iliia (Nozdrin), a confessor of the Patriarch of the Russian Orthodox Church, seems to be a particularly popular figure, perhaps because of his religious wisdom, perhaps because of his personal acquaintance with President Putin.[104]

In summary, Rasputin was not a monk or priest and probably not a *Khlyst*, Alexandra's lover, a German agent, or the evil all-powerful ruler of the Russian Empire. Nicholas and Alexandra continued to rule the Russian Empire, not Rasputin. By the end of 1916, the empire's greatest problem was not that it was governed by an evil manipulator but that, as a result of the relentless hardships of world war, temporary food and fuel shortages, and poor decisions by Nicholas, it was becoming increasingly ungovernable.

---

103. Barrett Seaman, "Good Heavens! An Astrologer Dictating the President's Schedule?" *Time*, May 16, 1988, 24.

104. Mikhail Rubin, et al. "Kremlevskii starets: Rasskaz o tom, kak rossiiskaia vlast' uvleklas' mistitsizmom," *Proekt*, May 29, 2019, https://www.proekt.media/narrative/starets-iliy-nozdrin/.

2. THE MYTH OF TREASONOUS CONSPIRACY CAUSING THE RUSSIAN MONARCHY'S FALL

All around there is treason, and cowardice, and deceit.[1]

—*Tsar Nicholas II*

This is not a mutiny, comrade admiral, but a revolution![2]

—*Anonymous sailor to Admiral Robert Viren*

Figure 2.1: Nicholas II under house arrest in Tsarskoe Selo, March–August 1917.

On February 22, 1917, Tsar Nicholas departed to resume his duties as commander-in-chief of the army at General Headquarters in Mogilev (today a city in Belarus, fifty miles from the Russian border).[3] Increasingly hated and isolated (Rasputin was dead), Alexandra lived outside Petrograd in Tsarskoe Selo (Tsar's Village). Nicholas had to travel to Tsarskoe Selo to be with her and their children.

The war took an emotional toll on Nicholas. Former prime minister Vladimir Kokovtsov, who visited him in Tsarskoe Selo in January, found him struggling to recall simple details, his face worn and wrinkled. Nicholas insisted that he was merely tired, though Kokovtsov believed Nicholas on the verge of a serious illness.[4]

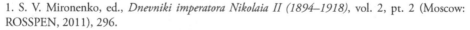

1. S. V. Mironenko, ed., *Dnevniki imperatora Nikolaia II (1894–1918)*, vol. 2, pt. 2 (Moscow: ROSSPEN, 2011), 296.

2. Evan Mawdsley, *The Russian Revolution and the Baltic Fleet* (New York: Barnes and Noble Books, 1978), 13.

3. Mogilev was roughly three hundred miles east southeast of Moscow and roughly five hundred miles south of Petrograd.

4. Vladimir Kokovtsov, *Iz moego proshlago: Vospominaniia 1903–1919 gg.*, 2 vols. (Paris: Izd. zhurnala Illustrirovannaia Rossiia, 1933), 2:403.

In his correspondence with Alexandra, Nicholas often mentioned how much he missed her and their children.[5] Yet military headquarters offered respite from the charged atmosphere in Petrograd, where some relatives pressured him to distance himself from Alexandra and to implement governmental changes advocated by the Duma. Sensing the tsar's growing isolation, the British ambassador Sir George Buchanan broke with diplomatic protocol and, on January 12 (N.S.), urged him to appoint a head of government enjoying the trust of the Duma. "Break down the barrier that separates you from your people," he urged, "and regain their confidence." Nicholas shot back: "Do you mean that I am to regain the confidence of my people or that they are to regain my confidence?"[6]

Nicholas was hopelessly out of touch. He had no idea that mass demonstrations commenced on February 23 and swelled to several hundred thousand striking workers, mutinying military personnel, and other disgruntled inhabitants of Petrograd (Map 2.1). In his diary, he blamed deceit and betrayal.[7] Alexandra blamed an international conspiracy.[8] This myth became widespread among Russian monarchists and antisemites in Russia and abroad.

Alexandra as the "Eyes and Ears of the Tsar"

Alexandra continued to encourage Nicholas to reject concessions to public demands. On February 22, she wrote that the Russian people "must learn to fear you." She went on: "Love is not enough. A child that adores his father must still have fear to anger, displease, or disobey him." The Russian people, she added, needed decisive treatment, "especially now."[9]

That very day mass unrest was brewing. On January 9, 1917, one hundred thousand Petrograd workers had gathered to commemorate the anniversary of Bloody Sunday—when troops in 1905 had fired on peaceful demonstrators, killing some two hundred and triggering the first Russian Revolution.[10] Arrests of radical activists on January 27 had prevented a demonstration planned for February 14, though ninety thousand workers went on strike and processed through Petrograd. From February 20, rumors spread of impending bread rationing. Lack of fuel prompted factory

5. Joseph T. Fuhrmann, ed., *The Complete Wartime Correspondence of Tsar Nicholas II and the Empress Alexandra, April 1914–March 1917* (Westport, CT: Greenwood Press, 1999), 688–93.

6. George Buchanan, *My Mission to Russia and Other Diplomatic Memories* (London: Cassel and Company, 1923), 45–6.

7. Mironenko, *Dnevniki*, 296.

8. Fuhrmann, *Wartime Correspondence*, 702.

9. Fuhrmann, *Wartime Correspondence*, 687.

10. David Mandel, *The Petrograd Workers in the Russian Revolution, February 1917–June 1918* (Leiden: Brill, 2018), 73.

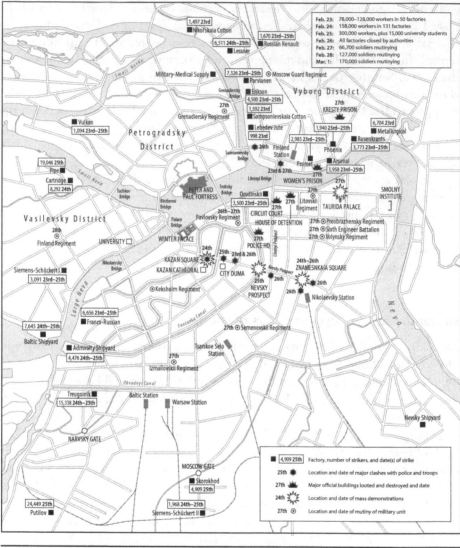

Map 2.1: Petrograd, February 1917

layoffs the following day. On February 22, tens of thousands of workers laid down their tools.[11] On February 23, International Women's Day, the number of protesters swelled dramatically (Map 2.1). Thousands of women went on strike and shouted: "Down with the war! Down with high prices!"[12] Students, workers, and other city

---

11. Jonathan W. Daly, *The Watchful State: Security Police and Opposition in Russia, 1906–1917* (DeKalb, IL: Northern Illinois University Press. 2004), 197–201.

12. Jonathan Daly and Leonid Trofimov, eds., *Russia in War and Revolution, 1914–1922: A Documentary History* (Indianapolis: Hackett Publishing Company, 2009), 36.

residents filled the streets in numbers that took revolutionary party activists—and government officials—by surprise.

Nicholas seemed all but oblivious. His diary entries were, as always, brief and unemotional:

> February 23, Thursday.
>
> Woke up in Smolensk[13] at 9:30 a.m. It was cold, clear, and windy. Devoted all free time to reading a Fr[ench] book on Julius Caesar's conquest of Gallia. Arrived in Mogilev at 3 p.m. Was met by General Alekseev[14] and the general staff. Spent one hour with him. The house seemed empty without Aleksei. Had lunch with all the foreigners and our people. Did writing in the evening and took tea with everyone.[15]

On February 24, Alexandra wrote to Nicholas about disorders in Petrograd:

> Yesterday there were rows [i.e., brawls] on the V. Ostrov [Vasil'evsky Island] & Nevsky [Prospect] because the poor people stormed the bread shops—they smashed Filipov['s bakery] completely & the Cossacks were called out against them.

She added that disorders were continuing. At the time, she was anxiously tending to her children, who were suffering from the measles—in those days, a serious illness.[16] The following day, Nicholas replied without mentioning the disorders. His diary entry for that day was also unremarkable.[17]

On February 25, most of Petrograd's factories closed. Up to three hundred thousand workers filled the streets, along with thousands of students and others, most peaceful, though attacks against police and other government officials multiplied. Crowds set fire to police stations.

Alexandra grew more worried. She blamed the increasing disorders on hooligans: "Young boys & girls running about and screaming that they have no bread, . . . if it were very cold they wld. [*sic*] probably stay in doors [*sic*]." (Frigid temperatures had given way to warmer weather: 41–43°F.) Sharing the view of a military officer, she suggested that one reliable cavalry regiment could have easily restored order.[18]

---

13. About 130 miles northeast from Mogilev.

14. Mikhail Alekseev (1857–1918) was Nicholas II's chief of staff at military headquarters.

15. Mironenko, *Dnevniki*, 294.

16. Fuhrmann, *Wartime Correspondence*, 690–91.

17. Mironenko, *Dnevniki*, 295.

18. Fuhrmann, *Wartime Correspondence*, 692–93.

Nicholas Opts for Repression

Nicholas wrote on February 26: "I hope Khabalov[19] knows how to stop these street rows quickly. Protopopov[20] ought to give him clear & categorical instructions." He also hoped that Nikolai Golitsyn, the third prime minister in a year, would "not lose his head."[21] Yet his diary entry for that day was serene: he attended church, received visitors, took a walk, and played dominoes.[22]

Nicholas believed his troops could master the situation. After all, military units back from the Russo-Japanese War in 1905 had pacified the rebellious country.[23] Indeed, Khabalov cabled Alekseev at headquarters on February 26 that Petrograd was returning to calm.[24] War Minister Mikhail Beliaev reassured Nicholas that the disorders "would be suppressed."[25] Even the following day, while Khabalov warned Nicholas that mutiny was spreading among the troops, Beliaev reassured him that the government was maintaining "complete calm."[26]

Acting on Nicholas's orders, Khabalov mobilized troops from several guard regiments, including the Pavlovsky, the Volynsky, and Nicholas's old favorite, the Semenovsky. The troops shot at the largely unarmed crowds, killing 170–200 people on and around Nevsky Prospect—a slaughter comparable to Bloody Sunday. The troops involved in the shootings were elite soldiers training to become noncommissioned officers (NCOs). Their bullets delivered a simple message: protesters risked death.

Calm returned to the streets of Petrograd, but it was the calm before the storm. Some of the soldiers had shot into the air. Some of the demonstrators had regrouped and reappeared, throwing rocks and pieces of ice at their tormentors.[27]

The events of February 26 in Petrograd showed that many protesters were prepared to risk death, while the troops were not always willing to fire at them. Many soldiers in the capital were older reservists, unhappy about being called up for active duty, crowded into barracks intended for a fraction of their number, and viewing NCO-trainees as careerists. As a result, one eyewitness called them "kindling wood near a

---

19. Sergei Khabalov was commander of the Petrograd military district.

20. Aleksandr Protopopov was interior minister.

21. Fuhrmann, *Wartime Correspondence*, 695–96.

22. Mironenko, *Dnevniki*, 295.

23. Daly, *Watchful State*, 197.

24. A. A. Sergeev, ed., "Fevral'skaia revoliutsiia 1917 goda (Dokumenty stavki verkhovnogo glavnokomanduiushchego i shtaba glavnokomanduiushchego armiami severnogo fronta)," *Krasnyi arkhiv* 2(21) (1927): 3–78 (here: 5).

25. A. S. Lukomskii, *Vospominaniia Generala A. S. Lukomskogo*, 2 vols. (Berlin: Otto Kirchner, 1922), 124.

26. Tsuyoshi Hasegawa, *The February Revolution, Petrograd 1917* (Leiden: Brill, 2018), 463.

27. Hasegawa, *February Revolution*, 265.

powder keg."[28] Some soldiers fraternized with civilians and many realized they might soon have to shoot at them.

About a hundred Pavlovsky Guards seized weapons and marched out to stop the carnage, clashing with mounted policemen. The commander of the Pavlovsky Regiment, Colonel E. N. Eksten, managed to calm the mutiny, but as soon as he left the barracks, angry crowds murdered him.[29] The fate of the revolution was now in the hands of the people of Petrograd and the ordinary soldiers of the Petrograd garrison.

On February 26, Mikhail Rodzianko, chairman of the Duma, cabled alarming news to Nicholas:

> Popular unrest that began in Petrograd is assuming a spontaneous character and threatening proportions. Its cause is a shortage of baked bread and poor flour supplies that are eliciting panic, but most especially the complete distrust of the authorities. . . . Such sentiments will undoubtedly drive events, which it will be possible to suppress temporarily at the cost of shedding blood of peaceful citizens but not indefinitely. . . . The war cannot be won under these conditions.[30]

Rodzianko urged Nicholas to share power with popular political figures. Perhaps he was deliberately seeking to frighten Nicholas. He often used emotional language at the expense of factual detail. Moreover, Petrograd was still under government control. But that control was about to evaporate, and Rodzianko gave the tsar something available to him from no one else: a situation analysis. He made several points: the government was helpless, popular unrest was extensive and growing, a violent clampdown could slow but not halt its spread, and the army itself was increasingly affected by the unrest, to the point that winning the war would become impossible.

Rodzianko was probably right. Had Nicholas quickly appointed a government of "public confidence," he might have diffused the rapidly escalating revolutionary crisis. Nicholas refused. "That fat man [*tolstiak*] Rodzianko," he apparently remarked to the minister of the imperial court, Count V. B. Frederiks, "has again written me all sorts of nonsense, to which I will not even reply."[31] What he did instead was to give orders to suspend the Duma until April.[32]

---

28. Richard Pipes, *The Russian Revolution* (New York: Alfred A. Knopf, 1990), 178.

29. Semion Lyandres, *The Fall of Tsarism: Untold Stories of the February 1917 Revolution* (Oxford: Oxford University Press, 2013), 98n2.

30. Mikhail Rodzianko to Nicholas, February 26, 1917, Arkhivy shkole, http://school.rusarchives.ru/revolyutsiya-1917-goda/telegramma-predsedatelya-gosudarstvennoi-dumy-rodzyanko.html.

31. Pavel Schegolev, ed. *Padenie tsarskogo rezhima: Stenograficheskie otchety doprosov i pokazanii, dannykh v 1917 g. v Chrezvychainoi Sledstvennoi Komissii Vremennogo Pravitel'stva*, 7 vols. (Leningrad: Gosudarstvennoe izdatel'stvo, 1924–1927), 5:38.

32. Pipes, *Russian Revolution*, 278.

Everything broke apart on February 27. The same Volynsky unit that had shot at protesters the day before held back now. They shouted at their commander, Major I. S. Lashkevich, "Enough blood!" He read out Nicholas's directive to use military force. The soldiers killed him.[33] Order broke down because the military in Petrograd no longer remained loyal to the government or the monarch. The revolution triumphed because of, in the words of Richard Pipes, "the most stupendous military revolt in recorded history."[34] But the solidarity between the crowds and revolting soldiers was equally essential.

As mutinous soldiers and NCOs fanned out among the regiments, some encountered sympathy and support. Revolutionary activists also sought to foster mutiny. Most mutinous soldiers chose not ideology but morality: whether or not to kill those they believed were simply ordinary suffering people. But, as Laura Engelstein has noted, "the spread of mutiny was not a peaceful process." The mutineers attacked and killed commanding officers. They seized arms and munitions. They pressured their comrades to join with them, sometimes threatening them with violence.[35]

Workers ransacked nearby armories, amassing weapons and ammunition.[36] Crowds broke into prisons, freeing all inmates, including regular criminals. The Circuit Court building was set on fire, policemen were lynched, and stores were looted. One eyewitness recalled that "thousands of criminals stormed out of the prisons and looted nearby clothing stores, leaving the streets littered with prison garb."[37]

Also, on February 27, Khabalov reported to Nicholas (through Alekseev) that "the majority of regiments, one after another, betrayed their duty, refusing to fight against the rebels."[38] In his diary, the tsar mentioned the disorders: "Regrettably, the troops also began to participate. It is a disgusting feeling to be so far and only receive sketchy bad news!"[39] He still believed that military repression was the right and effective answer. If the Petrograd garrison could not do its job, other reliable troops would.

On that fateful day, Nicholas dismissed all requests for political concessions—from General Nikolai Ruzsky, the commander of the Northern Army Group; Rodzianko (again); and Nicholas's brother, Grand Duke Michael. It is striking just how modest these requests were: not even to grant the Duma authority to appoint a government, but on the tsar's own authority to appoint "a ministry of confidence," that is, government officials enjoying public trust. Then came a telegram from the head of Nicholas's own government, Prince Golitsyn, informing him that the government was powerless to halt the "anarchy" and pleading for Nicholas to appoint a government

33. Hasegawa, *February Revolution*, 278.

34. Pipes, *Russian Revolution*, 280.

35. Laura Engelstein, *Russia in Flames: War, Revolution, Civil War, 1914–1921* (New York: Oxford University Press, 2018), 111.

36. Engelstein, *Russia in Flames*, 111.

37. Daly, *Watchful State*, 205–6.

38. "Fevral'skaia revoliutsiia," *Krasnyi arkhiv* 2(21): 15–16.

39. Mironenko, *Dnevniki*, 295.

enjoying public confidence. Nicholas's chief of staff Alekseev met with him at least twice pleading, on his knees, as he later claimed, to heed Golitsyn's entreaty. Alekseev told Nicholas de Basily, a member of the staff of Nicholas's diplomatic chancellery at General Headquarters: "Again, I did everything possible to convince him to take the road to salvation at last. Again, I ran against a wall."[40] Nicholas's stubborn refusal to grant any political concessions on February 27 confirms that devotion to autocracy was a core belief—not a view imposed on him by Rasputin or Alexandra.

Indeed, on that very day, Nicholas appointed General Nikolai Ivanov commander of the Petrograd military district and charged him with crushing the rebellion—just as he had suppressed a mutiny at the Kronstadt naval base in 1907. Nicholas invested him with dictatorial powers over all the ministers and ordered his battle-hardened and well-equipped battalion to march immediately to Tsarskoe Selo. Furthermore, Alekseev obediently ordered all the main commanders to rush their most reliable troops to assist Ivanov. Bloodshed seemed inevitable.

Organizational centers of the revolution began to coalesce in Petrograd. In the Taurida Palace, where the Duma met, many dozens of socialists formed the Provisional Executive Committee of the Soviet of Workers' Deputies. The body, quickly renamed the Petrograd Soviet, expanded to include not just worker deputies from the Duma but also various socialist activists and elected worker, soldier, and sailor deputies who rivaled Duma politicians in prestige and popularity.

Leaders of the suspended Duma got together the following day, February 28, also in the Taurida Palace, to form a Provisional Committee with Rodzianko as chair. Its members cabled frontline commanders that they were replacing the former cabinet in order to restore state and public order. Nevertheless, they were hesitant, contacting Nicholas for permission to form a new government.[41]

Many historians agree that Khabalov's actions were poorly planned and uncoordinated. Perhaps in the final days of February, he could have rallied loyal troops and restored order. By March 1, however, it seems that turning back, stopping the revolution, had become all but impossible. There were several reasons for this. First, the Petrograd Soviet provided some organizational cohesion to the revolutionary forces; second, the existential threat of a punitive expedition could have rallied the arms-bearing people of Petrograd to collective defense; third, there was no guarantee "the contagion" would not spread to troops sent to suppress it; and, finally, the revolutionary wave extended beyond the capital.

Indeed, while the February Revolution is primarily associated with Petrograd, one of its most significant aspects is how quickly it spread further. On February 28, troop mutinies began in Tsarskoe Selo, close to the imperial residence at Alexander Palace.[42] The palace itself was heavily guarded by special troop detachments

---

40. Hasegawa, *February Revolution*, 463, 466, 465n15.

41. Pipes, *Russian Revolution*, 289.

42. E. N. Burdzhalov, *Russia's Second Revolution: The February 1917 Uprising in Petrograd*, trans. and ed. Donald J. Raleigh (Bloomington, IN: Indiana University Press, 1987), 282–83.

subordinated to the palace commandant, but they were no match for thousands of armed workers and mutinous soldiers.

On the night of February 28, the revolution spread to the naval base of Kronstadt, an island fortress about eighteen miles directly west in the Gulf of Finland. Like the rebellious soldiers in Petrograd, the sailors in Kronstadt acted spontaneously. The Kronstadt governor-general, Admiral Robert Viren, a strict disciplinarian hated by many sailors, was forcibly brought to Anchor Square. He warned the rebels that two loyal regiments arriving from Finland would crush the mutiny. "This is not a mutiny, comrade admiral, but a revolution!" answered one of the sailors. Viren was bayoneted to death. Several dozen commissioned and non-commissioned officers in Kronstadt were also murdered.[43] No aid came from Finland. Instead, unrest and mutiny spread throughout the Baltic Fleet, including its headquarters in Helsingfors (now called Helsinki), Finland. In Petrograd, turmoil raced from regiment to regiment; in Helsingfors, it spread from ship to ship.[44] Days after urging Nicholas to accept compromise with the Duma leaders, the Baltic Fleet commander, Admiral Adrian Nepenin, who had just resigned his post, was killed by rebellious sailors.

In Moscow, the food supply situation was better than in Petrograd, and local officials declared a state of siege on February 27. It did not help. Strikes, rallies, clashes with the police, and troop mutinies delivered Moscow to the revolution in just a few days.

The fate of the monarchy was in the hands of rebellious people, not conspirators or punitive expeditionary forces.

Getting to Abdication

In the meantime, oblivious of many of these developments and hopeful about the success of General Ivanov's expedition, Nicholas departed for Tsarskoe Selo on the morning of February 28. He traveled on his own train. Seeking to avoid Nicholas's coming into direct contact with Alexandra and perhaps fearing for his safety in proximity to Petrograd, members of the Provisional Committee of the Duma and their subordinates spread rumors that mutinous troops had seized the rail line on his path. Nicholas, therefore, demanded a rerouting of his train.[45] By the evening of March 1, his train had arrived about two hundred miles southeast of Petrograd in Pskov, the headquarters of the Russian Northern Army Group led by General Ruzsky and his chief of staff Yuri Danilov (Map 2.2). Nicholas did not yet know that in just a few hours, he would no longer be the tsar.

43. Mawdsley, *Russian Revolution and the Baltic Fleet*, 13, 14.
44. Mawdsley, *Russian Revolution and the Baltic Fleet*, 16–18.
45. Lyandres, *Fall of Tsarism*, 143, 151; Rex Wade, *The Russian Revolution, 1917*, 3rd ed. (Cambridge: Cambridge University Press, 2017), 51; Hasegawa, *February Revolution*, 482–84.

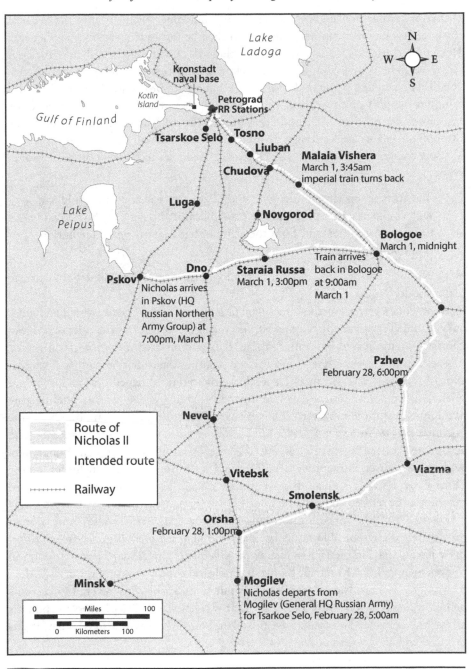

Map 2.2: Nicholas II en route to abdication in Pskov

Several key decision-makers influenced this outcome. Nicholas gave the order to crush the revolution by military means, but then he lost touch with events. Generals Alekseev and Ruzsky tried to implement the order but found it difficult. Alekseev had recently recovered from a heart attack, and Ruzsky was at the point of exhaustion. They wanted to preserve the monarchy but also to prosecute the war. They were willing to support punitive measures but only if they were likely to prove effective. Yet they came to believe that military repression could spark a civil war—dooming all hope for victory and perhaps turning their own soldiers against them. General Alekseev recognized as much in a telegram that Nicholas received upon his arrival in Pskov:

> The army is too closely tied with the life of the rear and one could say with confidence that unrest in the rear will cause the same in the army. It is impossible to demand from the army to fight calmly while revolution is unfolding in the rear.[46]

With Nicholas on the train and out of the loop, the commanders knew they had to make fast decisions.

Another key player was the Provisional Committee of the Duma, which had gradually assumed government responsibilities, including control of the railroads. From February 26, its soon-to-be-chair, Rodzianko, communicated with Generals Alekseev, Aleksei Brusilov, Aleksei Evert, and Ruzsky, assuring them that he had things under control. His goal was to cancel General Ivanov's punitive expedition and convince Nicholas to appoint "a ministry of confidence"—with a widely trusted public figure like himself as prime minister.[47] On February 28, however, Rodzianko argued that Nicholas had to authorize a "responsible ministry"—a government formed by and accountable to the legislature, as was the case in most constitutional monarchies. Rodzianko enlisted the support of three grand dukes for this plan, including Grand Duke Pavel, Nicholas's uncle. But when they asked Alexandra to sign the proposed manifesto, she refused and called it idiotic.[48]

Disturbed by the spreading revolution, Ruzsky and Alekseev also came around to the idea of a responsible ministry. Their thinking may have been akin to adopting a retreat tactic in the face of enemy encirclement. The monarchy faced "political encirclement." It had to retreat by making political concessions and do it fast. Alekseev ordered General Ivanov's forces to stay put, and Ruzsky withdrew reinforcements he had earlier sent to Ivanov. Now "all" that was left was to brief Nicholas upon his arrival and convince him to endorse this plan. Since Alekseev was in Mogilev, it was up to Ruzsky in Pskov to do so.

---

46. "Fevral'skaia revoliutsiia," *Krasnyi arkhiv* 2(21): 39.
47. Hasegawa, *February Revolution*, 274–75, 463.
48. Hasegawa, *February Revolution*, 476–77.

Tsar and general met on March 1 at 10:00 p.m. in the imperial train, which had been turned back from its progress toward Petrograd and had stopped in Pskov (Map 2.2). Nicholas was informed that the revolution had spread beyond Petrograd and that General Ivanov's punitive expedition had been suspended. He nevertheless rejected Ruzsky's proposal to authorize the Duma to form a new government, declaring that it would go against his conscience and his oath to God.[49] At 11:00 p.m., General Alekseev cabled Nicholas, urging him to agree to Ruzsky's proposal for the sake of the war effort. An imperial manifesto granting the Duma authority to form a government had already been drafted at General Headquarters. Alekseev's telegram tipped the scales. Around 12:30 a.m., on March 2, Nicholas signed the manifesto. With a stroke of a quill, Russia became a constitutional monarchy. To the deeply religious Nicholas, breaking his oath to God was an apocalyptic event. Ruzsky then went to bed, exhausted, probably feeling that he and Alekseev had saved the monarchy and the empire.

But the night—or the nightmare—was just beginning. A rude awakening came at 3:30 a.m. Rodzianko was requesting a telegraphic conversation. When Ruzsky informed him that Nicholas agreed to permit the Duma to form a new government, Rodzianko's response was staggering:

> His Majesty and yourself do not realize what is happening here. One of the most horrible revolutions has occurred that will not be easy to put down. . . . The popular passions have flared up so much that it will scarcely be possible to contain them; the troops are completely demoralized; they not only do not obey; they kill their officers.[50]

Rodzianko added that the hatred toward the dynasty had radically escalated and that Nicholas's abdication in favor of his son under the regency of his brother, Grand Duke Michael, was now a definite demand of the people and the troops.

This was not just Rodzianko's reading of the situation. The previous night, the Provisional Committee of the Duma in Petrograd had reached pivotal decisions of its own: to form an official Provisional Government (of which Rodzianko was not even a member), to work in concert with the newly formed Petrograd Soviet's Executive Committee, and to seek Nicholas's abdication.

In the early morning of March 2, General Alekseev was informed of the conversation between Ruzsky and Rodzianko. By 10:00 a.m., he seems to have made up his mind that nothing short of Nicholas's abdication could prevent further revolutionary unrest. Also, around 10:00 a.m., Ruzsky entered Nicholas's train car to inform him of his overnight conversation with Rodzianko. Predictably, Nicholas hesitated. He said

---

49. S. N. Vil'chkovskii, "Prebyvaniie Gosudaria Imperatora v Pskove, 1-e marta 1917 goda, po rasskazu general-ad"iutanta N. V. Ruzskago," *Russkaia Letopis'* 3 (1922): 167–70.

50. "Fevral'skaia revoliutsiia," *Krasnyi arkhiv* 2(21): 56.

he was ready to abdicate for the sake of Russia but worried that "the people" would see this as the abandonment of his duties.[51]

Then at 10:30 a.m., a circular telegram arrived from Alekseev, which had been sent to the other frontline commanders urging them to approve Rodzianko's abdication proposal and to send their own pleas to the tsar if they agreed with it.[52]

Nicholas waited for the commanders' responses. He took lunch and then walked silently on the railroad platform. At 2:30 p.m., Ruzsky, accompanied by other generals, brought Nicholas the telegrams. They expressed, in various ways, the sentiments of General Brusilov (Southwestern Front):

> [A]t this moment, the only way to save the situation and make it possible to continue fighting the external enemy, without which Russia will perish, is to give up the throne in favor of the Lord Heir Prince.[53]

Later that day, General Vladimir Sakharov and Admiral Adrian Nepenin of the Baltic Fleet added their imploring voices to those of their fellow commanders.[54]

Nicholas read the telegrams and let two other generals who came with Ruzsky speak. Both supported the abdication. A long silence followed. Then Nicholas made a sign of the cross and declared his decision to abdicate the throne in favor of Aleksei. It was around 3:00 p.m.

"What else could I do?" he said shortly thereafter to the members of his stunned entourage. "They have all betrayed me, even Nikolasha" (Grand Duke Nicholas).[55] Nicholas's diary confirms his sense of shock and betrayal: "All around there is treason, and cowardice, and deceit."[56] George Katkov was surely right to conclude that "the generals believed they were taking part in an action to save the monarchy and maintain the dynasty."[57] Yet in narrow and deluded Nicholas's mind, treason and betrayal, not massive popular rebellion, forced him to give up power. Alexandra vehemently agreed. She could not bring herself to recognize the simple fact that vast numbers of Russians, at least in the capital, no longer wished Nicholas to remain tsar.

Since social-scientific opinion polls did not exist at the time, it is impossible to say what proportion of the population—in Petrograd or elsewhere—wanted Nicholas to step down. But hundreds of thousands of people had come into the streets in the

---

51. Vil'chkovskii, "Prebyvaniie Gosudaria," 178.

52. "Fevral'skaia revoliutsiia," *Krasnyi arkhiv* 2(21): 67.

53. "Fevral'skaia revoliutsiia," *Krasnyi arkhiv* 2(21): 73.

54. "Fevral'skaia revoliutsiia," *Krasnyi arkhiv* 2(21): 74; "Fevral'skaia revoliutsiia 1917 goda (Dokumenty stavki verkhovnogo glavnokomanduiushchego i shtaba glavnokomanduiushchego armiami severnogo fronta: Okonchanie)," *Krasnyi arkhiv* 3(22) (1927): 3–70 (here: 12).

55. Marc Ferro, *Nicholas II: Last of the Tsars* (New York: Oxford University Press, 1994), 200.

56. Mironenko, *Dnevniki*, 296.

57. George Katkov, *Russia 1917: The February Revolution* (New York: Harper & Row, 1967), 429.

capital demanding radical change. Moreover, the security police had been attuned to growing resentment against the war and the monarchy. They intercepted private correspondence and surveyed the popular mood, but these surveys, however detailed, were anecdotal and usually lacked analysis. Moreover, they never made it past the desks of the police department director and the interior minister. As Protopopov admitted later, "I wished to calm the emperor and empress."[58]

The imperial couple continued to live in a dream world. It is hard to imagine that any analytical report could have changed their minds. Like their belief in the holiness of Rasputin, their belief in the Russian people's devotion to themselves was a matter of faith.

The elaborate public ceremonies, the letters from loyal monarchists, the seeming obedience of the troops, and occasional personal interactions with wounded soldiers reinforced the belief of Nicholas and Alexandra that the people loved them. "All adore you & *only* want bread," Alexandra assured Nicholas on February 26.[59] In the days that followed, she declared: "There is no revolution here. What we have is the revolution concocted by the Duma, and it is treason!"[60] When confronted with undeniable evidence of the people's and the troops' hostility, she complained, on March 2, that it was "hideous": the Guards Equipage (a marine battalion that participated in the revolutionary events in Petrograd) "understand absolutely nothing; a microbe sits in them."[61] On March 3, before she finished her letter, she learned that Nicholas had signed the abdication manifesto. The news devastated Alexandra, but she finished the letter declaring that Nicholas would return to the throne, "brought back by your people, to the glory of your reign." She called General Ruzsky "Judas." The following day she heard false rumors that Kaiser William II of Germany had been killed and his son wounded in a revolution. She blamed the Freemasons (below): "one sees all over the Freemasons in everything."[62]

Conspiracies in the Air . . .

Many people, and not just the imperial couple, believed that a treacherous conspiracy had destroyed the Russian monarchy. Like many potent myths, this narrative had elements of truth in it.

Revolutionary activists and organizations had conspired for decades to overthrow the Russian monarchy. The revolutionary wave of 1905 had brought them tantalizingly close to this goal. The Social Democratic Party (with its Bolshevik, Menshevik,

---

58. Daly, *Watchful State*, 201.

59. Fuhrmann, *Wartime Correspondence*, 694.

60. Hasegawa, *February Revolution*, 477.

61. Fuhrmann, *Wartime Correspondence*, 699.

62. Fuhrmann, *Wartime Correspondence*, 702.

and other factions), the Socialist-Revolutionary Party, anarchists, and other revolutionary activists and organizations worked tirelessly in the intervening years to foment popular unrest. By 1909, however, these radical groups had fallen on hard times. In part, they lost membership thanks to Russia's booming economic growth and suffered continuous police repression.

Yet politically and socially, Russia was far from stable. The bloody massacre of hundreds of mineworkers, who had been protesting their working conditions in a Siberian goldfield in April 1912, breathed new life into the labor movement. Intermittent strikes continued for the next two years, culminating in summer 1914 in a general strike in Petrograd. Nevertheless, the police and administrative authorities gained emergency powers and quickly suppressed political unrest as the war began. Even the six Bolshevik members of the Duma were arrested, despite their parliamentary immunity, and exiled to eastern Siberia.[63] By early 1917, revolutionary activists in Petrograd were few and lacked organization and cohesive strategy.

Rumors of plots—to remove Nicholas from power, force him to abdicate in favor of Aleksei, replace him with Grand Duke Nicholas, or confine Alexandra to a convent—continuously circulated in Petrograd before and after Rasputin's assassination. They undoubtedly reached the imperial couple.

Some of the rumors involved Freemasons (or Masons). Introduced in the second quarter of the eighteenth century but outlawed in 1822, loosely autonomous Freemasonic lodges were reestablished in Russia after the Revolution of 1905. Like Freemasons in Europe, North America, and elsewhere, Russian Masons were typically devoted to liberal causes. Around 1909–1911, a Masonic organization called the Supreme Council of the Peoples of Russia brought together members of different political parties who favored republicanism (that is, the abolition of the monarchy). The organization promoted anti-monarchical sentiments, solidarity, and coordination among its members.[64] Several members of the Provisional Committee of the Duma and the Petrograd Soviet were Masons. But just like the leaders of the main revolutionary parties, Masonic politicians neither orchestrated nor even anticipated the revolution.

Details of rumored plots are murky, but most did not yield anything of substance. Among the most elaborate was that of the so-called Committee of Five, which planned to capture Nicholas using troops from the Reserve Cavalry Division. The ringleader, Aleksandr Guchkov, headed the moderate liberal Octobrist Party. Nikolai Nekrasov and Mikhail Tereshchenko, two Masons, later joined the Provisional Government. They discussed placing Aleksei on the throne with Grand Duke Michael as regent. They also considered installing General Aleksei Manikovskii (a Mason[65]) as

---

63. Daly, *Watchful State*, 159–64.

64. Hasegawa, *February Revolution*, 180.

65. Tsuyoshi Hasegawa, personal communication, April 8, 2020.

a temporary leader with emergency powers.[66] These plans came to naught, though; on February 28, the conspirators sent two regiments, which could have intercepted Nicholas's train had he continued moving toward Tsarskoe Selo.[67]

Some "representatives of Duma and public circles" seemingly had approached General Alekseev a few months before the revolution to inquire if he would support a coup to remove Nicholas. Alekseev answered no but did not report the incident.[68] As mentioned above, members of the Provisional Committee of the Duma, with Rodzianko's knowledge, obstructed the movement of Nicholas's train in part to prevent his reunification with Alexandra in Tsarskoe Selo. Likewise, once Ruzsky concluded that political concessions could stave off revolution, he, on his own initiative, recalled reinforcements he had sent to General Ivanov. Finally, pro-monarchist sources indicate that Ruzsky was rude to Nicholas in Pskov.[69]

Still, it would require a great leap of imagination to view all these actions as one grand treasonous conspiracy against Nicholas and, even more so, a conspiracy against the monarchy. Most ringleaders and main participants wanted to preserve the Russian monarchy in some form, not destroy it. Even Rodzianko's opponents in the Duma, like the moderate Guchkov or the left-liberal Constitutional Democratic Party leader Pavel Miliukov, wanted the Romanov dynasty to continue; they just wanted a different tsar—one who would preside over a constitutional system. At that point in the revolution, apart from several Masons and republicans in the Provisional Committee of the Duma, all the key decision-makers were monarchists. However, hundreds of thousands of rebellious people in Petrograd and beyond were not, and millions more apparently did not care. That is what sealed the monarchy's fate.

The Abdication Drama

Nicholas's decision to abdicate did not spell an immediate end to the Russian monarchy. In fact, it gave hope to monarchists that this ancient institution could survive in a refashioned form. Few people in Russia had strong negative feelings, specifically toward Aleksei. In this scenario, Aleksei, still a boy, would not be able to make any political decisions, shielding the dynasty from critics. Meanwhile, his designated regent, Grand Duke Michael, was a convinced proponent of constitutionalism.

Nicholas himself killed that scenario. At 9:00 p.m., on March 2, he met with two Duma deputies, the liberal Guchkov and the conservative Vasilii Shulgin, who came

---

66. Hasegawa, *February Revolution*, 493; Aleksandr Guchkov, *Aleksandr Ivanovich Guchkov rasskazyvaet: Vospominaniia predsedatelia Gosudarstvennoi dumy i voennogo ministra Vremennogo pravitel'stva* (Moscow: TOO Red. Zhurnala "Voprosy istorii," 1993), 21.

67. Lyandres, *Fall of Tsarism*, 278.

68. A. I. Denikin, *Ocherki russkoi smuty*, 5 vols. (Paris: J. Povolozky, 1921–1926), 1:35.

69. M. Kleinmikhel, *Iz potonuvshego mira* (Berlin: Glagol, 1923), 213.

to seek his abdication. He shocked them by declaring that he no longer wanted his son Aleskei to be tsar. Aleksei's doctor, Professor Fedorov, had explained that Aleksei would require constant protection and care. Acting out of fatherly feelings and contrary to established legal norms of imperial succession, Nicholas changed the abdication manifesto to designate his brother Michael as the next tsar and charged Prince Georgii L'vov, the chairman of the United Committee of the Union of Zemstvos and the Union of Towns (Zemgor), an association of institutions of local self-government created in 1915 to assist with the war effort, with forming a new government.[70]

Ironically, that very day Prince L'vov became the head of a government not appointed by Nicholas but selected by the Provisional Committee of the Duma, in consultation with the Petrograd Soviet. The newly constituted Provisional Government supplanted the monarchy on March 2 (even though Grand Duke Michael did not abdicate until the next day). It was far more radical than the Provisional Committee of the Duma.[71] Its leaders felt obligated to develop a working relationship with the revolutionary Petrograd Soviet and therefore included one of its key members—the socialist Alexander Kerensky. His ability to bridge the political gap between the Petrograd Soviet and the Provisional Government and ensure some coordination between the two meant that Kerensky immediately began to gain power and influence. Rodzianko, on the other hand, was excluded from the Provisional Government, as even his Duma colleagues had significantly radicalized. In fact, "the Provisional Government consciously severed its institutional ties with the Duma and the Duma Committee, seeking to persuade the insurgent masses that its legitimacy stemmed from the revolution itself."[72] Even so, the Petrograd Soviet viewed the Provisional Government as too moderate and offered it only conditional support.

The Provisional Government split on the question of the monarchy. Its foreign minister and informal leader, Miliukov, advocated a constitutional monarchy. So did Guchkov, the minister of war. Others hoped for a republic, including the increasingly powerful Kerensky (Justice), as well as Nekrasov (Transportation), Tereschenko (Finance), and Aleksandr Konovalov (Trade and Industry). All four were Masons.[73] Other members of the Provisional Government agreed that the idea of Grand Duke Michael becoming tsar was so unpopular that there was no point in championing it. Indeed, on March 2, Miliukov went to make an informal announcement of the creation of the Provisional Government to the revolutionary crowd. They cheered as

70. Vasilii Shul'gin, *Dni. 1920* (Moscow: Sovremennik, 1989), 256, 258.

71. A. B. Nikolaev, "Vremennyi komitet Gosudarstvennoi dumy: Khronika zasedanii 20–30 marta 1917 g.," *Tavricheskie chteniia*, ch. 1 (2017): 238–55.

72. Tsuyoshi Hasegawa, "The February Revolution," in *Critical Companion to the Russian Revolution, 1914–1921*, ed. Edward Acton, Vladimir Cherniaev, and William G. Rosenberg (Bloomington, IN: Indiana University Press, 1997), 59.

73. Hasegawa, *February Revolution*, 179.

he attacked the old regime, especially when he mentioned that Kerensky would join the Provisional Government. Then someone asked him about the fate of the dynasty. Miliukov replied that Aleksei would be the new tsar under the regency of Grand Duke Michael. The crowd erupted with indignant shouts: "This is the old dynasty!" "Down with the dynasty!" "Long live the republic!"[74]

Figure 2.2: Soldiers in Petrograd, late February 1917. The first banner reads: "Through struggle you will attain your rights"; the second: "Down with the monarchy. Long Live the Republic."

On March 3, Guchkov and Shulgin also got a taste of the popular sentiment in Petrograd. As they arrived at the train station with Nicholas's revised abdication manifesto and made speeches about "the New Emperor Michael II," the reaction was mixed. One crowd, consisting mostly of soldiers, responded with shouts of "hooray," probably more in response to the news that Nicholas was no longer tsar than because they supported Michael. But when Guchkov spoke to a crowd of railroad workers, the reaction was hostile.[75]

The last act of Russia's monarchical drama occurred on the morning of March 3. The Provisional Government met with Grand Duke Michael. Prince L'vov and Rodzianko presented the majority view that Grand Duke Michael should not assume the throne since they did not believe they could ensure his safety. As much as he might have desired to mount the throne in normal times, Michael declined to take power

74. Daly and Trofimov, *Russia in War and Revolution*, 51.

75. Shul'gin, *Dni*, 288–94.

until a democratically elected Constituent Assembly should determine Russia's form of government.[76]

The full truth that the members of the Provisional Government did not admit to Grand Duke Michael, although they probably had it in the back of their minds, was that not only his safety but also their own could not be guaranteed. If the revolutionary people of Petrograd (and the Petrograd Soviet) angrily rejected the scheme to preserve the monarchy through Grand Duke Michael, who could guarantee they would not then turn against the Provisional Government itself, had it tried to implement this scheme?

The growing popular hostility toward the Russian monarchy ran parallel to the growing popular hatred of the hierarchical order the monarchy symbolized and sanctioned. To rapidly growing numbers of people, this order appeared not merely insulting to human dignity but deadly and destructive. The roots of this hostility went back at least to Bloody Sunday in 1905, when it became clear to many working people in Saint Petersburg and beyond that their lives did not matter to the government and the tsar, and some members of the lower classes began to call the tsar "Nicholas the Bloody."

Contempt for the lives and needs of ordinary people was nothing new in imperial Russia, but it was manifested in countless new ways during the Great War. Lofty wartime declarations about the need to recapture the ancient Byzantine capital of Constantinople from the Turks rang hollow among those in the army who suspected that Constantinople mattered more to the tsar than their own lives. Officers enforced hierarchy and discipline among peasants and workers in uniform through verbal insults and corporal punishment.[77] In Russian, as in most European languages, there are two forms of the second-person pronoun "you": the formal and respectful "vy," and the informal, familiar, and sometimes contemptuous "ty." People in positions of authority under the old regime notoriously used "ty" as an expression of disrespect, much to the anger and resentment of ordinary people. Such insults were many. In Kronstadt, for example, a sign at the entrance to Petrovsky Park read: "No admittance to lower ranks and dogs."[78] The massacres of February 26 served as another proof that the tsar and the imperial government were willing for peaceful protestors to die and soldiers to become killers of fellow Russian subjects as the price to pay for maintaining order.

Revolutionary crowds took out their hostility not only on representatives of the old regime but also its symbols, including double-headed eagles, statues of prerevolutionary heroes, portraits of the tsar, official buildings, musical instruments, works of art, place-names and nameplates, imperial emblems, jails and courthouses, and other

76. Hasegawa, *February Revolution*, 606.
77. Mawdsley, *Russian Revolution and the Baltic Fleet*, 5.
78. Mawdsley, *Russian Revolution and the Baltic Fleet*, 5.

tokens and icons of the crumbling order in what the historian Richard Stites termed a "war on luxury," and a "war on signs."[79]

Treason and Conspiracy Myths

A robust and nuanced discussion among historians of the Russian Revolution continues to shed more light on the degree of spontaneity versus organization in the February Revolution.[80] But those who believed in the revolution's conspiratorial origins did not need such debates.

It was psychologically difficult for convinced Russian monarchists to accept the idea that their cherished monarchical institution and its symbolization in the person of Nicholas II was broadly despised and rejected in 1917. Many, therefore, sought explanations involving treason and conspiracy behind the monarchy's downfall. The treason myth had psychological appeal because it cast the tsar as an innocent victim of those choosing the path of disloyalty and dishonor. As noted earlier, this is how Nicholas himself perceived the circumstances of his abdication. In the 1920s, émigré monarchist historians elaborated on this sentiment.[81]

The publication in 1936 of General Vladimir Voeikov's memoir, *With the Tsar and Without the Tsar*, powerfully boosted the treason myth. As court commandant, Voeikov had worked closely with Nicholas in Mogilev, on the imperial train, and in Pskov. The book reprinted the telegrams of Alekseev, Ruzsky, and Rodzianko, as well as Nicholas's manifestos. Voeikov added commentary that, while not rooted in evidence, sounded believable because he was an eyewitness participant. Voeikov asserted that Alekseev and other military commanders were "obedient followers" of Rodzianko's orders. By their treason, they "deprived the tsar of one of the main foundations of the all-Russian throne," by which he meant the military. "Judas betrayed Christ and repented, returning the thirty pieces of silver," he continued, "while our generals and admirals betrayed the tsar and did not repent."[82] Voeikov did not merely deny the widespread triumph of revolutionary sentiment in Russia but offered an alternative explanation. Educated people exulted, he claimed, because they were "fooled by the

---

79. Richard Stites, *Revolutionary Dreams: Utopian Vision and Experimental Life in the Russian Revolution* (New York: Oxford University Press, 1989), 61–71.

80. Michael Melancon, "Rethinking Russia's February Revolution: Anonymous Spontaneity or Socialist Agency?" *The Carl Beck Papers in Russian and East European Studies*, no. 1408 (June 2000); Semion Lyandres and Andrei Borisovich Nikolaev, "Contemporary Russian Scholarship on the February Revolution: Some Centenary Observations," *Revolutionary Russia* 30 (2017): 158–81; Hasegawa, *February Revolution*, 52–60.

81. N. A. Pavlov, *Ego Velichestvo Gosudar' Nikolai II* (Paris: Société N. P. Karabasnikoff, 1927); M. K. Diterikhs, *Ubiistvo tsarskoi semi'i chlenov Doma Romanovykh na Urale* (Moscow: Skify, 1991).

82. Vladimir Voeikov, *S Tsarem i bez Tsaria: Vospominaniia poslednego dvortsovogo komendanta gosudaria imperatora Nikoaliia II* (1936; repr., Moscow: Voennoe izdatel'stvo, 1995), 16–17, 240.

propaganda of the Jewish press." Meanwhile, public activists "fell under the influence of the Masonic ideal of creating a new international human being free from all restraints" and forgot that they were Russian and their motherland was Russia. As for "the lowest classes," an impulse to loot and steal "came easily to them."[83]

Another witness to the revolution echoed Voeikov's beliefs—General Aleksandr Spiridovich, chief of Imperial Court security until 1916, found himself in Petrograd during the revolutionary days. To Spiridovich, the generals who urged the tsar to abdicate were traitors. All they had to do, according to Spiridovich, was to say, "I am a soldier," and refuse to provide any advice regarding matters in which they lacked competence.[84] Although the book was published decades later, it undoubtedly reflected widespread views in the Russian emigration.

Spiridovich's argument shows the ever-expanding scope of the treason myth. According to this way of thinking, virtually any unauthorized action or even expression of opinion not sanctioned by the tsar could be considered treasonous. Believing in such an expansive interpretation of treason made believing in conspiracies much easier. In 1931, an émigré historian, Sergei Mel'gunov, carefully studied conspiracies allegedly in the works before the February Revolution, including several involving Masons. Although he concluded that the revolution resulted from a fusion of discontent among both ordinary people and educated elites and fraternization between the people and the army in the face of extraordinarily few vociferous defenders of the monarchy,[85] the book triggered the Russian émigré community to hunt for Masons among Duma politicians and military leaders involved in the February Revolution. In the absence of any evidence of direct Masonic organizational involvement in Nicholas's abdication and the collapse of the monarchy, imaginative theories proliferated.

The most influential conspiracy theory actually preceded the monarchy's downfall by about fifteen years. It was advanced in one of the most notorious forgeries of all time, the so-called *Protocols of the Elders of Zion*. This pamphlet purported to present a diabolical plan, hatched at an alleged meeting of Jewish leaders, to take over the world by destabilizing the political, economic, and social systems of European countries.[86] Scholars later demonstrated that two-fifths of the text was plagiarized from an 1864 book by French lawyer and satirist Maurice Joly, *Dialogue aux enfers entre Machiavel et Montesquieu ou la politique de Machiavel au XIXe siècle* (*Dialogue in Hell between Machiavelli and Montesquieu or the Politics of Machiavelli in the 19th Century*), while other parts reflected influences of Hermann Goedsche's 1868 antisemitic novel,

---

83. Voeikov, *S Tsarem*, 266.

84. Aleksandr Spiridovich, *Velikaia Voina i Fevral'skaia Revoliutsiia, 1914–1917*, 3 vols. (New York: Vseslavianskoe izdatel'stvo, 1960–1962), 3:300.

85. Sergei Mel'gunov, *Na putiakh k dvortsovomu perevorotu (Zagovory pered revoliutsiiei 1917 goda)* (Paris: Rodnik, 1931), 223–24.

86. Steven Marks, *How Russia Shaped the Modern World: From Art to Anti-Semitism, Ballet to Bolshevism* (Princeton, NJ: Princeton University Press, 2003), 149–55.

Biarritz (translated as *To Sedan*), which borrowed heavily from Joly but invented an assembly of "world rabbis" who met in a Prague cemetery to discuss "their successes since their last meeting in furthering their secret plan for world domination."[87]

The origins of the *Protocols* are murky. For many years scholars believed its author was an employee of the Russian security police, the Okhrana. This attribution seems incorrect, though the true author remains shrouded in mystery. Whoever it was, the person "supercharged European ideas, then exported them westward in more potent form," which, "like other works of Russian thought . . . gave off an aura of mystical, higher truth to foreign audiences."[88] The *Protocols* identified the Russian autocracy as "our only serious enemy in the world, not counting the Papacy."[89]

The protocols were first mentioned in 1902 in a conservative Saint Petersburg newspaper *Novoe vremia* (New Times) by a prominent antisemitic columnist, Mikhail Menshikov, and first published the following year in another conservative newspaper *Znamia* (Banner) by Pavel Krushevan, a notorious antisemite. They gained more traction after their publication in a 1905 book by Sergei Nilus, a self-styled mystic.[90]

As Daniel Pipes has argued, the *Protocols'* appeal can be explained in part by their vagueness. The work contains few specific names and dates; the protagonists are alleged to target and undermine a broad range of established institutions, including the monarchy and parliamentary democracy, churches and law courts, the press, and banks.[91] The book describes not a specific conspiracy but a conspiracy matrix allowing anyone prone to conspiratorial thinking to fill in the blanks based on particular anxieties, fears, or traumatic events.

The fall of the monarchy and the establishment of the Provisional Government, some of whose members were Freemasons, fit into this matrix. As will be discussed in Chapter 5, the seizure of power by the Bolsheviks also fit, especially since several Bolshevik leaders were Jews.[92] The fact that many Jewish liberal and revolutionary activists actually opposed the Bolsheviks did not matter, nor did the fact that Bolshevik activists played a relatively minor role in triggering the February Revolution, nor indeed that Jewish members of the Bolshevik leadership had renounced their Jewishness. Nevertheless, the Bolsheviks' abhorrent decision to execute Nicholas and members of his family in 1918 was taken as proof that the Jewish conspirators prevailed over the Russian tsar in accordance with the *Protocols'* alleged goals.

---

87. Maurice Joly, *The Dialogue in Hell between Machiavelli and Montesquieu: Humanitarian Despotism and the Conditions of Modern Tyranny*, ed. and trans. John Waggoner (Lanham, MD, and Oxford: Lexington Books, 2003), 357.

88. Marks, *How Russia Shaped the Modern World*, 154.

89. *Protokoly sionskikh mudretsov (po tekstu S. A. Nilusa): Vsemirnyi tainyi zagovor* (Berlin: Presse, 1922), 98.

90. Marks, *How Russia Shaped the Modern World*, 152–53.

91. Daniel Pipes, *Conspiracy: How the Paranoid Style Flourishes and Where It Comes From* (New York: Free Press, 1997), 85.

92. Richard Pipes, *Russia under the Bolshevik Regime* (New York: Alfred A. Knopf, 1994), 256.

Many diehard monarchists who fled Russia after the revolution took these con-spiratorial beliefs with them.[93] They found sympathetic audiences abroad. Few were more influential than Henry Ford, the founder of the Ford Motor Company and inventor of the assembly line production method, who published articles on the sup-posed global Jewish conspiracy in his own *Dearborn Independent* newspaper and the book *The International Jew: The World's Foremost Problem* (1920). Ford claimed in his writings that Nicholas was removed from power by the Jews: "In Russia," he wrote, "the Jews sprang immediately into official positions and have succeeded in remaining there. It began with Kerensky compelling the tsar to lay aside his crown; it continues with Trotsky and his armies at the throat of Europe."[94] The reason Ford singled out Kerensky, not Rodzianko, Ruzsky, or Alekseev, was because of the mythi-cal belief some hold even today that Kerensky was Jewish. Like most Russian liberals and socialists, Kerensky abhorred antisemitism and supported Jews who faced perse-cution. But he came from a family of Russian priests, and, apart from rumors, there is no historical evidence that he was Jewish.[95] (As will be discussed in Chapter 5, Ford was even more preoccupied with Leon Trotsky, a Bolshevik of Jewish origin, for he saw in the Bolsheviks and their vision of world revolution the embodiment of a sup-posed Jewish conspiracy to dominate the world.)

Among Russian émigrés, Nikolai Markov was one of the most vocal champions of the treason and conspiracy myth. As a notorious right-wing Duma deputy, he had polished his rhetorical skills in frequent antisemitic diatribes from its podium. In *The Wars of Dark Forces* (1928–1930), he declared that top Russian generals, together with Rodzianko and Guchkov and other Duma politicians, were traitors but added even Interior Minister Protopopov to that list. Protopopov's failure to maintain order in Petrograd was, according to Markov, "treasonous." He admitted he had no evi-dence that Protopopov was a Mason but considered it "highly likely." Markov's rabid antisemitism also required no evidence. Although he admitted that nearly every major actor in the February Revolution was Russian, he nevertheless insisted that "the hands were Russian, but the brains were Jewish."[96] He also blamed the Masons. "The gener-als played the revolution using Masonic sheet music," he declared. And behind the Masons? The Jews.[97]

---

93. See, for example, Alexandre Nechvolodov, *L'Empereur Nicolas et les Juifs: Essais sur la révolution russe dans ses rapports avec l'activité universelle du judaïsme contemporain* (Paris: Étienne Chiron, 1924).

94. Henry Ford, *The International Jew: The World's Foremost Problem* (Dearborn, MI: Dearborn Publishing, 1920), 171.

95. Boris Kolonitskii, "Aleksandr Kerenskii kak 'zhertva evreev' i 'evrei,'" *Evreiskii Obozrevatel*, February 2008, http://www.jewukr.org/observer/eo2003/page_show_ru.php?id=2347.

96. N. Markov, *Dumskie rechi. Voiny temnykh sil* (Moscow: Institut russkoi tsivilizatsii, 2011), 362–65.

97. Markov, *Dumskie rechi*, 589–90.

Such thinking abounded in Russia after the collapse of the Soviet Union in 1991,[98] as monarchism became a resurgent ideology and mindset in some circles.[99] Several books appeared blaming Masons and the Jews for the Russian Revolution.[100] Others emphasized betrayal and treason more broadly.[101]

In recent years, Russian monarchism has become political. In 2015, Nataliia Poklonskaia, a Putin supporter, former prosecutor, Duma deputy, and ardent monarchist, asserted that Nicholas's abdication manifesto was invalid because he had not followed the proper procedures. "They did not have the time to legalize Nicholas II's abdication in 1917. He is still our emperor,"[102] ran one provocative headline. Konstantin Dobrynin, deputy chair of the Constitutional Legislation Committee of the Federation Council (Russia's upper parliament chamber), retorted: "the Anointed One," meaning Nicholas II, had the authority to abdicate any way he saw fit.[103] One could imagine such a debate among Russian monarchists a century ago.

The centennial anniversary of the February Revolution occasioned a flurry of documentaries, publications, and conferences in Russia that again raised questions of treason and conspiracy surrounding Nicholas's abdication. The Patriarch of the Russian Orthodox Church declared that the February Revolution was guided by "dark forces" without specifying who they were.[104] Speaking at one conference, Viacheslav Nikonov, the grandson of Vyacheslav Molotov (Stalin's foreign minister), a long-serving Duma deputy, a national talk show co-host, chair of the Duma Committee on Education, and chair of the history department of Moscow State University, declared: "There can be no feeling of pride associated with the February events and

98. Eliot Borenstein, *Plots against Russia: Conspiracy and Fantasy after Socialism* (Ithaca, NY: Cornell University Press, 2019).

99. Maija Turunen, "Orthodox Monarchism in Russia: Is Religion Important in the Present-Day Construction of National Identity?" *Religion, State, and Society* 35, no. 4 (2007): 319–34; Natalia Mamonova, "Naïve Monarchism and Rural Resistance in Contemporary Russia," *Rural Sociology* 81, no. 3 (September 2016): 316–42.

100. Oleg Platonov, *Ternovyi venets Rossii* (Moscow: Russkii vestnik, 2000); and numerous other books published by "The Institute of Russian Civilization" in the "Russian Resistance" series.

101. P. Multatuli, *Gospod' da blagoslovit reshenie moe… Imperator Nikolai II vo glave deistvuiushei armii i zagovor generalov* (Saint Petersburg: Satis, 2002); V. Khrustalev, "Fevral'skaia revoliutsiia i otrechenie Nikolaia II, ili voenno-politicheskii zagovor," in *Otrechenie imperatora Nikolaia II: Vospominaiia i dokumenty*, ed. V. Khrustalev (Moscow: Prozaik, 2018), 7–48.

102. Aleksandr Dobrovol'skii, "Otrechenie Nikolaia Vtorogo v 1917-m ne udosuzhilis' uzakonit'," *Moskovskii komsomolets*, July 17, 2015, https://www.mk.ru/social/2015/07/16/otrechenie-nikolaya-vtorogo-v-1917m-ne-udosuzhilis-uzakonit.html.

103. "Sovfed: 'Nikolai II mog otrech'sia khot' gvozdiem na liste zheleza," *Moskovskii komsomolets*, July 16, 2015, https://www.mk.ru/politics/2015/07/16/sovfed-nikolay-ii-mog-otrechsya-khot-gvozdem-na-liste-zheleza.html.

104. Viktor Shnirel'man, "Revoliutsia 1917 g.—zagovor inovertsev i inorodtsev? Eskhatologicheskii vzgliad na russkuiu revoliutsiiu," *Scando-Slavika* 64, no. 1 (2018): 64–94 (here: 79).

the subsequent abdication of the czar Nicholas II. Rather, we should remember these events with a feeling of regret or even shame. The czar fell victim to an elitist conspiracy which he failed to prevent."[105] Nikonov's high political and social status reflects the belief among Russian government officials that revolutions against tyranny have conspiratorial rather than popular origins. This view reaches deep into Russian society. According to one survey, the number of people in Russia who believe that the Russian Revolution resulted from "a conspiracy of the enemies of the Russian people" increased from 6 percent in 1990 to 20 percent in 2017.[106] The myth lives on.

105. Dmitry Babich, "February Revolution of 1917: Good Intentions, Tragic Fates?" *Sputnik International*, October 2, 2017, https://sputniknews.com/columnists/201702101050558449-february-revolution-1917-good-intentions-tragic-fates/.

106. Shnirel'man, "Revoliutsia," 85.

3. The Myth of Lenin and the Bolsheviks as Secret German Agents

> And the cursed Bolshevik
> In an instant did his deed:
> Bowed down to the black bird,
> Sowed sedition, opened fronts,
> Dug a pit for all of Russia...
> Yet his efforts are in vain:
> The German lackeys will fail.[1]
>
> —*Anti-Bolshevik poster poem, 1917*

At the end of 1916, of all the revolutionary organizations in Russia, the Bolshevik Party was probably the weakest. It alone opposed the war, which was not a way to gain favor with the authorities. Arrests, secret police informants, and economic dislocation had made it increasingly difficult for the party leadership to maintain organizational and operational authority. Its flagship newspaper, *Pravda* (Truth), was shut down, cutting off its revenue stream. The party ranks shrank to a few thousand activists. The socialist revolution they believed in seemed nowhere on the horizon. In early 1917, Vladimir Lenin spoke to radical youths in Switzerland and recognized this grim reality when he remarked that his generation was unlikely to live long enough to see decisive battles of the coming proletarian socialist revolution in Europe.[2]

Yet, in the year that followed, the Bolsheviks staged one of the most remarkable comebacks in political history. After the collapse of the monarchy in February 1917, the Bolshevik leaders, among other exiled revolutionaries, returned to Russia, which Lenin called "the freest country in the world."[3] The party ranks swelled, their publications proliferated, their party organization grew increasingly robust, and in October 1917, the Bolsheviks seized power from the Provisional Government and established the regime that, with some modifications, survived until 1991.

---

1. I. Ia. Bilibin, "O tom, kak nemtsy bol'shevika na Rossiu vypuskali," 1917, https://upload.wikimedia.org/wikipedia/commons/0/03/O_tom_kak_nemtsy_bolshevika_na_Rossiyu_vypuskali.jpg.

2. Nadezhda Krupskaia, *Vospominaniia o Lenine* (Moscow: Partizdat, 1933), 259.

3. Vladimir Lenin, "The Tasks of the Proletariat in the Present Revolution," in *Collected Works*, 4th ed., 45 vols. (Moscow: Progress Publishers, 1960–1967), 24:19–26 (here: 22).

Figure 3.1: Vladimir Lenin (left) in Stockholm, on his way to Petrograd, April 13, 1917.

Leaders in the Provisional Government and other revolutionary parties observed the Bolsheviks' rise to power with a mix of denial, bewilderment, and dismay. Many refused to believe that such a small organization could become so successful in such a short period without outside help. And why would the Bolsheviks weaken the Russian army with anti-war rhetoric at the very moment when German troops were advancing on the Eastern Front? To those seeking simplistic narratives, the answer appeared obvious: the Bolsheviks were German agents and spies for Kaiser William II, helping him knock Russia out of the Great War. The Provisional Government spent a vast amount of its modest resources striving to hobble the Bolsheviks and investigating their ties to Germany. This chapter takes a closer look at these ties and discusses the consequences of the Provisional Government's obsession with the myth that the Bolsheviks were German agents.

Lenin and the Great War

The Great War found Lenin in Poronin, a small village in the Austro-Hungarian province of Galicia, a few miles from the picturesque town of Zakopane. Poronin was close to the Russian border, allowing communication with Bolshevik organizations as well as occasional visits of party activists. Austria-Hungary declared war on Russia six days after Germany, on July 24/August 6, 1914,[4] and Lenin was arrested soon afterward. He was a Russian subject, and his activities looked like Russian espionage to the police. It took intervention from Austrian Social Democrats to have Lenin released and exiled to Switzerland. In February 1916, Lenin and his wife Nadezhda Krupskaia settled in Zurich, as did many Russian political émigrés unable to move around Europe or return to Russia.

Lenin's state of mind during the war was marked by revulsion, anger, bitterness, hatred, and growing isolation.[5] As a Marxist, believing that material forces and interests shape societies, he immediately turned to socio-economic causes to explain the war's origins. To Lenin, they were crystal clear: the class of industrial capitalists, "imperialists," as he often called them, plunged the world into the bloodiest war to date for the sake of maximizing its profits and control over markets, natural resources, and colonies. Industrial workers mercilessly exploited by the capitalist masters were now put in uniform and sent to kill one another and die for the sake of capitalist profits and imperialist acquisitions.

By the eve of the war, Marxist-influenced socialist and social-democratic parties of Europe were formidable political forces in parliamentary politics and trade-union organizations. In 1889, they had formed a worldwide communist association, the Second International. Among its core ideals was antimilitarism. Lenin could reasonably expect that many, if not all, socialists and social democrats of Europe would stand against the war once it began. The opposite happened as they rallied behind their respective governments and voted for military budgets in parliamentary assemblies.[6] Lenin saw this as a ghastly betrayal. Intellectually, he viewed Europe's socialists and social-democratic leaders as selling out fundamental principles of Marxism that stress the global solidarity of exploited people regardless of race or nationality. Politically, Lenin believed that they had become accomplices in the unprecedented, cynical slaughter of working people.

Admittedly, Lenin had never been inclined to treat his political adversaries with great respect. His private letters and articles were replete with condescending and derogatory expressions. People who knew him well confirmed his penchant to mock and insult anyone who disagreed with him in any way—even his closest party comrades.[7] Still, a look at Lenin's wartime writings reveals the depths of his traumatized revulsion toward the "social-chauvinists" who claimed they were defending the

---

4. Dates indicated thus: July 24/August 6, 1914, should be read as July 24 (O.S.)/August 6 (N.S.), 1914.

5. Neil Harding, *Lenin's Political Thought: Theory and Practice in the Democratic and Socialist Revolutions*, 2 vols. in one (Chicago: Haymarket Books, 2009), 2:16–40.

6. Harding, *Lenin's Political Thought*, 2:7–12.

7. Georgii Solomon (Isetskii), *Sredi krasnykh vozhdei, 1898–1923* (Moscow: Giperboreia, Kuchkovo pole, 2007), 320–21.

fatherland but in reality favored a "defence of the privileges, the advantages, the right to pillage and plunder, of one's 'own' (or any) imperialist bourgeoisie."[8] Lenin seemed to hate the patriotic socialists as much as he hated the imperialist rulers and capitalists. As he wrote in 1914, "To the socialist, it is not the horrors of war that are the hardest to endure . . . but the horrors of the treachery shown by the leaders of present-day socialism."[9] His state of mind during the war sheds light on decisions he would make in early 1917. They also help explain Bolshevik hostility toward other left-wing political activists in Russia, which helped them consolidate a one-party dictatorship after seizing power in October 1917. Even Joseph Stalin's hostility toward the Social Democrats in Weimar Germany, which prevented German Communists from joining in resisting Hitler's rise, can be traced back to Bolshevik experiences and attitudes during World War I.

In September 1915, thirty-eight left-wing socialists from several European countries, including several involved in the war, gathered in the cozy Swiss village of Zimmerwald to protest the war and rekindle the prewar antimilitaristic stance of the Second International. Lenin attended, but to him and other radicals, condemning the war—or even pursuing a negotiated settlement to the war—was not good enough. Lenin advocated turning "the imperialist war between the peoples into a civil war of the oppressed classes against their oppressors."[10] Instead of killing one another, industrial workers in uniform should turn their weapons against the real enemy—their own capitalist-controlled governments that were sending them to their deaths. This would create immediate momentum for a continent-wide socialist revolution and ultimately destroy capitalism in Europe and beyond. Lenin and the other radicals failed to rally a majority to support a statement to that effect, written by the Austrian socialist Karl Radek, though Lenin and his allies supported the final manifesto. It called on the entire socialist movement "to march side by side with other sections of the International."[11] The "Zimmerwald Left" remained, however, a minority voice on the radical fringe of the socialist movement, another reason for Lenin to feel angry and embittered. While he steadfastly held to his prediction of a revolutionary future for Europe, just when this future would become a reality seemed impossible to know.

In the meantime, the war dragged on, Lenin's isolation persisted, and money was tight. In a letter to a fellow Bolshevik in fall 1916, he admitted: "I need a way to earn money. Otherwise, all that will be left for me is to die, no kidding! The cost of living

8. Vladimir Lenin, "Socialism and War," in *Collected Works*, 21:307.

9. Vladimir Lenin, "The European War and International Socialism," in *Collected Works*, 21:20.

10. Vladimir Lenin, "The Draft Resolution Proposed by the Left Wing at Zimmerwald," in *Collected Works*, 21:348.

11. R. Craig Nation, *War on War: Lenin, the Zimmerwald Left, and the Origins of Communist Internationalism* (Durham: Duke University Press, 1989), 90.

is devilishly high and there is nothing to live on."[12] At some point during that year, other Bolsheviks tried to raise funds for Lenin with only modest success.[13]

One place in Zurich that offered peace and enjoyment for free was the public library. He became one of its most loyal patrons, even ensuring that his lunchtime coincided with the library's lunch break.

One day in February 1917, when Lenin and Krupskaia had just finished lunch, and Lenin was about to return to the library, an acquaintance barged in with extraordinary news: "There is a revolution in Russia!" The couple rushed to read all they could in the latest newspapers.[14] Even though Lenin learned about the February events in Petrograd from the press, his role in the events that followed cannot be underestimated. His energies were now devoted to finding a way to leave "damned Switzerland." During one sleepless night, he thought of flying in an airplane (something civilians rarely did in those days). What seemed enticing at night appeared quite unfeasible in the daylight. He thought of asking Swedish socialists to furnish him with a passport. Sweden was a neutral country that bordered Russia. Posing as a Swede carried risks, however, since Lenin did not speak Swedish. A mute Swede, perhaps? Krupskaia thought it was too risky: "What if you fall asleep, dream of Mensheviks, and start cursing: 'Bastards! Bastards!' That's the end of your cover."[15] The Mensheviks were fellow revolutionaries, in fact, fellow Marxists who had assumed a more moderate political position (as discussed in Chapter 7), earning Lenin's scorn.

Lenin was not alone in this feverish desire to reach Russia. Thousands of émigré revolutionaries—like Trotsky in New York City and Stalin in Siberian exile—wanted the same thing. Those like Lenin who opposed the war could not hope to convince Britain or France to grant them transit to Sweden; this left the option of traveling through Germany.

Germany Assists Lenin

The German government took a great interest in social and political developments in Russia. It was never Germany's intention to fight a protracted war against the Triple Entente, an alliance of Britain, France, and Russia. Ever since the first months of the war, when Germany's Schlieffen Plan failed to neutralize France quickly, the German leadership actively sought ways to break up or at least weaken the Entente. In military terms, despite successes in the east against Russia, Germany's main targets had been in the west. The Battle of Verdun (1916) devastated but did not break the French army.

---

12. Lenin to A. G. Shliapnikov, after October 3, 1916, in Vladimir Lenin, *Polnoe sobranie sochinenii*, 5th ed., 55 vols. (Moscow: Politizdat, 1958–1965), 49:302.

13. Solomon, *Sredi krasnykh vozhdei*, 353.

14. Krupskaia, *Vospominaniia*, 260.

15. Krupskaia, *Vospominaniia*, 262.

In early 1917, the Germans hoped unrestricted submarine warfare in the Atlantic would make Britain sue for peace before the United States could do anything about it. But the German leadership also showed a keen awareness of its enemies' other, non-military vulnerabilities. All of the Entente powers were empires. None appeared as fragile as Germany's ally, the Austro-Hungarian Empire, but each had weaknesses to exploit.

Germany worked to undermine British imperial dominance from Ireland to the Middle East, even actively promoting jihad—a holy war by Muslims against their British colonial masters—all coordinated by an office in Berlin in charge of "Seditious Undertakings against Our Enemies."[16] Several high-level operatives with intimate knowledge of Islam and the Middle East, as well as competence in Arabic and Turkish, worked feverishly to inflame anti-British sentiment across the Islamic world. As for the Russian Empire, several non-military tactics were employed. Intermediaries were to reach out to Nicholas to convince him to sign a separate peace but failed to gain any traction. Contrary to rumors mentioned in Chapter 1, Nicholas remained committed to the Entente as steadfastly as to his monarchical powers and prerogatives. Yet, as Russian troops retreated from the empire's western provinces, nationalist stirrings and unrest among ethnic minorities offered attractive destabilizing opportunities. In the words of George Katkov:

> German embassies in neutral countries were constantly besieged by a crowd of Finnish nationalists, Polish counts, Ukrainian clerics, Caucasian princes and highwaymen, and revolutionary intellectuals of every description, who wanted to establish liberation committees, publish nationalist propaganda, and work for some independent and free national state which they fondly hoped would result from the partition of the Russian Empire.[17]

One can detect sarcasm in Katkov's observation, but the national awakening in Poland, Ukraine, Finland, and other western territories of the Russian Empire was real.

No less real were Russian socialist parties, the Socialist-Revolutionaries and the Social Democrats (the Mensheviks and the Bolsheviks) in particular, and the suffering and exploitation of Russian soldiers, peasants, and industrial workers whose interests the revolutionaries championed. To capitalize on their discontent and outrage, the Political Section of the German General Staff targeted hundreds of thousands of Russian POWs with secessionist and socialist propaganda. But Political Section officials were constantly alert to other options.

---

16. Sean McMeekin, *The Berlin-Baghdad Express: The Ottoman Empire and Germany's Bid for World Power* (Cambridge, MA: Belknap Press of Harvard University Press, 2012), 93.

17. George Katkov, *Russia 1917: The February Revolution* (New York: Harper & Row, 1967), 73.

In March 1915, German diplomats received a memorandum from Dr. Alexander Helphand, also known as Aleksandr Parvus. Born Israel Lazarevich Gel'fand in Russia to a Jewish artisan family, Parvus received a doctorate in political economy in Germany, participated in the Russian Revolution of 1905, and served a term of exile in Siberia. His socialist beliefs did not prevent Parvus from accumulating a significant fortune in commerce and enjoying a prosperous lifestyle. In his memorandum, Parvus did not declare that he abandoned his beliefs. Instead, he simply argued that Germany's goals for Russia overlapped with the goals of those who sought to promote revolution. His fundamental premise was that Russia would not be able to fight Germany effectively if mired in revolutionary turmoil. This was not just a theoretical argument. Parvus proposed a specific program to boost socio-economic and, ultimately, revolutionary unrest among Russian industrial workers.[18] He also claimed that he had an established network of agents inside Russia to make it happen; all he needed was money. The German Foreign Ministry was interested enough to provide Parvus with millions of Russian rubles and German marks for revolutionary propaganda. In late 1915, after promising to trigger revolution in Russia by January 1916, he received more money still.[19]

Figure 3.2: Aleksandr Parvus, 1905.

Parvus met Lenin in the summer of 1915 in Switzerland, but, apparently, the two did not get along. To Lenin, Parvus was a "social-chauvinist" who sacrificed his commitment to international socialism for the advancement of German national power. To Parvus, Lenin's goal of turning the Great War into a civil war in Europe sounded more far-reaching than the goal of promoting revolution in Russia.[20] Moreover, his German government sponsors would hardly like the idea of using government funds to assist a group of fringe radicals eager to ignite civil war all over Europe, including Germany itself.

Another "social-chauvinist" who helped keep the German government alert to Lenin was Karl Moor, a socialist member of the Bern Great Council. He had helped Lenin settle in Switzerland at the beginning of the war and also worked as an informant for the Austrian and German General Staffs.[21]

---

18. "Preparations for a Political Mass Strike in Russia," in *Germany and the Revolution in Russia, 1915–1918: Documents from the Archives of the German Foreign Ministry*, ed. Z. A. B. Zeman (London: Oxford University Press, 1958), 140–52.

19. Katkov, *Russia 1917*, 86–87.

20. Katkov, *Russia 1917*, 81.

21. Katkov, *Russia 1917*, 74.

Thus, by the time Lenin made inquiries about the possibility for him and his comrades to cross Germany by train, the German government was well aware of his activities and his beliefs. A number of people claimed that sending Lenin to Russia through Germany was their idea. It was certainly floated in various communications between Berlin and German diplomatic representatives in Denmark, Sweden, and Switzerland. Parvus joined the chorus, arguing that supporting the Bolsheviks could knock Russia out of the war in three months. (He also wanted five million more German marks for revolutionary propaganda.)[22] What is important is that an initially skeptical Lenin became convinced that there was no other way for him to reach Russia.

The Swiss socialist Robert Grimm and, more importantly, Fritz Platten, Lenin's Swiss ally of the Zimmerwald Left, helped arrange with the liberal Swiss Foreign Minister, Arthur Hoffmann, for Lenin and other Russian socialists to receive transit documents across Germany.[23]

The German decision to let Lenin and other Bolsheviks pass through Germany was not an endorsement of Lenin's beliefs, which in early 1917 still centered on transitioning from the Great War to a civil war on a European scale. German officials simply believed that Lenin's immediate activities in Russia would be consistent with German interests. The German decision was not part of a well-developed master plan to topple the Provisional Government, bring the Bolsheviks to power, and ignite a new, more radical phase of the revolution in Russia. It was impossible at the time to predict how effective Lenin and his supporters would be, and the German leadership had not abandoned the hope of reaching a settlement with the Provisional Government. At the very least, it hoped the Bolsheviks would help destabilize Russia socially, weaken the Provisional Government politically, and render the Russian army less effective militarily.[24]

The Bolsheviks' Train Ride

On March 27/April 9, 1917, Lenin and other socialists embarked from Zurich on what turned out to be one of history's most momentous train rides. Still, the German train was no Orient Express. Waiting for them at the Swiss-German border were second- and third-class train cars, relatively comfortable but not luxurious. The Russians traveled in one carriage; their German guards in a second. A chalk line separated the two carriages and symbolized the German-Russian "border," crossed only by the neutral Fritz Platten, who was the sole intermediary between the Russians and the

---

22. Catherine Merridale, *Lenin on the Train* (New York: Metropolitan Books/Henry Holt, 2017), 135–40.

23. Robert Service, *Lenin: A Political Life*, vol. 2: *Worlds in Collision* (Bloomington, IN: Indiana University Press, 1991), 151.

24. Zeman, *Germany and the Revolution in Russia*, 94.

Map 3.1: Lenin's journey from Zurich to Petrograd, April 1917

Germans. At the Swiss border, most of their food was confiscated because of a wartime law against exporting food items.[25] The travelers realized that getting enough to eat would be a problem. Germany was running short on food because of the British naval blockade.

Lenin's traveling party consisted of thirty-two people and included his wife, Nadezhda Krupskaia, and his dear friend (and possibly lover) Inessa Armand. Also among the traveling companions were Lenin's close associate and member of the Zimmerwald Left, Grigorii Zinoviev, with his ex-wife, his current wife, and a son; and some non-Bolsheviks invited in order to provide "cover" so that other political parties would share in any appearances of impropriety,[26] including six members of the Bund, a secular Jewish socialist movement, and three supporters of Trotsky.[27]

Most members of the group were bound by shared radical beliefs and nearly millenarian expectations of the coming international revolution. Lenin quickly gave evidence of his eventual governing style: he physically tossed a Social Democrat off the train, thinking him a spy; tried to "exile" Radek's girlfriend to a farther compartment because she was being too loud; and threatened to punch a German labor leader who wanted to meet with him in Stuttgart. Aware of his fastidiousness and acknowledging him as a leader, the other travelers insisted that Lenin and his wife enjoy a single, second-class compartment to themselves. Meanwhile, the others squeezed into seven remaining compartments (two second class and five third class).[28] Those traveling in the compartment next to Lenin annoyed him with their constant banter and singing. Lenin established sleeping hours for everyone and banned smoking in the compartments and corridors. This turned the toilet into a point of contention since a large number of people wanted to use it for smoking, which caused complaints among those who wanted to use it for other purposes but had to stand in the same line as the smokers. Lenin came up with a ticket system giving priority to nonsmoking toilet users. They were entitled to "first-class" tickets, while the smokers were given "second-class" tickets and were told to yield to the former.[29] A faction of dissenters led by the chain-smoking Karl Radek retorted that smokers' physical needs were greater and that they were entitled to the "first-class tickets," not the other way around. Radek also laughed at Lenin, "declaring that his imperious dispositions in the carriage 'fitted him to assume the leadership of the revolutionary government.'"[30] Little did either know that just a year later, Lenin would be responsible for designing and implementing the

25. Service, *Worlds in Collision*, 152; Merridale, *Lenin on the Train*, 147–48.

26. Dmitri Volkogonov, *Lenin: A New Biography*, trans. and ed. Harold Shukman (New York: Free Press, 1994), 120; Sean McMeekin, *The Russian Revolution: A New History* (New York: Basic Books, 2017), 121.

27. Richard Pipes, *The Russian Revolution* (New York: Alfred A. Knopf, 1990), 391.

28. Service, *Worlds in Collision*, 152–53; Merridale, *Lenin on the Train*, 149.

29. Merridale, *Lenin on the Train*, 151–52.

30. Service, *Worlds in Collision*, 153.

world's largest countrywide rationing system for thousands of goods and services and tens of millions of people.

Legend to the contrary, the train that transported Lenin and other Russian radicals across Germany was not sealed. Some German soldiers entered the train car from the platform, curious to inspect the Russian radicals. In Berlin, the passengers were allowed to disembark. They spent twenty-four hours in the German capital, though little is known of what they did there.[31] The train ride across Germany was followed by a boat ride to Sweden, brief stopovers in Malmo and Stockholm, another train up north to the border crossing point, a sleigh ride across the frozen river between Sweden- and Russian-controlled Finland, and yet another train ride that ended in the triumphal arrival in Petrograd at the Finland Station.

Lenin Delirious?

When Lenin arrived in Russia, after seven days' travel, on April 3/16, revolution was on his mind—but not only revolution in Russia. He declared that Europe at large was now on the verge of upheaval. While he did not always publicly emphasize the importance of a global transition from an imperialist war between nations to an international civil war, such was his paramount hope and goal. The Russian Revolution, he believed, would play a vital role in the forthcoming worldwide transition from capitalism to socialism. In order to do so, however, it had to become more radical. As noted above, Lenin's ideas were a minority view at Zimmerwald, and so they were also among fellow Bolsheviks in revolutionary Petrograd.[32]

The Bolsheviks in Russia were not robotic followers of Lenin's orders. They closely collaborated with other socialists during the February Revolution, and their relatively small numbers made collaboration a tactical necessity. But even after the revolution, many Bolsheviks were thrilled by its outcome and predisposed toward working together with Mensheviks (orthodox Marxists) and Socialist-Revolutionaries (broadly popular but peasant-oriented socialists) in the Petrograd Soviet and beyond. This meant that their militant anti-war position softened as well. The Petrograd Soviet declared its desire for the war to end quickly and on fair terms, without annexations or indemnities, but it also expressed support for the Provisional Government's goal of peace through victory.

To Lenin, this was nothing but "social-chauvinism." "It is simply shit!"—was his reaction to the news from the Petrograd Soviet. "I repeat: shit."[33] One can only imagine his angry reaction to articles supporting a defensive war in the recently reconstituted

---

31. Merridale, *Lenin on the Train*, 149, 159–60; Pipes, *Russian Revolution*, 392.

32. Rex Wade, *The Russian Revolution, 1917*, 3rd ed. (Cambridge: Cambridge University Press, 2017), 72–73.

33. Merridale, *Lenin on the Train*, 132.

Pravda. From the moment Lenin arrived at the Finland Station, he began spreading his message of revolution, not the revolution that had already occurred, but the revolution that was—in his mind—about to sweep across Europe and destroy empires and capitalism everywhere. His first speech took place just outside the station. Numerous rallies followed. Neither Bolshevik supporters nor other Bolshevik leaders were convinced that it was time for an international socialist revolution.

Lenin had to recalibrate. His declaration known as the "April Theses" demanded: peace through a socialist revolution; no support for the Provisional Government; transition to "the republic of soviets," where power would belong to the proletariat and the poorest peasants; abolition of the police, army, and bureaucracy; the merger of all banks into one; and nationalization of all land. Most of these demands related to Russia, albeit in an international context.[34] Lenin gave his vision a trial run on the balcony of Petrograd's Kshesinskaia Mansion, which the Bolsheviks had appropriated following the February Revolution.[35] He then presented his demands at a gathering

Figure 3.3: Lenin delivers his April Theses in a speech to Soviet deputies.

34. Lenin, *Polnoe sobranie sochinenii*, 31:113–18.

35. The mansion had belonged to Mathilde Kshesinskaia, a prima ballerina and a mistress of the future tsar Nicholas II before his marriage to Alexandra.

of Soviet deputies and published his speech in *Pravda* on April 20/May 7. Among the Bolsheviks, the reception was mixed; among their opponents and adversaries, it was contemptuous.[36]

Grigorii Plekhanov, the founder of Russian Marxism, dismissed Lenin's April Theses as "delirium" divorced from specific realities. Russia was still an underdeveloped country, far from completing its phase of capitalist growth, not to mention far from transitioning from capitalism to socialism. Plekhanov also rejected equating Russia's position and interests in the war to those of aggressive Germany.[37] Pavel Miliukov, who served as foreign minister in the Provisional Government, told the French ambassador, Maurice Paléologue, that Lenin was booed when championing his "pacifist" cause and that he would never survive this embarrassment.[38]

Instead, Miliukov's days as foreign minister were numbered. On April 18/May 1, he issued a diplomatic note recommitting Russia to honoring its treaty obligations.

Figure 3.4: Anti-Bolshevik rally in Petrograd. "The Fatherland is in danger. The blood we shed demands war until victory. Comrade soldiers, immediately to the trenches. Return Lenin to Wilhelm."

---

36. Service, *Worlds in Collision*, 165–69.

37. D. S. Anin, ed., *Oktiabr'skii perevorot: Revoliutsiia 1917 goda glazami ee rukovoditelei: Vospominaniia russkikh politikov i kommentarii zapadnogo istorika* (Moscow: Sovremennik, 1991), 170–78.

38. Merridale, *Lenin on the Train*, 229.

Many of these obligations had been secret and included Allied consent to Russia's seizure of the Dardanelles from Turkey, the waterway connecting the Sea of Marmara with the Aegean Sea. This agreement contradicted a consensus reached between the Petrograd Soviet and the Provisional Government that Russia's war goals should not include territorial annexations. To Miliukov, a historian by training, possession of the Dardanelles meant control over Constantinople—the ancient capital of the Orthodox Christian Byzantine Empire—and turning Russia into a Mediterranean power. But this plan caused popular outrage. Many Russians rejected the idea of risking their lives for the Dardanelles.[39] Massive anti-war rallies broke out, followed by counterrallies, at some of which the Bolsheviks were accused of being German agents.

The most important tactical insight behind Lenin's April Theses was his recognition that the Bolsheviks at the time were "a weak minority." This meant that propaganda work—and patience—were of paramount importance.[40] "The masses," wrote Lenin, "will overcome their mistakes by experience."[41]

Mass misery and mass slaughter were such experiences in May–July 1917. While living conditions continued to deteriorate in the rear, War Minister Alexander Kerensky was busy planning a major offensive in the Austro-Hungarian province of Galicia. Kerensky was aware of the growing anti-war sentiment in the Russian army but gambled that success would quickly boost morale and improve Russia's military position. A successful offensive would have resulted in a major defeat for Austria-Hungary and the recapture of Galicia's main city of Lvov (now Lviv, Ukraine). Instead, it followed the familiar seesaw pattern of the Great War: initial victory followed by the regrouping of enemy forces and a counterattack that obliterated the earlier triumphs.

Tens of thousands of casualties, as well as mutinies and desertions, accompanied the Russian retreat. When news of yet another military failure reached Petrograd, an armed uprising—the "July Days"—broke out. On July 16–20/August 3–7, armed workers, soldiers, and sailors marched against the Provisional Government, demanded that all power be given to the soviets, and attacked government forces in the capital, leaving as many as four hundred dead.[42] While many of the rioters were Bolshevik supporters—and Bolshevik activists and leaders at all levels supported and even incited them—Lenin and other top leaders hesitated to "own" the rebellion.[43] It was not yet clear in July how Bolshevik supporters could be organized and what tactics could be pursued going forward. One thing was clear: what looked like delirium to Lenin's critics in April was an increasingly popular stance in July. Initially dismissive of the Bolsheviks, the Provisional Government realized it was now facing a formidable

---

39. Wade, *Russian Revolution*, 82–84.
40. Service, *Worlds in Collision*, 167.
41. Lenin, *Polnoe sobranie sochinenii*, 31:115.
42. Wade, *Russian Revolution*, 184.
43. Wade, *Russian Revolution*, 181–84.

enemy. The government responded not by seeking to deal with the political, social, and economic problems boosting the Bolsheviks' popularity but instead by denouncing them as traitors to Russia and agents of Germany.

The Question of Money

It is indisputable that the German government assisted Lenin and other Bolsheviks in their efforts to reach Russia as quickly as possible. But did it also provide them with financial support, and if so, did it continue after Lenin's return to Russia?

In Stockholm, on his way to Russia, Lenin refused to meet with Parvus, sending Karl Radek instead. Afterward, Parvus traveled to Berlin and met privately with the German state secretary, Arthur Zimmermann.[44] Lenin himself met with a trusted comrade, Yakov Ganetsky (b. Jakub Fürstenberg and also known as Hanecki). Back in 1914, Ganetsky had helped Lenin flee Austria-Hungary for Switzerland and soon moved to Copenhagen, where he became a managing director of Parvus's *Handels og-Exportcompagniet*, a firm that sold German goods in neutral countries and through intermediaries to Russia. Given Russia's prewar dependence on German products, this was a highly profitable business involving various items, intermediaries, supply chains, and occasional smuggling operations. In early 1917, the Danish authorities expelled Ganetsky for violating Danish laws on trading in pharmaceuticals, forcing him to relocate to Stockholm. In Sweden, Ganetsky continued working for Parvus while collaborating with another Bolshevik, Wacław Worowski, who became Parvus's company representative in Stockholm.[45] With Lenin's blessing, Ganetsky and Worowski joined with Radek to form the Foreign Bureau of the Bolshevik Central Committee.

Lenin corresponded more frequently with Ganetsky/Fürstenberg than with anyone else, aside from Inessa Armand. Also, some evidence suggests that Ganetsky's business dealings were subsidized by the German government.[46] Ganetsky and Worowski visited Petrograd in the spring and met with Lenin to discuss party matters. Ganetsky's commercial dealings and the intricate network of financial transactions he engaged in for that purpose, along with his status as Lenin's confidant, were ideal for funneling German money into Bolshevik hands. But there is no hard proof that this happened. Lenin's letter asking Ganetsky for three thousand rubles in April 1917 has survived;[47] so did his notice to Ganetsky that two thousand rubles "were received" from his

---

44. Pipes, *Russian Revolution*, 392.

45. Merridale, *Lenin on the Train*, 196–97; Semion Lyandres, "The Bolsheviks' 'German Gold' Revisited: An Inquiry into the 1917 Accusations," *Carl Beck Papers in Russian and East European Studies*, no. 1106 (1995): 98–99; Volkogonov, *Lenin*, 109–19.

46. Volkogonov, *Lenin*, 119, 122.

47. Lenin to Jakub Ganetsky, April 1, 1917, in *Collected Works*, 43:624.

representative, Mecheslav Kozlovskii.[48] Finally, one scholar has argued that Ganetsky was so committed to the revolutionary movement that he would not have engaged in business "for any other principal purpose than aiding the revolutionary cause."[49] Of course, all of this is merely circumstantial evidence. There is no proof that Lenin received large amounts of money from Ganetsky or other operatives. We do know that, after crossing the border from Sweden into the Russian Empire, Lenin's traveling party was interrogated for hours by Russian officials. Some, including Lenin, were strip-searched. They hated the experience, but it yielded nothing suspicious.[50]

The Provisional Government Goes After the Bolsheviks

Members of the Provisional Government had been tipped off about possible Bolshevik ties with the Germans by the French minister of munitions, Albert Thomas, in late April/early May. Thomas was visiting Russia to boost support for the war. He was a socialist but also an ardent supporter of the war effort. Soon after Thomas's departure, the French military mission in Petrograd shared with Foreign Minister Mikhail Tereshchenko sixty-six intercepted telegrams sent in April–June between Ganetsky and his agents in Russia, as well as several Bolsheviks. Tereshchenko, in turn, passed them to other senior officials. Since rumors about the Bolsheviks' German ties had been circulating for months, the intercepts, which, as we shall see below, were quite opaque, looked suspicious enough to alert Russian military counterintelligence and require an official investigation.[51]

On June 24/July 7, Provisional Government members received a briefing on the suspicious telegrams but did not find the evidence strong enough to warrant their publication. In the meantime, the minister of justice, Pavel Pereverzev, expanded the scope of the investigation, ordering surveillance of individuals mentioned in the telegrams and the preparation of a list of Bolshevik leaders to be arrested. The Central Counterintelligence Division, Intelligence Division of General Headquarters, and Military Censorship were also brought on board, and more potentially incriminating telegrams were intercepted.[52]

During the July Days unrest in Petrograd, when the Provisional Government was at its weakest, Pereverzev decided to make public what he believed were the most damning documents accumulated during his investigation. As a member of the

---

48. Lenin, *Polnoe sobranie sochinenii*, 49:437, 438.

49. Michael Futrell, *Northern Underground: Episodes of Russian Revolutionary Transport and Communications through Scandinavia and Finland, 1863–1917* (London: Faber and Faber, 1963), 192.

50. Merridale, *Lenin on the Train*, 207–9.

51. Lyandres, "'German Gold' Revisited," 7.

52. Lyandres, "'German Gold' Revisited," 7–9.

Provisional Government, he could not openly go against its earlier decision to keep the telegrams secret, so he orchestrated a leak. On July 4/17, he passed the documents to Grigorii Aleksinskii, a former-Bolshevik-turned Menshevik who had long campaigned against suspected German agents in the revolutionary milieu. The next day, Aleksinskii published a summary of the telegrams in the newspaper *Zhivoe slovo* (The Living Word) under a telling title: "Lenin, Hanecki [i.e., Ganetsky], & Co. Spies."[53] The myth that the Bolsheviks were German agents was now in full bloom. The introduction referred to intercepted telegrams and the interrogation of Ensign Dmitrii Ermolenko. Ermolenko was a German agent and claimed hearsay knowledge that Lenin was a German spy.[54]

Figure 3.5: "How the Germans Unleashed the Bolshevik on Russia," 1917. This poster features a Bolshevik propagandist with the newspaper *Pravda* in his pocket and a red banner proclaiming: "Down with everything." The Imperial German eagle (which has turned into a vulture) and German soldiers with champagne and foamy beer mugs expect the Bolshevik propaganda to stir up rebellion and hinder the war effort.

A few days later, Aleksinskii published the full text of the leaked documents. According to the record of Ermolenko's interrogation, he saw Lenin in Berlin in 1916 as he was getting ready to sign some devilish contract with the German General Staff. Ermolenko was a trained German agent, but documents from the German foreign

---

53. Robert Browder and Alexander Kerensky, eds. *The Russian Provisional Government 1917: Documents*, 3 vols. (Stanford, CA: Stanford University Press, 1961), 3:1365.

54. Lyandres, "'German Gold' Revisited," 1, 11.

ministry reveal that his assignment was to foment a nationalist uprising in Ukraine.[55] As to the telegrams, they left a lot to the imagination. Three examples follow.[56]

Telegram 6.

Saltsjobaden[57] May 7, 1917[58]
Rozenblitt[59] Petrovka 17[60] Moskva.
Wire immediately quantity received of original pencils [and] quantity sold[.] exact account send in writing[.] telegraph address Saltsjobaden FÜRSTENBERG.

Telegram 10.

Stockholm May 8, 1917
KOLLONTAI[61] Ispolnitel'nyi Komitet[62] Tavricheskii,[63]
KOZLOVSKII Sergievskaia 81[.][64] Redaktsiia Pravdy[.][65] Petrograd.
Stetskevich[66] searched everything confiscated Tornio[.][67] protest insist immediate forwarding to us all of the confiscated items[.] received [we] not a single letter[.] have Volodia[68] wire [us] whether [we] should send telegrams for *Pravda* and what should be their length[.] GANETSKII.

---

55. George Katkov (with the assistance of Michael Futrell), "German Political Intervention in Russia," in *Revolutionary Russia*, ed. Richard Pipes (Garden City, NY: Anchor Books, 1969), 73.

56. Lyandres, "'German Gold' Revisited," 27, 31, 83.

57. Saltsjobaden was a seaside resort near Stockholm and the closest telegraphic office to where Ganetsky/Fürstenberg was residing.

58. Dates given in N.S. Original number details (telegram number, word count, time of sending) have been omitted.

59. Probably Iulii V. Rozenblat (or Rozenblitt), a Moscow business associate of Fürstenberg and Kozlovskii. See Lyandres, "'German Gold' Revisited," 26n14.

60. A building in central Moscow in the commercial district.

61. Alexandra Kollontai was a prominent Bolshevik activist and the only one to rally immediately to Lenin in April.

62. Executive Committee of the Petrograd Soviet.

63. The Taurida Palace in Petrograd, seat of the Petrograd Soviet and the Bolshevik Party headquarters.

64. Sergievskaia (now Tchaikovsky Street) abutted the Taurida Palace in Petrograd. Kozlovskii's law practice was housed at 81 Sergievskaia. He shared it with the prominent Social Democrat Nikolai D. Sokolov, the secretary of the Petrograd Soviet Executive Committee.

65. The editorial board of the Bolshevik newspaper *Pravda*.

66. Maria Steckiewicz was a Bolshevik supporter close to Ganetsky/Fürstenberg and Lenin's family. She helped arrange Lenin's return to Russia.

67. Finnish border town where Steckiewicz was stopped and searched on May 6/19 on her way to Stockholm.

68. Nickname for Vladimir Lenin.

Telegram 57.

Stockholm. from Petrograd July 5, 1917.
FÜRSTENBERG Grand Hotel Stockholm.
NESTLE sends no flour[.] request[.] SUMENSON. E.M. SUMENSON.[69]
Nadezhdinskaia 36.[70]

Might some of these words be encoded? Could "telegrams to *Pravda*" mean German money remittances to *Pravda*? Could "pencils" denote German gold? Was Nestle flour really Nestle flour or German Reichsmarks? The possibilities were endless.

Those who believed that the Bolsheviks were German agents thought the telegrams proved their guilt. The historian Semion Lyandres, however, has carefully analyzed the sixty-six extant telegrams and found in them no evidence demonstrating German efforts to finance the Bolsheviks. According to him, the transactions mentioned, such as those excerpted above, appear to have been purely commercial, while political reports and notifications in some of the telegrams seem not to have been related to money.

After the July Days, the Provisional Government appointed an investigative commission to look at Pereverzev's evidence. Two weeks later, the commission charged several Bolsheviks, including Lenin, with espionage—spying on behalf of Germany—and high treason.[71] The espionage charge was surely spurious. High treason was closer to the mark, however, given the Bolsheviks' strategic commitment to political subversion, its subsequent overthrow of the Provisional Government in October, and eventual abandonment of one-third of European Russia to Germany. Ultimately, the commission sought to prove that the Bolsheviks were doing Germany's bidding in organizing the July Days. Arrests followed. Ganetsky's operatives in Russia, Sumenson and Kozlovskii, were arrested. So was Trotsky. Government officials apparently hoped the arrests would sow confusion and panic among the Bolsheviks, while the interrogation of suspects would help the prosecution build a stronger case.

At first, the arrests appeared to strengthen the Provisional Government's position. Lenin, joined by Grigorii Zinoviev, went into hiding outside Petrograd, where they lived in a thatched shelter and pretended to be Finnish seasonal workers (Figures 3.6a and 3.6b). Eventually, they relocated to Finland, where Russian officials had no executive authority. The Bolsheviks started issuing inconsistent disavowals. Lenin denied having financial ties with Ganetsky—a lie that was obvious not only to the investigators but also to many revolutionaries around him. Ganetsky, in turn, admitted publicly in Stockholm that the commercial proceeds from his trading business were used to support revolutionaries in Poland but not in Russia. This was a remarkable admission given that Kozlovskii, his company's chief representative in Russia, had

---

69. Evgeniia Sumenson handled the finances of Ganetsky's firm, Handels og-Eksportkompagniet. On July 5/18, she was arrested. See Lyandres, "'German Gold' Revisited," 18n2.

70. A fashionable apartment building in central Petrograd.

71. Lyandres, "'German Gold' Revisited," 1, 11, 113n52.

been a member of the Social-Democratic Party of Poland and Lithuania since 1900.[72] Ganetsky probably hoped that if Kozlovskii confessed to receiving money from him, he could then claim that the money was from his own company, not the Germans, and intended for social-democrats in Poland, not for the Bolsheviks in Petrograd. Ganetsky was right to be alarmed—the following day after her arrest, Sumenson admitted to Russian counterintelligence that Ganetsky had given her instructions to give Kozlovskii money on demand and without receipts.[73]

Figure 3.6a and 3.6b: Lenin in disguise for fake passport and place of his concealment, August 1917.

A Smoking Gun?

On December 3, 1917 (that is, after the Bolsheviks had come to power), German foreign minister Richard von Kühlmann sent a telegram to Kaiser William II stating, "It was not until the Bolsheviks had received from us a steady flow of funds through various channels and under different labels that they were in a position to be able to build up their main organ *Pravda*, to conduct energetic propaganda, and appreciably to extend the originally narrow basis of their power."[74] Unless von Kühlmann was lying to the Kaiser, this all but proves German financial support for the Bolsheviks.

By the end of 1917, the German government and the Kaiser himself had reasons to fear that the Bolsheviks were perhaps too successful. The example they set in Russia, the ideas they embraced, and the operational contacts they had with the radical German left were beginning to threaten Germany's own stability.[75]

---

72. Katkov, *Russia 1917*, 109–10, 113; Lyandres, "'German Gold' Revisited," 24n12.

73. Olga Ivantsova, ed., *Sledstvennoe delo Bolshevikov: Sbornik dokumentov v dvukh knigakh*, Kniga 2, chast' 1 (Moscow: ROSSPEN, 2012), 565.

74. Zeman, *Germany and the Revolution in Russia*, 94.

75. Pierre Broué, *The German Revolution, 1917–1923*, trans. John Archer, ed. Ian Birchall and Brian Pearce, intro. Eric D. Weitz (Leiden and Boston: Brill, 2005), 116–21.

Given Lenin's willingness to accept German assistance in reaching Russia, it is reasonable to assume that Lenin would accept and—if Kühlmann is to be believed—did accept money the Bolsheviks desperately needed in the spring and summer of 1917, even if it came from German sources. But receiving assistance from the German government, whether logistical or financial, did not turn Lenin and other Bolsheviks into German agents willing to follow German orders. The Bolsheviks remained committed revolutionaries. The goals they pursued were their own and at great variance with Germany's goals. As George Katkov put it, "It is obvious from Kühlmann's report to the Kaiser that in giving their support to the Communists the Germans were giving a 'grant in aid' to an independent subversive movement and not financing political agents and spies working on instructions."[76]

In other words, if provided, German financial support likely helped the Bolsheviks get out their message, strengthen their organization, and ultimately take power in Russia, not on behalf of the German government but in order to bring about a worldwide socialist revolution, one that would have toppled the German government, according to Lenin, if only it had succeeded beyond the borders of Russia.

Failure to Heed Yearnings for Peace: The Provisional Government's Greatest Mistake

In late August, everything changed for the Bolsheviks. Kerensky had been negotiating with the supreme commander of the army, General Lavr Kornilov, to restore order in Petrograd should radical activists get out of hand. The two men did not fully trust each other or have the same ideas about potential disorder. They also had opposite personalities: Kornilov was tough, unexcitable, not very smart, of lower-class origins; Kerensky was flighty, brilliant, in love with his own rhetoric, from an upper-middle-class family. It seems that Kornilov would have liked to shut down the Petrograd Soviet completely, whereas Kerensky only wanted to reduce its power over the government. Because of a series of miscommunications, Kerensky concluded that Kornilov was planning a coup d'état and, therefore, ordered his removal from office. Kornilov responded by ordering troops to "take Petrograd."[77] Kerensky turned to the Petrograd Soviet for help in organizing the city's defense. This led to the release of several Bolsheviks arrested in conjunction with the German money and espionage investigation. In September and October, the popularity of the Bolsheviks in both Petrograd and Moscow increased dramatically, and on October 25/November 7, 1917, they toppled the Provisional Government and arrested most of its members

---

76. George Katkov, "German Foreign Office Documents on Financial Support to the Bolsheviks in 1917," *International Affairs* 32, no. 2 (April 1956): 181–89 (here: 186).

77. Wade, *Russian Revolution*, 202–4.

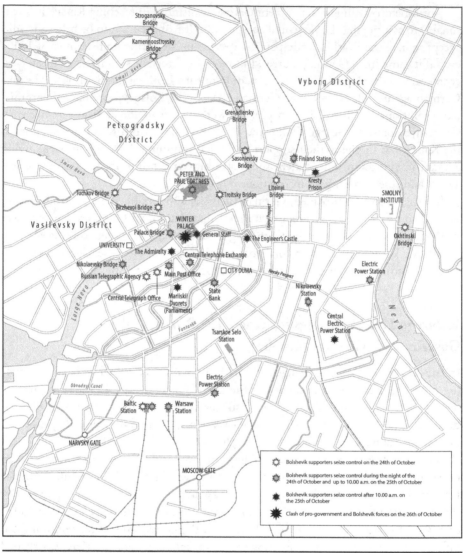

Map 3.2: Petrograd, October 1917

(Map 3.2). The Bolsheviks then established a one-party dictatorship that lasted seventy-three years.

After the collapse of the Soviet Union in 1991, historians could finally consult the Provisional Government's investigative files, which were published in 2012 in three massive volumes. They contain, in addition to the telegrams discussed above, interrogation records of defendants and various witnesses and meticulous searches of banking records and financial transactions. However, there was no absolute proof of German funding of the Bolsheviks.[78] We will never know whether the Provisional Government could have convicted any of the Bolsheviks in a court of law on the basis of the evidence it had collected. The case was scheduled to go to trial in the Petrograd District Court in late October.[79] But, because of the Bolshevik takeover, the trial never took place.

In its effort to prosecute the Bolsheviks as German agents and spies, the Provisional Government scored several tactical wins. The Bolshevik party leadership had to go into hiding, sowing confusion among rank-and-file members of the party. Those who believed the Bolsheviks were unpatriotic could now say so with greater confidence. But these tactical wins evaporated as the Provisional Government limped from one crisis to another in the fall. Also, they meant little compared to the consequences of refusing to recognize and address the roots of the Bolsheviks' resurgence. As sincere liberals of the old school, fixated on due process and procedural integrity, the Provisional Government failed to implement swift and sweeping land reform to alleviate the peasants' lack of agricultural holdings. It failed to hold prompt democratic elections to the Constituent Assembly, which was supposed to build the foundations of a new Russian constitutional order.

Honoring their military commitments and realizing that any peace made while the Germans were not defeated would be draconian, the Provisional Government failed to respond to the growing popular yearning for peace. It would never negotiate a separate peace with Germany, even though such a step would have stolen the Bolsheviks' most popular proposal. At the very least, the government could have taken cues from the actions of its allies. In spring 1917, the French commander-in-chief, General Robert Nivelle, attempted an offensive on the Western Front that was supposed to create "a rupture" in the frontline and achieve a major victory for the Allies. Instead, a major slaughter occurred with massive French casualties followed by mutinies affecting roughly half the French divisions on the Western Front.[80] Nivelle was replaced by General Philippe Pétain, who defused the mutinies by offering French troops extended leaves and furloughs and refraining from any major offensives until the arrival of American troops. Pétain's careful treatment of the French army stands in marked contrast with the nationalist stubbornness and inflexibility of the Provisional Government that first dismissed the Bolsheviks and their supporters as a minor nuisance, then declared them "unpatriotic," and finally became more preoccupied with exposing their real and imagined ties to Germany than with the disastrous consequences of continuing the war.

---

78. Ivantsova, ed., *Sledstvennoe delo Bolshevikov*.

79. Lyandres, "'German Gold' Revisited," 93.

80. Leonard V. Smith, *Between Mutiny and Obedience: The Case of the French Fifth Infantry Division During World War I* (Princeton, NJ: Princeton University Press, 1994), 119.

The Myth of Foreign Agency

Blaming Germany and the Bolsheviks for the Provisional Government's woes was a recurring theme in writings by eyewitnesses and other commentators of the time. Kerensky himself insisted that "had Lenin not had the backing of the entire material and technical power of the German propaganda machine and espionage service, he never would have succeeded in destroying Russia."[81] Likewise, Pavel Miliukov expressed his belief that Lenin made a straightforward deal with the Germans to take Russia out of the war on humiliating terms in exchange for assistance in seizing power.[82] Winston Churchill added eloquence to oversimplification and outright error. The Germans, he wrote, "turned upon Russia the most grisly of all weapons. They transported Lenin in a sealed truck like a plague bacillus from Switzerland to Russia." Churchill added, however, that Lenin was driven by Marxist beliefs as well as a sense of vengeance.[83]

The so-called Sisson documents gave a major boost to the "Bolsheviks as German agents" myth. Edgar Sisson was a Petrograd representative of "The Committee on Public Information," a U.S. wartime propaganda agency. Sisson obtained documents from various sources in spring 1918 before returning to the United States to head the Committee's Foreign Section. He was convinced the documents were genuine, and the Wilson administration released them to the press in September 1918. The committee published a pamphlet called "The German-Bolshevik Conspiracy" with sixty-eight documents collected by Sisson in Russia.[84]

Reporting on the release of the Sisson documents, the *New York Times* was quick to conclude that "the present heads of the Bolshevist government—Lenin and Trotsky and their associates—are German agents . . . [and] the present Bolshevist government is not a Russian government at all, but a German government, acting solely in the interests of Germany, and betraying the Russian people, as it betrays Russia's natural allies, for the benefit of the Imperial German Government alone."[85]

In the decades that followed, the Sisson documents were sometimes cited as evidence that Bolsheviks were German agents. Sisson himself insisted on the documents' authenticity in his memoir published by Yale University Press in 1931.[86] It took the superb scholarly training (and political status) of George F. Kennan to argue

---

81. Aleksandr F. Kerensky, *The Catastrophe: Kerensky's Own Story of the Russian Revolution* (San Francisco: Borodino Books, 2017), 173.

82. Katkov, "German Documents," 186.

83. Winston Churchill, *The World Crisis*, 5 vols. (London: T. Butterworth, 1923–1931), 5:73.

84. United States, Committee on Public Information, Edgar Grant Sisson, and National Board for Historical Service, *The German-Bolshevik Conspiracy* (Washington, DC, 1918).

85. "Documents Prove Lenine and Trotzky Hired by Germans," *New York Times*, September 15, 1918, E1.

86. Edgar Sisson, *One Hundred Red Days: A Personal Chronicle of the Bolshevik Revolution* (New Haven, CT: Yale University Press, 1931).

successfully that most of the Sisson documents were forgeries.[87] Kennan's article came out in 1956, and the myth of Bolsheviks as German agents steadily declined thereafter.

In conspiracy-prone circles, asserting that the Bolsheviks were German agents and spies has never had the same ring as claiming that they were agents of a "Judeo-Masonic" conspiracy, a myth discussed in Chapter 5. Still, after the collapse of communism and the opening of the Russian archives, the myth was occasionally revived as the Russian press was eager to explore topics that had been taboo for decades.

Another resurgence of interest in Bolshevik-German ties coincided with the one-hundredth anniversary of the Russian revolution in 2017. A Russian film director, Vladimir Khotienko, produced an eight-part film called *The Parvus Memorandum*. A truncated six-part version was renamed *The Demon of the Revolution* and aired in November 2017 on the government-controlled Russia 1 TV channel, just in time for the centennial of the Bolshevik overthrow of the Provisional Government. A further revised and even shorter version was released in 2019 as a feature film, *The Lenin Factor*. But even in this cinematic effort, it is Parvus, not the Germans, who, as the main character and villain, orchestrates Lenin's return to Russia and the Russian Revolution itself. Parvus declares that his goal is Russia's destruction, but Lenin tries to outmaneuver both Parvus and the Germans.

Channel 1, another leading government-controlled TV channel, featured an eight-part series called *Trotsky*, directed by Aleksandr Kott and Konstantin Statskii. Parvus and the Germans feature in the series as Leon Trotsky's supporters but appear less demonic and less central to the story of the Russian Revolution. The series recognizes disagreements between Lenin and Trotsky, but in a somewhat unconventional fashion—by showing Lenin and Trotsky fighting physically on a Paris rooftop. Both productions are not much concerned with historical accuracy but are filled with deep anxieties about the conspiratorial origins of revolutionary unrest. In the words of a critic: "Soviet films about the revolution emphasized the power of the people's spirit. Contemporary shows emphasize money."[88]

The centennial of the Russian Revolution also sparked a brief surge in blogosphere headlines highlighting Germany's role in its outbreak. Some strived for clickbait sensationalism. On November 4, 2017, an economist's post on the *Times of India* blog section was provocatively titled "The 1917 Russian Revolution Was a German Plot," yet the author concludes: "Was Lenin a German agent, as critics claim? Surely not. But without German assistance, he would not have come to power."[89]

---

87. George F. Kennan, "The Sisson Documents," *Journal of Modern History* 28, no. 2 (June 1956): 130–54.

88. Andrei Arkhangelskii, "Rol' nalichnosti v istorii," *Ogonek*, 44 (November 6, 2017): 34–35 (here: 35).

89. Swaminathan S. Anklesaria Aiyar, "The 1917 Russian Revolution Was a German Plot," *Times of India*, November 5, 2017, https://timesofindia.indiatimes.com/blogs/Swaminomics/the-1917-russian-revolution-was-a-german-plot/.

An unsigned article on the website of *Deutsche Welle* (German Wave), Germany's public international broadcaster, bore another catchy title: "How Germany Got the Russian Revolution off the Ground." The article inflated the role of Parvus in the Russian Revolution and argued that it unfolded in accordance with his plan, which was "a roadmap for what actually happened just a few months later. . . . Gelfand's cunning plan eventually bore fruit. On November 7, 1917, a coup d'état went down in history as the October Revolution."[90]

However, the clickbait prize should probably go to the *New York Times* op-ed page, which carried an article by Sean McMeekin, a historian, with the enticing title: "Was Lenin a German Agent?" The article did not provide a yes or no answer, although it referred to the evidence collected by the Provisional Government as "damning." McMeekin further argued that "No matter Lenin's real intentions, it is undeniable that he received German logistical and financial support in 1917, and that his actions, from antiwar agitation in the Russian army to his request for an unconditional cease-fire, served the interests of Russia's wartime enemy in Berlin."[91]

A lighter piece appeared on a quasi-official Russian website Russia Beyond titled: "Bolshevik Life Hacks—How to Raise Money for Revolution." Its author Oleg Yegorov offered four: "Rob a Bank," "Find Wealthy Friends," "Plot a Marriage of Convenience," and "Take Money Even from Your Enemies." All four tactics had historical roots in Bolshevik revolutionary activities. In relation to the last one, the article quoted historian Andrei Sorokin of the Russian State Archive on socio-political history: "The very fact of receiving funding from the Germans does not mean that the Bolsheviks were German agents. Most likely, they took the money without any strings attached, trying to use Germany for their purposes, just as Germany tried to use them for its own ends."[92]

Historians will never attain a *comprehensive* or *definitive* picture of Germany's role in the Russian Revolution (or of any other event in history). Traces of secret funding and other clandestine activities are often opaque, and the chances are that some of these secrets will never be fully revealed. But a lack of evidence should not be replaced by an overabundance of imagination. It is possible that the German, Russian, British, and French archives, which may house relevant classified materials, especially concerning intelligence operations, could yield more evidence of German monetary support for the Bolsheviks in 1917. Such findings would hardly undermine the established historical record that Bolsheviks' views, policies, and tactics were fully their own. While fascination with Parvus is likely to continue in some circles, a

---

90. "How Germany Got the Russian Revolution off the Ground," *Deutsche Welle*, November 20, 2017, https://www.dw.com/en/how-germany-got-the-russian-revolution-off-the-ground/a-41195312.

91. Sean McMeekin, "Was Lenin a German Agent?" *New York Times*, June 19, 2017, https://www.nytimes.com/2017/06/19/opinion/was-lenin-a-german-agent.html.

92. Oleg Yegorov, "Bolshevik Life Hacks—How to Raise Money for Revolution," Russia Beyond, September 5, 2017, https://www.rbth.com/history/326093-bolshevik-life-hacks-how-to.

major revival of the myth that the Bolsheviks were German agents is unlikely. Still, the notion that opposition political activists are unpatriotic agents of foreign powers doing their destructive bidding continues to persist and may even be on the rise in our contemporary world.

Testing new levels of absurdity and paranoia, a Russian law passed in 2012 states that any nongovernmental organization, or NGO, engaged in ill-defined "political activity" with any amount of foreign funding must register as "a foreign agent." Since then, this requirement has expanded to include the media and even individuals who publicly share their views and are "supported from abroad" or found to be "under foreign influence."[93] As a result, many public organizations and their leaders, as well as private individuals in Russia, especially after Russia's invasion of Ukraine on February 24, 2022, have curtailed their activities, suffered reduced funding, stopped working, faced more harassment (including arrest and imprisonment), or fled the country.

Similarly, in neighboring Belarus, the autocratic leader Alexander Lukashenko claimed that mass protests in cities throughout his country denouncing alleged fraud in the August 9, 2020, presidential election were being fomented by agents or citizens of other countries.[94]

Like the Provisional Government, political leaders sometimes draw comfort and tactical advantage in treating popular discontent as acts of foreign subversion, dismissing people's real needs, concerns, and grievances. They may be setting themselves up for unpleasant surprises.

---

93. Stefan Meister, "The Domestic and Foreign Policy Nexus: Politics, Threat Perception, and Russian Security Strategy," in *Routledge Handbook of Russian Security*, ed. Roger E. Kanet (Abingdon, UK: Routledge, 2019), 75–85 (here: 77–78).

94. Andrei Makhovsky, "Protests Swell in Belarus, Lukashenko Blames Foreigners," Reuters, August 14, 2020, https://www.reuters.com/article/us-belarus-election/protests-swell-in-belarus-lukashenko-blames-foreigners-idUSKCN25A0ZU.

4. The Myth that Princess Anastasia Survived the Assassination of the Imperial Family

I don't need to see her. I know.[1]
—*General Max von Hoffman, upon receiving news of Anastasia's possible survival*

On the night of July 16–17, 1918, in the Ural city of Ekaterinburg, secret police (Cheka) officials entered the Ipatiev House, a private home that had been commandeered by the Bolsheviks and converted in April into the maximum-security residence of the former Russian tsar and his family. The two-story stone house was surrounded by a tall wooden stockade and guarded twenty-four hours a day by dozens of security personnel. At around 1:30 a.m., the head of the Ekaterinburg Cheka, Iakov Iurovskii, awakened Nicholas II, Tsarina Alexandra, their five children (Olga, Tatiana, Maria, Anastasia, and Aleksei), three servants, and the court physician Dr. Evgenii Botkin. After washing and dressing, the eleven were led to the lower level and into a large room with no furniture. Two chairs were brought in at the tsar's request. He sat his hemophiliac son Alexei on one; Alexandra sat on the other. The rest were told to line up. In a few minutes, Iurovskii entered the room with ten armed men. He announced that the local authorities had ordered the tsar and his family shot. The gunmen immediately fired dozens of bullets at the hapless victims. Blood splattered everywhere. Some were finished off with bayonets. The lifeless bodies were then driven ten miles to the north and, in the middle of nowhere, stripped, burned, and cast into an abandoned mineshaft. The next night, however, they were retrieved, driven to a more remote site, disfigured with sulfuric acid, and

Figure 4.1: Grand Duchess Anastasia Nikolaevna of Russia, c. 1914.

---

1. James Blair Lovell, *Anastasia: The Lost Princess* (New York: St. Martin's Press, 1995), 121.

reburied.[2] (That same night, Alexandra's sister Elizabeth and several other Romanov family members were also murdered farther north in the Urals.)

Fräulein Unbekannt

On February 27, 1920, thousands of miles from Ekaterinburg, a woman threw herself from the Bendler Bridge into the Landwehr Canal in Berlin in an apparent suicide attempt and was rescued by a police sergeant. Neither the police nor the doctors could establish her identity, and she was placed in the Dalldorf Asylum. Referred to simply as "Fräulein Unbekannt" (Miss Unknown), she appeared to be suffering from partial amnesia and paranoia. She attracted the attention of another asylum patient, Clara Peuthert, a German who had lived in Russia and was suffering from a temporary nervous breakdown. She discovered that the mysterious stranger appeared mentally sane and was increasingly intrigued and drawn to her. The *Berliner Illustrirte Zeitung* had recently run a cover article on the assassination of the imperial family (and alleged survival of Anastasia), with pictures of its members.[3] Clara thought Fräulein Unbekannt bore a striking resemblance to Grand Duchess Tatiana. As the two ladies leafed through the article, Fräulein Unbekannt shared some comments and hints that confirmed Clara's suspicion.[4]

Once released, Clara Peuthert rushed to share her alleged discovery with Baron Arthur von Kleist, a Baltic German, and Captain Nicholas Schwabe, a Russian guard officer. In the early 1920s, Berlin was host to a large Russian émigré community. Those still loyal to the monarchy coalesced around the Supreme Monarchist Council, which sent several representatives to the asylum to investigate the matter. None was more prominent than Baroness Sophie Buxhoeveden. She had been Alexandra's lady-in-waiting and had been separated from the imperial family only when they were sent to Ekaterinburg. When the baroness, Clara, and Captain Schwabe entered Fräulein Unbekannt's room, she hid under her bed covers. The baroness spoke English as she had done to the grand duchesses but got no response. The baroness showed her an icon and a ring that must have been familiar to Grand Duchess Tatiana. Again, no reaction. When the baroness got a good look at the unidentified woman, she concluded that there was no resemblance between her and Tatiana.[5] "I did not say I was

---

2. Jonathan Daly and Leonid Trofimov, *The Russian Revolution and Its Global Impact* (Indianapolis: Hackett Publishing Company, 2017), x.

3. "Die Wahrheit über den Zarenmord," *Berliner Illustrirte Zeitung* 30, no. 43 (October 23, 1921): 665–67.

4. Greg King and Penny Wilson, *The Resurrection of the Romanovs: Anastasia, Anna Anderson and the World's Greatest Royal Mystery* (Hoboken, NJ: John Wiley and Sons, 2011), 90–91.

5. Arthur J. Olsen, "Anastasia: Grand Duchess or Grand Hoax?" *New York Times*, August 24, 1958, 19, 22; Lovell, *Anastasia*, 79–81; John Klier and Helen Mingay, *The Quest for Anastasia: Solving the Mystery of the Lost Romanovs* (Secaucus, NJ: Carol Publishing Group, 1997), 94–95; Robert K. Massie, *The Romanovs: The Final Chapter* (New York: Random House, 1995), 163.

Tatiana," said Fräulein Unbekannt a few days later. Eventually, she tacitly admitted to Captain Schwabe that she was Anastasia, and he believed her. The asylum's nurses later claimed that Fräulein Unbekannt had secretly confided to them that she was Anastasia even before Clara Peuthert's "discovery."[6]

Thus, one of the most spectacular celebrity myths of the twentieth century was born. Believing that "Anastasia" was truly the grand duchess required not only accepting certain evidence but also a lot of trust. "Anastasia's" supporters were emotionally attached to the person who claimed to have survived the Ekaterinburg tragedy. They seem to have felt that supporting "Anastasia's" claim could make the imperial family's tragedy a bit less horrific. Equally important was "Anastasia's" behavior, which bore signs of profound physical and psychological trauma, as almost everyone who encountered her agreed. Her suffering seemed more important to her than any desire to convince anyone of anything. Little in her actions, especially at this early stage, suggested a strategic calculation on her part.

However, if the fervor of "Anastasia's" supporters was understandable, so was the outrage of those who did not believe her to be the real grand duchess. One can easily imagine their indignation at what they believed was a cynical and horrendous lie and an insult to the true victims' suffering. The stage was set not just for years but for decades of fierce confrontation, in which both sides accused one another of nefarious motives and considered themselves to be righteous champions of the imperial Romanov family, its memory, and the truth.

The Bolsheviks as Murderers and Mythmakers

One could argue that at the heart of many survivor myths lies an instinctive unwillingness to accept a horror or tragedy too extraordinary and unprecedented to fathom. Denial is a common way to respond to catastrophic reality and offers fertile ground for the construction of mythical "alternative realities." Yet the Bolsheviks themselves greatly contributed to the mythmaking around the Ekaterinburg tragedy by initially denying that the entire imperial family was slaughtered along with Nicholas.

The first announcement of the Romanov execution appeared in various official communiqués on July 18. It read:

> Recently Ekaterinburg, the capital of the Red Ural, was seriously threatened by the approach of the Czecho-Slovak bands.[7] At the same time a counter-revolutionary conspiracy was discovered, having for its object

---

6. Klier and Mingay, *Quest for Anastasia*, 95; Peter Kurth, *Anastasia: The Riddle of Anna Anderson* (Boston: Little Brown and Company, 1983), 15; King and Wilson, *Resurrection of the Romanovs*, 88–89, 91.

7. Discussed in Chapter 6.

the wresting of the tyrant[8] from the hands of the Council's authority by armed force. In view of this fact, the Presidium of the Ural Regional Council decided to shoot the ex-Tsar, Nicholas Romanov. This decision was carried out on July 16.

The wife and son of Romanov have been sent to a place of security.[9]

The official Bolshevik announcement, which appeared in the London *Times* four days later,[10] was, thus, a mixture of truth, falsehoods, and omissions. It correctly stated that Nicholas was executed, falsely claimed that Aleksandra and Aleksei were in a secure place, that a conspiracy to free them was afoot, and was silent on the fate of the Romanov girls. Also questionable was the claim that the decision to execute Nicholas had been taken by the Ural regional soviet.

Historians have analyzed the murder of the imperial family for decades and are divided on nearly every aspect of the execution, including its importance.[11] One hotly contested topic is whether the execution was ordered or sanctioned in Moscow. It is known that some Ural Bolsheviks longed to kill the imperial family. The Central Bolshevik authorities, by contrast, hoped to stage a grandiose show trial with Leon Trotsky as prosecutor.[12] Upon learning that Tobolsk, Siberia, where the family had been held from August 1917 until April 1918, was insecure, Iakov Sverdlov, a senior Bolshevik in Moscow, arranged to transfer them to Ekaterinburg.[13]

Circumstantial evidence points to Moscow's hand in the massacre. Filipp Goloshchekin, a military commissar of the Ural region and an old friend of Sverdlov, had stayed with him on a visit to Moscow earlier in July, allegedly to discuss the fate of the imperial family, including the possibility of trying the tsar or other actions should it prove necessary for Bolshevik forces to abandon Ekaterinburg.[14] A surviving telegram

---

8. That is, the former emperor, Nicholas Romanov.

9. George Gustav Telberg and Robert Wilton, *The Last Days of the Romanovs* (New York: George H. Doran Company, 1920), 322.

10. "Ex-Tsar Shot," *Times*, July 22, 1918, 6.

11. Robert Service, *The Last of the Tsars: Nicholas II and the Russian Revolution* (New York and London: Pegasus Books, 2017), chap. 17; Laura Engelstein, *Russia in Flames: War, Revolution, Civil War, 1914–1921* (New York: Oxford University Press, 2018), 397–98; Sheila Fitzpatrick, *The Russian Revolution*, 4th ed. (Oxford: Oxford University Press, 2017), 46.

12. Mark Steinberg and Vladimir Khrustalev, eds., *The Fall of the Romanovs: Political Dreams and Personal Struggles in a Time of Revolution* (New Haven, CT: Yale University Press, 1995), 287–88.

13. Steinberg and Khrustalev, *Fall of the Romanovs*, 183–87; "Soveshchanie starykh bol'shevikov po voprosu prebyvaniia Romanovykh na Urale," February 1, 1934, Tsentr dokumentatsii obschestvennykh organizatsii Sverdlovskoi oblasti (Center for Documentation of Public Organizations of the Sverlovsk Region), f. 41, op. 1, d. 150, l. 4.

14. Steinberg and Khrustalev, *Fall of the Romanovs*, 290–93; Orlando Figes, *A People's Tragedy: The Russian Revolution, 1891–1924* (New York: Penguin Books, 1998), 638–39.

from the Ural regional soviet sent on July 18 asks Moscow "to sanction" the language of the announcement of Nicholas's execution.[15] Such a request makes it unlikely that the execution itself was carried out unsanctioned. Finally, Trotsky later admitted that "the execution of the Tsar's family was needed not only to frighten, horrify, and dishearten the enemy, but also in order to shake up our own ranks, to show them that there was no turning back."[16]

In any case, the Bolshevik leaders publicly declared their approval of Nicholas's execution. But why not that of the entire family? Perhaps the Bolsheviks worried that such news would anger the people and harden their adversaries' resolve.[17] Likewise, the German government expressed concern for the fate of the German-born Alexandra and her children.[18] Increasingly under attack by domestic opponents, the last thing the Bolsheviks wanted was a resumption of hostilities with Germany. As late as 1922, Soviet commissar of Foreign Affairs Georgii Chicherin asserted that "the fate of the young daughters of the Tsar is at present unknown to me. I have read in the Press that they are now in America."[19] These denials surely inspired hope that some of the family members might still be alive.

Adding to such hopes were witnesses claiming to have seen Alexandra and her children traveling north by train *after* the massacre.[20] Nicholas's mother, Dowager Empress Maria Feodorovna, after a safe return to her home country of Denmark, continued to believe that her son and his family were still alive. Rumors also circulated that Nicholas and his family had been sighted in England, the French Riviera, and Rome.[21] On February 17, 1919, the London *Times* Tokyo correspondent reported that Nicholas II's death in Ekaterinburg had been staged, that he was being held prisoner in the Kremlin, and that his family was interned in the nearby Troitse-Sergiev Monastery. According to the report, Lenin was planning to transfer power to the tsar after the destruction of the bourgeoisie.[22] As a *Boston Globe* reporter eventually put it, "rumors and Romanovs are going together like vodka and caviar."[23]

15. Steinberg and Khrustalev, *Fall of the Romanovs*, 335–37.

16. Engelstein, *Russia in Flames*, 398.

17. Figes, *People's Tragedy*, 641.

18. Service, *Last of the Tsars*, 258–59.

19. Wendy Slater, *The Many Deaths of Tsar Nicholas: Relics, Remains, and the Romanovs* (London: Routledge, 2007), 52.

20. Steinberg and Khrustalev, *Fall of the Romanovs*, 295.

21. Robert K. Massie, *Nicholas and Alexandra* (New York: Ballantine Books, 2000), 522, 529; Slater, *Many Deaths*, 86.

22. "Tsar Legend," *Times*, February 17, 1919, 9.

23. Melvyn Johnson, "The Romanovs: Were They Murdered?" *Boston Globe*, April 2, 1972, B42.

What the Whites Found Out

Ekaterinburg fell to anti-Bolshevik forces on July 25, nine days after the massacre. The Bolsheviks had left the city in great haste, and the Ipatiev House still contained scattered furniture, pins, toothbrushes, combs, icons, and books. The basement walls bore traces of bullets; the floor had dents from bayonets.[24] Soon thereafter, a Provisional Ural Government was established in Ekaterinburg with both democratically minded and authoritarian leaders.

Legally trained officials commissioned by the Provisional Ural Government concluded that only Nicholas and Aleksei had been executed. After Admiral Aleksandr Kolchak established himself as Supreme Ruler of anti-Bolshevik forces in November 1918, he appointed a military commander, General Mikhail Diterikhs (sometimes spelled Dietrichs), to oversee the investigation. A believer in a Bolshevik-Jewish-Masonic conspiracy, Diterikhs picked Nikolai Sokolov, a court investigator and an ardent monarchist, to lead the probe.[25]

Sokolov had a conspiratorialist mindset of his own, but his approach was driven by a search for evidence. He scrutinized the Ipatiev House, collected masses of circumstantial evidence (such as an official requisition order for sulfuric acid), and interrogated Bolshevik guards (including the head of the Ipatiev House guard). Sokolov concluded that all members of the imperial family and their entourage had been murdered, but he failed to extinguish survivor myths for one simple reason: no bodies were found. (Only a severed finger and Doctor Botkin's denture turned up in a nearby mine.) Sokolov believed that the bodies had been burned to ashes in the forest.[26] Still, the absence of the bodies coupled with Bolshevik official denials ensured a perpetual stream of pretenders who gave the survivor myths staying power.

There were, for example, several "Alekseis." Anti-Bolshevik investigators debunked Aleksei Putsiato's claim to be Aleksei Romanov in 1919 by enlisting the Romanov children's French teacher, Pierre Gilliard, who did not recognize him.[27] In 1925, Soviet secret police agents shot another "Aleksei," along with a "Grand Duchess Maria."[28] Yet another "Aleksei" appeared in 1927 in Chelmno, Poland, and attracted international attention.[29] In 1949, psychiatrists in Petrozavodsk, northeast of Leningrad, examined a labor camp inmate, Filipp Semenov. He not only resembled the grand duke but

---

24. Edvard Radzinskii, *Imperator i muzhik* (Moscow: AST, 2014), 643–47.

25. Klier and Mingay, *Quest for Anastasia*, 67–68; Nikolai Sokolov, *Ubiistvo tsarskoi semii* (Moscow: Algoritm, 2017), 13–14.

26. Radzinskii, *Imperator*, 649–58.

27. Slater, *Many Deaths*, 87–88.

28. Slater, *Many Deaths*, 81–83; Mariia Malysheva and Vladimir Poznanskii, "'Prishlos' uslyshat' o svoem tsarskom proiskhozhdenii,'" *Istochnik*, 6 (1995): 21–29.

29. "Russians Hail Boy as Lost Czarevitch," *New York Times*, August 24, 1927, 13.

also had detailed familiarity with court protocol and the layout of imperial palaces.[30] Female pretenders also emerged. In 1920, the Soviet authorities arrested Nadezhda Vasilieva, who claimed to be Grand Duchess Anastasia. She died in a mental asylum in 1971. In the 1950s, Marga Boodts convinced several German royals that she was Grand Duchess Olga.[31]

"Anastasia's" Hopes

Yet no other Romanov survivor myth came close to captivating the popular imagination as the myth born in the Dalldorf Asylum in 1921. After Fräulein Unbekannt's release, Baron von Kleist offered her a room in his Berlin apartment, but their relations soured. Then, in 1922, a police inspector, Albert Gruenberg, took her in. He reconstructed her story: "Anastasia" survived the execution of her family in Ekaterinburg. A guard, Alexander Tchaikovsky, discovered her unconscious but alive and carried her to his house. He traveled with her and his family in a peasant cart to Romania. She bore Alexander's child, and they married in a Catholic church. They abandoned the child at an orphanage, and Alexander died in Bucharest during a street fight. "Anastasia" made her way to Berlin, seeking her mother's sister, Princess Irene. Full of despair, she threw herself into the Landwehr Canal.[32]

The story of "Anastasia's" miraculous survival was deeply moving to some and implausible to others. What is remarkable is that nothing about it could be confirmed by any historical records. No proof exists that Alexander Tchaikovsky served as an Ipatiev House guard or even lived in Ekaterinburg. No record confirms his presence, marriage, or death in Bucharest, nor is there an adoption record for his child.[33] The birth of the child was a particularly troubling aspect of the story to some monarchists. If it was true, then a direct heir to the Russian throne might still be found in a Romanian orphanage nullifying endless succession debates among more distant Romanov relatives and their supporters.

There was another major problem. "Anastasia" refused to speak Russian. She and her supporters pointed to a profound psychological trauma she felt when speaking Russian. Yet she also had no knowledge of English, a native language of her mother, and her German was not native either. Supporters blamed memory loss due to brain damage. Thus, both her memories and her lack of memories served as proofs for her claims. A similar reflex enabled her supporters to dismiss "memories" that were patently false or absurd, for example, that Leon Trotsky had once visited

---

30. Radzinskii, *Imperator*, 714–18.

31. Massie, *Romanovs*, 145–47.

32. Olsen, "Anastasia"; Massie, *Romanovs*, 164–65.

33. Massie, *Romanovs*, 164–65.

the imperial family before the revolution, breaking some china and upsetting the emperor.[34]

It is difficult to tell how much of "Anastasia's" story Inspector Gruenberg believed, but he took a step intended to solve her mystery once and for all. He invited Princess Irene of Hesse-Darmstadt, Alexandra's sister, for a discreet visit. During the encounter, Princess Irene declared that "Anastasia" was not her niece and did not bear any resemblance to her. Yet later, she admitted: "She *is* similar. She *is* similar. But what does that mean if it is not she?"[35]

Irene's reaction reveals the terrible dilemma faced by those who had known the real Anastasia and then met the claimant: How to categorically reject someone who may have changed over the years and apparently suffered from devastating traumas? How could anyone be certain that person was a liar and a cheat? And if there was even a slight chance that she was who she claimed to be, how could anyone deny her that chance to reassert her identity after all the horrors she had been through? "Anastasia's" supporters pointed to such hesitations as evidence of that identity, but surely it was above all evidence of the humane unwillingness to make a terrible mistake.

"Anastasia's" encounter with another aunt was much more promising. In 1925, Grand Duchess Olga, one of Nicholas II's two sisters, visited her in Berlin for three days running. Olga lived in Denmark, like her mother, the Dowager Empress Maria. The visit occurred after "Anastasia" had recovered from an inflammatory illness involving major surgery. Olga spoke Russian; "Anastasia" responded in German, but Olga was profoundly moved. She had fond recollections of her time with Nicholas's daughters before the revolution and leaned toward accepting the claimant as the real Anastasia.[36]

Grand Duchess Olga did not act entirely on her own. The Danish envoy in Berlin, Herluf Zahle, had been instructed by the dowager's brother, Prince Valdemar of Denmark, to investigate the claimant's story and, in the meantime, provide her with the necessary support. He became wholeheartedly convinced that the claimant was, in fact, Anastasia. Unfortunately, his reports to the Danish royal family remain classified to this day. Also unavailable is the report of Aleksei Volkov, Alexandra's servant, whom Zahle brought to Berlin to help establish the claimant's identity before Olga's visit.[37]

Two other people assisted Olga. As mentioned above, the Romanov children's French teacher, Pierre Gilliard, had been forcibly separated from the Romanov family in Ekaterinburg. He stayed in Russia, however, and married Alexandra Tegleva, a maid to the grand duchesses. Three years later, he returned to his native Switzerland

---

34. Massie, *Romanovs*, 169–70; King and Wilson, *Resurrection of the Romanovs*, 103, 199.

35. Lovell, *Anastasia*, 86; Massie, *Romanovs*, 167–68.

36. Massie, *Romanovs*, 174.

37. Lovell, *Anastasia*, 94–96.

and became a professor of French at the University of Lausanne.[38] One cannot think of anyone more closely and recently familiar with the Romanov daughters to either verify or invalidate "Anastasia's" claims. Gilliard and Tegleva first met with "Anastasia" three months before Grand Duchess Olga's visit, but at that time, she was physically incapable of interacting with them because of her illness. Still, Tegleva had a chance to look at her feet. Anastasia had a particular malformation of the joints at the root of her toes, more so on the right foot than on the left. And so, according to Tegleva, did the claimant. Like Olga, Tegleva was deeply moved by meeting Anastasia again and seemed to believe it was she. Gillard was more restrained, especially after meeting with other Russian émigrés in Berlin and realizing how much "Anastasia" could have learned from them about the royal family. Still, he allegedly declared: "We are going away without being able to say that she is *not* Grand Duchess Anastasia Nikolaevna."[39] Thus, in 1925, "Anastasia" came close to having her claim recognized by the Romanov family.

Hopes Crushed

The warming up to "Anastasia" ended abruptly. Several factors were at play. First, she sought to contact another member of the Hesse-Darmstadt dynasty, Alexandra's brother, Grand Duke Ernest Ludwig. She claimed that she had seen "Uncle Ernie" as recently as 1916 when he had visited Russia to convince the imperial family to negotiate a separate peace with Germany.[40] This was a bombshell. No record of such a journey existed, and it is doubtful it ever took place. Even a rumor that Ernest Ludwig had had contacts with Germany's enemy during the war would have tarnished his reputation among German conservatives. But this allegation also irked Russian monarchists since it substantiated liberal charges that the imperial family, especially Alexandra, was prone to German influence and not sufficiently patriotic. Thus, "Anastasia's" bombshell confused the Russian monarchists and turned members of the Hesse-Darmstadt dynasty into her bitter enemies.

Second, there was the question of money. "Anastasia" later declared that she had told Olga about sizeable amounts of money Nicholas II kept for them in the Bank of England as dowries. Later she named the amounts: five million rubles for each daughter. Supposedly, Nicholas gathered his daughters shortly before the end and told them that if they were separated, they could count on that money, even though it was kept in someone else's name. In whose name, "Anastasia" could not remember. But Olga

38. Helen Rappaport, *The Romanov Sisters: The Lost Lives of the Daughters of Nicholas and Alexandra* (New York: St. Martin's Press, 2014), 379; Klier and Mingay, *Quest for Anastasia*, 99–100.

39. Massie, *Romanovs*, 172–73; King and Wilson, *Resurrection of the Romanovs*, 127–28.

40. Lovell, *Anastasia*, 96–97; B. V. Ananich and R. Sh. Ganelin, "Emperor Nicholas II, 1894–1917," in *The Emperors and Empresses of Russia: Rediscovering the Romanovs*, ed. Donald J. Raleigh, comp. A. A. Iskenderov (Abingdon, UK: Routledge, 2015), 398.

undoubtedly relayed that information to her other relatives. Once money was mentioned, the question of the claimant's identity and the money's rightful recipient was no longer a matter merely of sentimental feelings.[41]

The skeptical view of "Anastasia" hardened. She was no longer seen as a helpless, confused, and deeply traumatized person with an unclear past but as a cunning and greedy manipulator who craved glory and riches and tarnished the sacred memory of the real Grand Duchess Anastasia. Olga stopped writing to her. The Danish envoy Zahle was ordered to terminate all contacts. Gilliard made public statements denying ever believing "Anastasia" was truly Anastasia. He called the claimant "a vulgar adventuress" and even co-authored a book entitled *The False Anastasia*.[42]

The Romanovs grew even more suspicious when one of Anastasia's staunchest supporters, Harriett Rathlef-Keilmann, published a book in her defense. A successful artist born to a prominent Jewish family in Riga, Rathlef fled Russia after the revolution and settled in Germany. For many months she spoke with "Anastasia," helped with her living arrangements and health needs, and took detailed notes of their encounters. Rathlef's book was serialized in early 1927 in the German tabloid, *Berliner Nachtausgabe* (The Berlin Night Edition). The book turned "Anastasia" into an instant celebrity and not just in Berlin. Her story was reported in newspapers on both sides of the Atlantic.[43]

Then came the final blow. In April, the *Berliner Nachtausgabe* published the results of a private investigation establishing that "Anastasia" was, in reality, a demented munitions factory worker from Poland, Franziska Schanzkowska (b. Francisca Anna Czenstkowska),[44] who suffered a devastating explosion at work and went missing around the same time that Fräulein Unbekannt was rescued from the Landwehr Canal. Several witnesses confirmed her identity, including members of her own family.[45]

Botkin to the Rescue

In this dark hour for "Anastasia," she gained a new supporter whose closeness to the real "Anastasia" rivaled that of Gillard and Tegleva: Gleb Botkin. He was the son of

41. Lovell, *Anastasia*, 106.

42. Pierre Gilliard and Constantin Savitch, *La fausse Anastasie, histoire d'une prétendue grande-duchesse de Russie* (Paris: Payot, 1929).

43. William Clarke, *The Lost Fortune of the Tsars* (New York: St Martin's Press, 1994), 124; Lovell, *Anastasia*, 119–20; Michael Farquhar, *A Treasury of Deception: Liars, Misleaders, Hoodwinkers, and the Extraordinary True Stories of History's Greatest Hoaxes, Fakes, and Frauds* (New York: Penguin, 2005), 217.

44. Robert S. Meisner, *Steinkreuze, Kreuzsteine und andere Sühnemale zwischen Inn und Salzach* (Norderstedt: BoD – Books on Demand, 2021), 119.

45. Lovell, *Anastasia*, 123–24; Coryne Hall, *Little Mother of Russia: A Biography of the Empress Marie Feodorovna (1847–1928)* (New York: Holmes and Meier, 2001), 356.

Dr. Botkin, who had remained with the imperial family throughout their exile to give Aleksei the constant medical attention he needed. Gleb's father perished together with the Romanovs, a hero whose act of professional and personal sacrifice is often overlooked. His daughter Tatiana and son Gleb knew Nicholas's children well, and Gleb, in particular, had played with Anastasia for years. They had remained in Tobolsk after their father had departed to Ekaterinburg. Both children eventually escaped Soviet Russia.[46]

Gleb arrived in the United States in 1922. As he later recalled: "Wherever I went, I heard of rescued Grand Duchesses. I even met some of them. It came to the point when every announcement of another 'discovery' of a rescued Grand Duchess caused me to fly into fits of anger."[47] But at the urging of Tatiana, he traveled to Europe in 1927 to meet "Anastasia." He claimed he recognized her immediately. She spoke of "his funny animals." This was a reference to the animal pictures Gleb used to draw for Anastasia (Figure 4.2), most recently in Tobolsk. To Gleb, this was the ultimate proof that the claimant was Anastasia, even though, in his earlier statements, he admitted that he had been the first to mention the topic.[48] Still, he declared that "Anastasia"

Figure 4.2: One of Gleb Botkin's "funny animal" drawings.

46. Lovell, *Anastasia*, 28–29, 125.

47. Gleb Botkin, "This *Is* Anastasia," *North American Review* 229, no. 2 (February 1930): 193–99 (here: 195).

48. King and Wilson, *Resurrection of the Romanovs*, 175.

remembered many minute details in the pictures that Gleb himself had forgotten.[49] Perhaps "Anastasia" had gained some of this knowledge from Gleb's sister Tatiana. In any event, for many years, Gleb remained "Anastasia's" ardent champion.

As time went on, the quality and accuracy of "Anastasia's" "memories" improved, which was not surprising given the vast and continuous stream of literature about the Romanov family that included memoirs and photographic essays. Some of her supporters claimed, like Gleb, that her intimate knowledge of Russian court life could not have come from public sources. For example, Lili Dehn, Alexandra's lady-in-waiting, was won over in 1957 by many details shared by "Anastasia," including her son's private nickname. Dehn presumably had forgotten that she had shared that information in her memoir in 1922.[50]

In the meantime, scandalous publicity was making "Anastasia's" situation increasingly precarious. While staying in a Bavarian castle courtesy of the Duke and Duchess of Leuchtenberg, she was besieged by endless curious visitors and began receiving death threats. She later described a meeting with Prince Felix Yusupov, one of Rasputin's assassins, who came from Paris to meet her. She claimed he stretched his trembling hands toward her and declared: "I killed Rasputin, and I will kill you for what your mother did to my country."[51] As so often with "Anastasia," the veracity of her story is impossible to confirm.

Gleb Botkin believed he found a solution to "Anastasia's" troubles—taking her to the United States, away from her enemies in Europe. He also found a new host willing to take her in: Anastasia's cousin, Princess Xenia. She was a daughter of Grand Duke Paul (a cousin of Nicholas II), who had married a wealthy American, William B. Leeds. Xenia recognized the claimant as Anastasia, whom she had last met before the war, and offered her the hospitality of her Long Island estate.[52] Upon arriving in America, "Anastasia" received much sympathetic publicity. In the meantime, Dowager Empress Maria died in Denmark in October 1928 without officially recognizing or rejecting her supposed granddaughter. Official rejection followed twenty-four hours later when the twelve members of the extended Romanov family and three members of the Hesse-Darmstadt family declared that "Anastasia" was not Nicholas and Alexandra's daughter.[53] Grand Duchess Olga and Princess Irene were the only signatories who had met the claimant. Princess Xenia was not asked to sign, nor was Grand Duke Andrew, who had met with "Anastasia" before she left Europe and declared that he recognized her.[54]

---

49. Botkin, "This Is Anastasia," 196, 198.

50. King and Wilson, *Resurrection of the Romanovs*, 217.

51. Lovell, *Anastasia*, 130–31.

52. Massie, *Romanovs*, 190.

53. Hall, *Little Mother of Russia*, 356.

54. Massie, *Romanovs*, 175.

While those who refused to accept "Anastasia's" claims increasingly ascribed to her the most cynical and vile ambitions, her supporters responded in kind. They asserted that Anastasia's relatives denied her identity to protect their own claims to the Romanov succession and wealth. Gleb put it most harshly in response to the above-mentioned public declaration: the "endless persecution of one of your own family," he wrote, was worse than the murder of the emperor and his family by "a gang of crazed and drunken savages."[55] Such a charge precluded reconciliation.

"Anastasia" in the Courts

In 1929, "Anastasia" granted power of attorney to an American lawyer, Edward Fallows, to search for Romanov family money and claim her share. Fallows set up the Grandanor Corporation (an acronym of Grand Duchess Anastasia of Russia) to solicit financial support for future court battles. Contributors were promised an attractive return on their investment. Fallows himself was supposed to receive a quarter of any amount under four hundred thousand dollars and 10 percent of the rest.[56] Speculative estimates of the last tsar's hidden wealth reached one billion dollars.[57] Fallows uncovered no evidence of substantial Romanov wealth because of British banking confidentiality rules, because Nicholas II seems to have moved his family funds from Britain to Russia during the war for patriotic reasons, and because the tsar's remaining monies in Germany were dissipated by postwar hyperinflation.[58]

Meanwhile, "Anastasia's" life in America was rocky. After she quarreled with Princess Xenia, the world-famous composer and pianist Sergei Rachmaninoff arranged for her to stay at a "comfortable hotel suite in Garden City, Long Island," where she registered as Mrs. Anderson, soon adding the first name Anna. The name stuck. Next, she lived with Annie B. Jennings, "a wealthy Park Avenue spinster eager to have a daughter of the tsar under her roof. For eighteen months, the onetime Fräulein Unbekannt was the toast of New York society, a fixture at dinner parties, luncheons, tea dances, and the opera."[59] Throughout, "Anastasia's" capricious character, stubbornness, bouts of anger, and paranoia further convinced her supporters that she was truly Alexandra's daughter. They also landed her, once again, in a mental institution.

Upon her release in 1932, she spent the next thirty-six years in Germany, moving from one city or province to another, eventually settling in the village of Unterlengenhardt in the Black Forest. While in Germany, she relied on support from Prince

---

55. Massie, *Romanovs*, 179, 183.

56. Clarke, *Lost Fortune of the Tsars*, 125.

57. Klier and Mingay, *Quest for Anastasia*, 121.

58. Clarke, *Lost Fortune of the Tsars*, 265–68.

59. Massie, *Romanovs*, 196–97.

Frederick of Saxe-Altenburg, a distant relative of the Romanovs.[60] In 1938, the Nazis tried and failed to establish her identity. On orders of the Nazi government, the Hannover police arranged a meeting between "Anastasia" and four of her alleged Schanzkowski siblings. After much hesitation, she agreed to the meeting, but only if Edward Fallows and Gleb Botkin were present. Upon seeing "Anastasia," Gertrude Schanzkowska started screaming: "Can you deny that you are my sister? Go on, say it. You cannot fool me." Yet the four siblings refused to sign an affidavit against "Anastasia," which could have led to her incarceration as an impostor under Nazi law.[61]

Later that year, with the encouragement of Fallows and Botkin, "Anastasia" took her identity battle to court. She contested the distribution of a small estate to Alexandra's Hessian family relatives. The validity of her suit depended on her identity, and it was up to the judiciary to resolve the mystery. The courts amassed a vast body of testimony from "Anastasia's" supporters and detractors, but also from doctors, forensic experts, graphologists, and criminologists—even a renowned anthropologist. Most of the expert testimony supported her case.[62] Suspended during the war, it was reviewed in German courts in the 1950s and 1960s. During this period, reporters and tourists frequently descended on "Anastasia's" cottage in the Black Forest to catch a glimpse or have tea with a "Grand Duchess." She, in turn, often preferred the company of cats, whose number in her home eventually surpassed sixty.[63]

Amid what became the longest-running legal case in twentieth-century German history, "Anastasia" wrote an autobiography, assisted by Prince Frederick and Roland Krug von Nidda, which appeared first in German, then in English.[64] In the English translation, she declared that, above all, she wanted her name and identity back. She added: "I hope to God the legal proceedings soon reach an end for I find it a dreadful strain trying to follow what is happening, and even then understanding only part of what is going on."[65] The Hessian descendants vigorously challenged "Anastasia's" claims, including most forcefully Lord Mountbatten, an uncle of Prince Philip, Queen Elizabeth II's husband, and Alexandra's nephew. He spent thousands of pounds on the case and successfully prevented the BBC from making a film that would have included an interview with "Anastasia." The courts ultimately ruled

---

60. Klier and Mingay, *Quest for Anastasia*, 114–5.

61. Klier and Mingay, *Quest for Anastasia*, 128–9.

62. Klier and Mingay, *Quest for Anastasia*, 158–62; Massie, *Romanovs*, 189–91; King and Wilson, *Resurrection of the Romanovs*, 220–35.

63. Klier and Mingay, *Quest for Anastasia*, 130–31, 140; "Is This Princess Alive: A Broadway Hit and a Visit to a Shack Spotlight the Dark Mystery of Anastasia's Fate," *Life*, February 14, 1955, 31–34.

64. Klier and Mingay, *Quest for Anastasia*, 143; Roland Krug von Nidda, *Ich, Anastasia, erzähle; Aufzeichnungen und Dokumente der Grossfürstin Anastasia von Russland* (Frankfurt am Main: H. Scheffler, 1957).

65. Anna Anderson, *I Anastasia: An Autobiography*, trans. Oliver Coburn, notes Roland Krug von Nidda (New York: Harcourt, Brace and Company, 1959), 263.

Figure 4.3: "Anastasia" and her husband, Dr. Jack Manahan.

that "Anastasia" could not prove her identity claim, and in 1970 the Supreme Court in Karlsruhe rejected her appeal.[66]

Two years earlier, "Anastasia" had left Europe again. Thanks again to help from Gleb Botkin, she settled in Charlottesville, Virginia, as a guest of a University of Virginia history professor and genealogist John Manahan, whom she had met in Germany in the 1960s. There she met Maria, the daughter of Grigorii Rasputin, who claimed to recognize her and invited her to Los Angeles for a fancy tea in her honor. She agreed, then declined, suspecting a publicity stunt. "Anastasia" and Manahan married and lived together as an increasingly eccentric couple (Figure 4.3), alienating their neighbors in part by the growing number of living and buried cats on their property. In 1984, "Anastasia" died of pneumonia. Her death certificate issued by the Commonwealth of Virginia granted her the identity she had claimed as Anastasia Nikolaevna Manahan, daughter of Tsar Nikolai and Alix of Hesse Darmstadt, occupation: "royalty."[67] Anastasia's body was cremated and, with it, seemingly any chance to resolve her mystery.[68]

"Anastasia" in Popular Culture

While "Anastasia" did not fare well in the courts, the court of public opinion and popular culture lavished her with attention. Her character's cinematic debut occurred in a 1928 Hollywood silent film, *Clothes Make the Woman*, starring Eve Southern

---

66. Klier and Mingay, *Quest for Anastasia*, 133; Frances Welch, *Romanov Fantasy: Life at the Court of Anna Anderson* (New York: W.W. Norton, 2007), 247–49; King and Wilson, *Resurrection of the Romanovs*, 236–38.

67. King and Wilson, *Resurrection of the Romanovs*, 253.

68. Klier and Mingay, *Quest for Anastasia*, 144; Emilee Hines, *Virginia Myths and Legends: The True Stories behind History's Mysteries*, 2nd ed. (Guilford, CT: Globe Pequot, 2016), 102–3.

and Walter Pidgeon. Other films followed.[69] In 1951, French playwright Marcelle Maurette's play, *Anastasia*, debuted in Paris.[70] In the story, an exiled Russian prince-turned-taxi-driver in Berlin uses Anna to extort money from the Romanov family. In her encounter with the dowager empress, she claims to be Anastasia, but in a plot twist, she runs off with an "idealistic, penniless doctor 'to find life—her real life.'" In 1953, the play was adapted for British television. The same year, in London, it was produced for the stage by Lawrence Olivier to great acclaim, followed by similar success in New York. The reviews were mostly positive, "not art, perhaps," as one critic put it, "but one grand show filled with heroes and heroines and the skullduggery of the most enchanting villain."[71]

The play was also made into a major motion picture in 1956, starring Ingrid Bergman as Anastasia (Figure 4.4), a role that won her an Oscar for Best Actress.[72] A soundtrack album, performed by the popular singer Pat Boone, was released the same year.[73]

Figure 4.4: 1956 *Anastasia* film release poster.

Maurette's play also inspired the creators of an operetta, *Anya*, in 1965. The music, by Rachmaninoff, "stands among the best of the decade, even amid the silliness," according to one assessment.[74] Then came two ballet productions in 1967 and in 1989 and another theater play: *I Am Who I Am* by Royce Ryton.[75]

---

69. Welch, *Romanov Fantasy*, 183; King and Wilson, *Resurrection of the Romanovs*, 204.

70. Marcelle Maurette, *Anastasia*, ed. Guy Bolton (New York: Random House, 1955).

71. Amnon Kabatchnik, *Blood on the Stage, 1950–1975: Milestone Plays of Crime, Mystery, and Detection* (Lanham, MD: Scarecrow Press, 2011), 12–14 (quotations: 13).

72. "Brilliant Return for Ingrid," *Life*, November 26, 1956, 75–76, 79–80, 82.

73. Lovell, *Anastasia*, 216–23.

74. Ethan Mordden, *Open a New Window: The Broadway Musical in the 1960s* (New York: Palgrave Macmillan, 2002), 87.

75. Lovell, *Anastasia*, 471–72.

Figure 4.5: Dimitri, Anastasia, Rasputin, poster for the 1997 animated film, *Anastasia*.

In the 1990s, Anastasia leaped across genres again and entered the world of animation with a Fox Animation Studio production— its debut film aimed at challenging Disney's hegemony—with Meg Ryan voicing the title character (Figure 4.5). (Oddly, Rasputin rises from the dead and comes after Anastasia.) An aggressive marketing campaign involved cross-promotion agreements with Burger King, Dole Foods, Hershey, Chesebrough Ponds, Shell Oil, and the U.S. Figure Skating Championships.[76] A video game followed, as well "Anastasia on Ice," in the words of the *Chicago Tribune*'s Chris Jones, "the only family ice show in history to be based on Bolshevik brutality."[77]

Recently, *Anastasia* made a comeback as a new musical, which opened in 2015 in Hartford, CT. A new villain is introduced, a political policeman (of the notorious Cheka) named Gleb Vaganov, and some Tchaikovsky music was added.[78] The musical ran for two years on Broadway and toured North America, then on to Holland, Japan, and Australia.[79]

Few other stories of the Russian Revolution gained such a high profile in popular culture.

Given the tragedy of the massacre at the Ipatiev House, it is understandable why some people found such treatment offensive, especially after Anastasia had been

76. Chris Petrikin, "Fox Draws out Big Guns in Toon Town Showdown," *Variety*, August 25, 1997, 9, 84.

77. Chris Jones, "'Anastasia' Impressive Bit of Family Fare," *Chicago Tribune*, September 25, 1998, 2.

78. Linda Buchwald, "'Anastasia,' All Grown Up with Somewhere to Go," *American Theatre*, June 3, 2016, https://www.americantheatre.org/2016/06/03/anastasia-all-grown-up-with-somewhere-to-go/.

79. Trilby Beresford, "'Anastasia' Musical to End Broadway Run in March," *Hollywood Reporter*, February 5, 2019, https://www.hollywoodreporter.com/news/anastasia-musical-end-broadway-run-march-1183201.

canonized as a martyr in 1981 by the Russian Orthodox Church Abroad.[80] But did artistic representations of the Anastasia myth help perpetuate it? Not necessarily. Just as likely, turning "Anastasia's" story into artistic performance blurred the boundaries between reality and fiction. With every new artistic rendition, the story looked increasingly like a parable rooted in broadly shared human emotions and experiences: separation and loneliness, hope and perseverance, fear and love, and a search for identity. The plays, ballets, and films did not assert the story's veracity. Instead, they made it truthful to human feelings, an accomplishment that can stand on its own.

"A New Anastasia"

Despite "Anastasia's" rise in popular culture, the historical truth behind her story remained as murky as ever. In 1963, Mrs. Eugenia Smith of Elmhurst, Illinois, approached a New York publisher with a remarkable manuscript—biographical notes by Grand Duchess Anastasia, allegedly written by a friend but later claimed as her own. Another "Anastasia"![81]

In order to ascertain the truthfulness of her story, the publisher imposed thirty hours of lie-detector testing, which Mrs. Smith passed with flying colors. Fearing that she might be sufficiently deluded to "beat" the lie detector, the publisher hired a highly respected psychiatrist who conducted four lengthy interviews with Mrs. Smith. This expert found "no evidence of delusion formation or other schizophrenic symptoms, nor of other psychosis."[82] Her book was, therefore, published as *Anastasia: The Autobiography of I.I.H., the Grand Duchess Anastasia Nikolaevna of Russia*.[83] *Life* magazine ran a cover story about Mrs. Smith and her book under the heading: "The record says she died—The legend says she lives."[84] Although "New Anastasia's" story bore some similarities to that of Anna Anderson, *Life* adduced graphological and anthropological evidence, as well as interviews with persons intimately familiar with the real Anastasia, suggesting that Mrs. Smith was an impostor.

Several letters to the editor followed. One sarcastically remarked: "Wouldn't it be a good idea for *Life* to arrange a family reunion of all the imperial Russian fakes in this world?"[85] Indeed, on December 31, 1963, a most remarkable encounter took place

---

80. Ari L. Goldman, "A Russian Sect Canonizes Nicholas II," *New York Times*, November 2, 1981, B1; Carey Goldberg, "After the Revolution, Comes 'Anastasia' the Cartoon," *New York Times*, November 9, 1997, A2.

81. Massie, *Romanovs*, 157–58.

82. "The Case of a New Anastasia: A Lady from Chicago Claims She is the Czar's Daughter," *Life*, October 18, 1963, 104A–12 (here: 109).

83. *Anastasia: The Autobiography of H.I.H., the Grand Duchess Anastasia Nikolaevna of Russia* (New York: R. Speller and Sons, 1963).

84. "New Anastasia," 104A.

85. Letter to the editor, *Life*, November 8, 1963, 27.

between "New Anastasia" and Michael Goleniewski, a former Polish secret service officer and onetime Soviet spy, now a spy for the CIA, claiming to be Tsarevich Aleksei.[86] "New Anastasia" and "Aleksei" "recognized" one another as sister and brother. "New Anastasia" soon changed her mind, but "Aleksei" continued to insist she was his sister.[87] "New Anastasia" died in 1997 in North Kingstown, Rhode Island.[88] She was "buried in Orthodox tradition" at the Holy Trinity Orthodox Monastery, Jordanville, New York.[89]

Uncertainty

Interest in "New Anastasia" peaked in the 1960s, but the controversy over the possible survival of some members of the imperial family was reignited in 1970 with the publication by an American journalist Guy Richards of an account of the Romanov family's rescue, followed by a second book on the same topic in 1975.[90]

A more serious take on the survival controversy was the publication of *The File on the Tsar* by two BBC journalists, Anthony Summers and Tom Mangold, in 1976. The book, a spinoff from a TV documentary, dismissed Richards's theories but freshly challenged the conclusions of the Sokolov investigation. The authors reached out to forensics experts who confirmed that neither sulfuric acid nor fire could have destroyed human teeth without a trace. As a result, they wrote, "there are about 350 missing teeth to account for."[91] They also pointed to the witness accounts of the alleged evacuation to Perm of Alexandra and her daughters. While Sokolov did not find these accounts credible, he preserved them, and they eventually became part of Harvard University's Houghton Library collections. Summers and Mangold cited a witness, Dr. Pavel Utkin, who recounted that in September 1918, he had been summoned to the Perm Cheka to treat a young woman supposedly beaten after an escape attempt. According to Doctor Utkin, "In a trembling voice, but quite distinctly, she answered me, word for word—as follows: 'I am the emperor's daughter Anastasia.'"[92]

---

86. Kevin Coogan, *The Spy Who Would Be Tsar: The Mystery of Michal Goleniewski and the Far-Right Underground* (Abingdon, UK: Routledge, 2022).

87. Massie, *Romanovs*, 159; Slater, *Many Deaths*, 100.

88. "Eugenia Smith Smetisko," *Providence Journal* (February 8, 1997): A8.

89. "Eugenia Smith," Find a Grave, accessed June 11, 2020, https://www.findagrave.com/memorial/33541170/eugenia-smith.

90. Guy Richards, *The Hunt for the Tsar* (Garden City, NY: Doubleday, 1970); Richards, *The Rescue of the Romanovs: Newly Discovered Documents Reveal How Czar Nicholas II and the Russian Imperial Family Escaped* (Old Greenwich, CT: Devin-Adair Co., 1975).

91. Anthony Summers and Tom Mangold, *The File on the Tsar* (New York: Harper and Row, 1976), 159.

92. Summers and Mangold, *File on the Tsar*, 337.

Summers and Mangold's book illustrates well the advantages and pitfalls of non-academic historical research. On the one hand, it is humbling to academics to be reminded that excellent questions and important insights can be offered by people outside their field. On the other hand, the authors' uncritical embrace of historical sources and their imaginative conclusions based on incomplete historical evidence resulted in sheer speculation. Concerning Anastasia, they wrote:

> We cannot conclude that all definitely died, for we have no proof. The evidence suggests one daughter made her escape, however brief, during the Perm period. It is feasible that events repeated themselves during the journey to Moscow, and someone may have survived. If we allow for the possibility that, after her first escape, the injured Anastasia was moved separately from the rest of her family, it is conceivable that Anastasia was such a survivor.[93]

In 1974, the authors were eager to test their theory by meeting with "Anastasia," who by then resided in Charlottesville, Virginia. She seemed to play along in her classic enigmatic way: "There was no massacre there . . . but I cannot tell the rest."[94]

Professional historians' reaction to *The File on the Tsar* was mixed. Richard Pipes dismissed the Perm survival story out of hand, holding it to be based upon "gossip, innuendo, unanswered questions."[95] However, French historian Marc Ferro allowed for the plausibility of the Perm survival story and suggested that "only a full confrontation of the Soviet archives with the relevant foreign archives could enable us to be more positive about what happened at Ekaterinburg than about Pope Joan" (a mythical early medieval female pope).[96]

It seemed that from that point on, the only way to put to rest speculations about the possible survival of Anastasia or any other members of the imperial family would be to do what the anti-Bolshevik investigators had failed to do—locate their actual remains.

Three Moments of Truth

At the time of the sparring over *The File on the Tsar*, unbeknownst to Summers and Mangold and to all the "Anastasias," "Alekseis," and other "surviving Romanovs," several Soviet nonacademic researchers were about to make a major historical discovery that became a moment of truth in the debates over the fate of the Romanov family. Reports of a hidden burial site had circulated in the Soviet Union for years, mostly

---

93. Summers and Mangold, *File on the Tsar*, 353.

94. Summers and Mangold, *File on the Tsar*, 239.

95. Richard Pipes, "The File on The Tsar," *New York Times*, December 12, 1976, BR1.

96. Marc Ferro, *Nicholas II: The Last of the Tsars* (Oxford: Oxford University Press, 1990), 284.

due to statements by those involved in the execution. Such stories sometimes contradicted each other and were never published, given tight Soviet censorship. However, enough people learned of them eventually to make curious minds wonder where the burial site could be. In the 1970s, a former criminal investigator and writer, Gelii Riabov, partnered with a geologist, Aleksandr Avdonin, and others to bring together the scattered references and attempt to find the burial site in the Koptiaki Forest outside of Ekaterinburg. In summer 1979, they succeeded, uncovering the mass grave

and excavating the remains (Figure 4.6). They kept their discovery secret, as well as a big discrepancy: according to Bolshevik and anti-Bolshevik investigators, eleven people had been murdered in the Ipatiev House, yet only nine sets of remains were found. Two had gone missing.[97]

It was only in 1989, two years before the collapse of the USSR and amid Mikhail Gorbachev's glasnost, or openness, campaign, that Riabov

Figure 4.6: Romanov family burial ground, 1918–1991, Koptiaki Forest.

and Avdonin found it possible to make their discovery public.[98] An official investigation with the requisite forensic expertise was undertaken to identify the remains. The experts utilized bone analysis and DNA testing, still in its early stages in the 1990s, and confirmed that the remains belonged to five members of the Romanov family, three members of their entourage, and Dr. Botkin. This was a turning point, a moment of truth, in the Anastasia mystery.

The Russian Orthodox Church leadership was slow to accept the findings, perhaps fearing that the remains were part of some elaborate hoax. In 1998, the Russian government buried the Romanov family remains in the Cathedral of Saints Peter and Paul in Saint Petersburg, the resting place of nearly all the Russian emperors and empresses from Peter the Great onward. Two years later, the entire family was canonized by the Russian Orthodox Church as *strastoterptsy*, "not as martyrs killed for Christ, but as sufferers killed 'in Christ.'"[99] Experts concluded

97. Klier and Mingay, *Quest for Anastasia*, 173–80.

98. Gelii Riabov, "Soshestvie v ad. Posmertnaia sud'ba Tsarskoi Sem'i: Fakty, domysly, spekuliatsii," *Kontinent*, no. 2 (148) (2011): 626–55.

99. Karin Hyldal Christensen, *The Making of the New Martyrs of Russia: Soviet Repression in Orthodox Memory* (Abingdon, UK: Routledge, 2018), 43.

variously that the missing remains belonged to Aleksei and Maria or to Aleksei and Anastasia.[100]

These allegations raised the tantalizing possibility that one or more of the Romanov children may have survived. Could the late Mrs. Manahan of Charlottesville, Virginia, who died of pneumonia in 1984, have been Grand Duchess Anastasia after all? Freelance writer James Lovell, "Anastasia's" biographer and supporter, eloquently made that case in *Anastasia: The Lost Princess* (1991).[101] Yet only a DNA test could answer this question beyond the shadow of a doubt. Of course, DNA could not be extracted from the ashes of Mrs. Manahan's cremated body. Yet five years before her death, "Anastasia" had undergone a surgical procedure at Martha Jefferson Hospital in Virginia involving the removal of part of her intestine. As a routine practice, the hospital preserved this tissue and after a court battle, permitted DNA extraction. Another DNA sample was extracted from surviving strands of "Anastasia's" hair. When tested in different labs, "Anastasia's" nuclear and mitochondrial DNA did not match the remains found in Ekaterinburg or of various descendants of Alexandra. Her mitochondrial DNA did, however, match that of Karl Maucher and Margarette Ellerik, descendants of Franziska Schanzkowska, the real individual behind "Anastasia," a remarkable woman in her own right. In their recent comprehensive study of the Anastasia myth, Greg King and Penny Wilson uncovered a vast amount of evidence that refuted "Anastasia's" supporters' implicit conviction that a person of humble background could not master the skills and knowledge necessary to perpetrate an elaborate royal claim.[102]

In a second moment of truth, science, therefore, had settled a long-standing mystery of the twentieth century. As historians who had believed Franziska's claim put it: "The world had been led to believe that evidence in her favor was overwhelming. How wrong we all were."[103] But the fact that two bodies were missing from the Romanov grave suggested the possibility that somehow the real Anastasia, Maria, or perhaps Aleksei, might have survived the Russian Revolution; if not "Anastasia," then at least one of the other Romanov claimants might have been telling the truth. Michael Occleshaw, a popular British author, seized upon this possibility, presenting circumstantial evidence that British intelligence had rescued Grand Duchess Tatiana in Ekaterinburg, spiriting her off to Great Britain, where she allegedly lived incognito for several years.[104]

---

100. Massie, *Romanovs*, 66.

101. James Blair Lovell, *Anastasia: The Lost Princess* (New York: St. Martin's Press, 1995).

102. Massie, *Romanovs*, 195–241; Klier and Mingay, *Quest for Anastasia*, 222–23; King and Wilson, *Resurrection of the Romanovs*, 267–89.

103. King and Wilson, *Resurrection of the Romanovs*, 328.

104. Michael Occleshaw, *The Romanov Conspiracies: The Romanovs and the House of Windsor* (London: Orion, 1993), 98–99, 178–9, 181–82.

A third moment of truth settled that question utterly. In summer 2007, Sergei Plotnikov and Leonid Vokhmiakov discovered another grave with two sets of human remains, seventy yards from the first one. Bone analysis and DNA testing confirmed that they belonged to Aleksei and one of his sisters, most likely Maria.[105] They were unable to receive a proper burial due to the Russian Orthodox Church's unsubstantiated doubts about their authenticity.[106]

Several writers and historians continue to entertain the theory that one or more Romanov children survived the massacre in Ekaterinburg. In a chatty 2012 book, Carlos Mundy and Marie Stravlo denied the reliability of the DNA tests performed on the bones "conveniently found" in Ekaterinburg in 1991.[107] Working with Veniamin Alekseev, a member of the Russian Academy of Sciences, Georgii Shumkin published documents from the archive of Grand Duke Andrew in 2014. In his carefully worded introduction, Alekseev suggested it was unlikely that the entire Romanov family perished in Ekaterinburg and urged readers "to reach their own conclusions."[108] Around the same time, Marc Ferro added his voice to the chorus.[109] "Historical reasoning," he stated, "can be more reliable than DNA tests."[110]

A Merciless Reality

In 1934, Iakov Iurovskii spoke to a gathering of old Bolsheviks in Ekaterinburg, which at the time was called Sverdlovsk, in memory of Yakov Sverdlov, an early Bolshevik leader. Like Trotsky, Iurovskii spoke of "the political necessity" to destroy the entire Romanov family:

105. Nadezhda Danilevich, "Kak iskali ostanki detei Nikolaiia II," *Moskovskii komsomolets*, August 25, 2007, 12; Luke Harding, "Bones Found by Russian Builder Finally Solve Riddle of the Missing Romanovs," *Guardian*, August 25, 2007, 3; Michael D. Coble, "The Identification of the Romanovs: Can We (Finally) Put the Controversies to Rest?" *Investigative Genetics* 2 (September 26, 2011), https://investigativegenetics.biomedcentral.com/articles/10.1186/2041-2223-2-20; "V SK raskryli podrobnosti rassledovaniia ubiistva tsarskoi semi," TASS, July 16, 2020, https://tass.ru/obschestvo/8988125.

106. Neil MacFarquhar, "Orthodox Church Blocks Funeral for Last of Romanov Remains," *New York Times*, February 14, 2016, A11.

107. Carlos Mundy and Marie Stravlo, *The Lost Romanov Icon and the Enigma of Anastasia* (London: Thames River Press, 2012), 169–74.

108. Veniamin Alekseev, "Predislovie," in *Kto Vy, gospozha Chaikovskaia? K voprosu o sud'be tsarskoi docheri Anastasii Romanovoi. Arkhivnye dokumenty 1920-kh godov*, ed. Georgii Shumkin (Ekaterinburg: Basko, 2014), 6, 16.

109. Marc Ferro *La vérité sur la tragédie des Romanov* (Paris: Tallandier, 2013).

110. Séverine Nikel, "Les filles du tsar n'ont pas été assassinées," *L'Histoire* 379 (September 2012): 13.

Not all people can politically appreciate and understand that these little ones would have grown up to become big ones and that each of them separately would have been a claimant to the throne, such that leaving them alive would have made them a constant banner, and even as corpses they would also have been a banner.[111]

Iurovskii's explanation of the reasons for the execution is clear and simple: the Romanovs were killed not because of what they did but because of who they were and not because they were a real threat but because they were a potential one. There was a logic to his argument, but it was an exterminationist logic. The Romanovs were, alas, far from the last victims of systematic "preemptive" extermination in the twentieth century.

---

111. "Soveshchanie starykh bol'shevikov po voprosu prebyvaniia Romanovykh na Urale," February 1, 1934, Tsentr dokumentatsii obschestvennykh organizatsii Sverdlovskoi oblasti, f. 41, op. 1, d. 150, l. 53.

5. The "Judeo-Bolshevik" Myth

> For decades, the Bolshevik-Jewish rulers from Moscow have been trying
> to set not just Germany, but the whole of Europe in flames.[1]
> —*Roman Catholic bishop Galen of Münster, 1941*

"Who would believe such nonsense?" might be the immediate response of most contemporary readers. If so, it is a hopeful sign that this particular myth—that the Bolsheviks were Jewish agents, funded by foreign forces, who sought world domination—has long exceeded its shelf life. Yet of all the myths discussed in this book, this myth remained highly virulent for decades after the Bolsheviks toppled the Provisional Government and seized power in October 1917. Before fading away, this myth contributed to the massive destruction of innocent life. Its history must not be forgotten. Nor is it completely dead.

A Planetary Revolution

Vladimir Lenin and the Bolsheviks believed the Russian Revolution had to sweep the entire earth. As discussed in Chapter 3, the most radical wing of European Marxists, associated with the Zimmerwald Left, believed that capitalism had exhausted its historical development and that the Great War provided an opportunity to begin the revolutionary transition from capitalism to socialism and eventually communism. In summer 1917, popular support for the Bolsheviks grew, while the Provisional Government's prestige and authority collapsed. Even as Lenin immersed himself in the volatile politics of post-monarchic Russia, he never lost sight of what he considered the bigger picture. The vision he had articulated in his April Theses had global, not Russian, roots. So did his arguments for the seizure of power in September and October.

---

1. Paul Hanebrink, *A Specter Haunting Europe: The Myth of Judeo-Bolshevism* (Cambridge, MA: Belknap Press of Harvard University Press, 2018), 147. Galen criticized the Nazi program of euthanizing disabled persons and its persecution of the Catholic Church, for which he was later beatified (the step prior to canonization as a saint). However, he never spoke out against the Nazi persecution and murder of Jews. See Beth A. Griech-Polelle, *Bishop von Galen: German Catholicism and National Socialism* (New Haven, CT: Yale University Press, 2002).

Lenin made this case to fellow party members in several letters, not in person.[2] Together with Grigorii Zinoviev, he had fled Petrograd after the July Days in 1917 as the Provisional Government sought to indict the Bolsheviks as German agents. Writing from secret hiding places, Lenin proposed seizing power immediately. His argument was multipronged. First, popular support for the Bolsheviks was on the rise—they had majority control in the Petrograd Soviet, now chaired by Leon Trotsky—but might begin to decline if they did not act soon. Second, should the German military take Petrograd, the conditions favorable to revolution would cease. Third, the Bolsheviks had a military command structure, arms, and the support of loyal army, navy, and Red Guard units.

Moreover, on October 16, the Petrograd Soviet

Figure 5.1: National Socialist (Nazi) propaganda poster, 1941: "This is the true and only goal of Bolshevik 'world revolution!'" The text beneath the image states: "The Jew fattened with the sweat and blood of the subjugated and enslaved peoples in Moscow and New York, in London and Johannesburg. With the pleasure of the slave owner, he will ensure that the bloodlust of his executioners destroys everything that opposes him if Europe is not united, from the polar cap to the Black Sea and from the Mediterranean to the Volga."

voted to create a Military Revolutionary Committee to defend Petrograd against a German advance. It was true that many of Lenin's fellow Bolsheviks, as Marxists, believed, like their Menshevik opponents, that predominantly rural Russia was not ready for a socialist revolution. Capitalism had to run its course, they argued, as it did in other industrially developed countries. Lenin would have none of this. If

2. Excerpts from these documents are in Jonathan Daly and Leonid Trofimov, eds., *Russia in War and Revolution, 1914–1922: A Documentary History* (Indianapolis: Hackett Publishing Company, 2009), 106–8.

Russia was not ready for socialism, other capitalist countries—most importantly, Germany—were ready.

"In Germany," wrote Lenin on October 1, "the beginning of a revolution is obvious, especially since the sailors were shot."[3] Lenin was apparently referring to mutinies in August in the German Imperial Navy, during the suppression of which seventy-five sailors in the North Sea port city of Wilhelmshaven were arrested and two executed. Lenin concluded his expostulation with the claim that an immediate seizure of power by the Bolsheviks would save hundreds of thousands of lives at the front, save the Russian Revolution, and promote world revolution. He estimated the chances of a "bloodless victory" as "ten to one."[4]

The first Bolshevik decree, issued hours after toppling the Provisional Government, avoided overt mention of the paramount goal of world revolution. It called for an immediate three-month armistice, followed by talks to establish a just and democratic (not a "socialist") peace, with relinquishment of all "annexed" territories in Europe and beyond. Tens of millions of Russians were war-weary. This very sentiment had catapulted the Bolsheviks into power. As Lenin later wrote: the masses, "worn out and tortured by four years' war, wanted only peace."[5] The fledgling Bolshevik regime was hanging by a thread and needed as much support as it could muster. Pacifism and peace-seeking were broadly social democratic and socialist values. In fact, it seems that the decree's apparent pacifism influenced the composition of Woodrow Wilson's Fourteen Points speech.[6]

Nevertheless, the Bolshevik leadership remained committed to world revolution. The decree itself, read carefully, suggested as much. Workers in all the belligerent countries, "by their comprehensive, decisive, and unabashedly energetic activism," it proclaimed, "will help us successfully achieve the cause of peace *along with* the cause of liberating working and exploited masses of population from all slavery and all exploitation."[7] Thus, the first Bolshevik decree, usually referred to as the Decree on Peace, was more precisely a decree on world revolution because such planetary liberation could not occur peacefully (as the Bolsheviks themselves admitted). Indeed, as Marxists, the Bolsheviks believed that the entire world—not only Russia—was destined to transition from capitalism to socialism and then to communism.

Thus, the Bolsheviks took every revolutionary stirring in Europe as a sign of the eagerly anticipated igniting of world revolution. In his prediction of revolution in Germany, Lenin was off by a year. On November 3, 1918, naval mutinies broke out in the North Sea port city of Kiel. Sailors and workers engaged in violent clashes with troops (Map 5.1). Peace, bread, and democratic reforms were their key demands. By

---

3. Daly and Trofimov, *Russia in War and Revolution*, 107.

4. Daly and Trofimov, *Russia in War and Revolution*, 108.

5. Edward Hallett Carr, *The Bolshevik Revolution, 1917–1923*, 3 vols. (New York: W.W. Norton, 1985), 3:10.

6. Carr, *Bolshevik Revolution*, 3:10.

7. *Dekrety sovetskoi vlasti*, 18 vols. (Moscow: Gospolitizdat, 1957), 1:12 (emphasis added).

Map 5.1: Revolutionary upheavals in Europe, 1918, 1919

early November, both Kiel and Wilhelmshaven were in the hands of revolutionary sailors, soldiers, and workers. Rebellion spread to other German cities, and the councils created by German workers and soldiers looked a lot like the soviets, which had emerged during the Russian Revolution.[8] One can imagine Lenin's fury when German "social-chauvinists," as he called mainstream German Social Democrats, opted

---

8. Robert Gerwarth, *November 1918: The German Revolution* (Oxford: Oxford University Press, 2020).

ВЛАДЫКА МИРА-КАПИТАЛ, ЗОЛОТОЙ КУМИР.

Недавно еще он грозно восседал на троне, окруженный вооруженными наемниками, а безоружные рабы шли для него работать... Но заря сознания осветила ум рабочего класса, он берет в руки оружие и Кумир будет низвергнут во всем мире.

Издательство Всероссийского Центрального Исполнительного Комитета Советов Рабочих, Красноарм., Крестьянских и Казачьих Депутатов.

Figure 5.2: "Master of the World—Capital, the Golden Idol," 1919. The commentary states: "Recently, it [the capitalist idol] sat menacingly upon its throne, surrounded by armed mercenaries, while its defenseless slaves headed off to work. But the dawn of consciousness has illuminated the mind of the working class, which will take up arms and overthrow the idol throughout the world."

for a parliamentary republic, not Bolshevik-style destruction of capitalism. In January 1919, the Bolsheviks briefly hoped that the ultra-left Spartacist League could rekindle revolution in Germany by seizing power in Berlin. When that failed, they saw a ray of hope for world revolution in Bavaria and Hungary, where socialists and Communists proclaimed short-lived soviet republics.[9] Those efforts, too, crumpled.

After their initial tactical reticence, when they declined to call world revolution by its name in the Decree on Peace, the Bolsheviks never again hesitated to declare their commitment to world revolution. In August 1918, Lenin wrote a letter to American workers. He declared the Bolshevik belief in the inevitability of the international revolution. Lenin admitted that it could take a long time for American workingmen to come to the aid of Soviet Russia. He was more optimistic about a near-term proletarian revolution in Europe. He concluded:

> Inevitably labor is approaching communistic, Bolshevistic tactics, is preparing for the proletarian revolution that alone is capable of preserving culture and humanity from destruction.
>
> We are invincible, for invincible is the Proletarian Revolution.[10]

9. Francis L. Carsten, *Revolution in Central Europe, 1918–1919* (Berkeley: University of California Press, 1972).

10. Jonathan Daly and Leonid Trofimov, eds., *The Russian Revolution and Its Global Impact: A Short History with Documents* (Indianapolis: Hackett Publishing Company, 2017), 111.

This confident certainty in the future triumph of world revolution found expression in hundreds of propaganda posters put out under official Soviet auspices, such as Figures 5.2 and 5.3.

The following year, on the third anniversary of the "proletarian dictatorship," a muscular factory worker is shown ready to stomp on economic and political leaders of the capitalist world, including Uncle Sam (Figure 5.3). The Soviet leaders even emblazoned their state seal with this ideal, featuring the globe and a rising sun as symbols of future planetary transition to communism.

Ideological commitment to world revolution was backed by strategic coordination and tactical support. When popular unrest was intensifying in Germany in October 1918, an ecstatic Lenin urged fellow Bolsheviks to provide German

Figure 5.3: "Labor will be the master of the world. Three years of proletarian dictatorship," 1920.

revolutionaries with grain, financial assistance, and a three-million-man military force. He declared: "We are all ready to die to help the German workers deepen the revolution they have begun."[11] In March 1919, the Bolsheviks brought together communist parties and movements from around the world to form the Third Communist International (Comintern), an organization whose main goal was to provoke communist revolution throughout the world, not only by means of propaganda campaigns but also through political, economic, financial, and military assistance.[12] Operational activities of the Comintern were often clandestine, but the organization itself and its main directives were anything but.

11. V. I. Lenin to Ia. M. Sverdlov and L. D. Trotskii, in Vladimir Lenin, *Polnoe sobranie sochinenii*, 5th ed., 55 vols. (Moscow: Politizdat, 1958–1965), 50:186.
12. Alexander Vatlin and Stephen A. Smith, "The Comintern," in *The Oxford Handbook of the History of Communism*, ed. Stephen A. Smith (Oxford: Oxford University Press, 2014), 187–202.

For example, the Russian poet and artist Vladimir Mayakovsky set out this vision in collaboration with the Russian Telegraph Agency (ROSTA) to create stencil-reproduced, pro-Bolshevik propaganda posters for the series of so-called ROSTA windows (like comic strips). The series proclaimed the Soviet vision of overturning the world in a global socialist revolution under the flag of the Comintern.

In sum, while the Bolsheviks were conspiring to topple established governments and market-based economic systems worldwide, this conspiracy was not secret. It was supposed to be driven not by clandestine plots but by hundreds of millions of people freely choosing communism over capitalism as humanity's best hope for progress and freedom from exploitation. The platform openly adopted at the First Congress of the Third International in 1919 in Moscow proclaimed that humanity had reached "the epoch of the breakdown of capital, its internal disintegration, the epoch of the communist revolution of the proletariat," which would step forward to "break the rule of capital, make wars impossible, abolish the frontiers between states, transform the whole world into a community where all work for the common good and realize the freedom and the brotherhood of peoples."[13] These optimistic predictions inspired enthusiastic hopefulness around the world. However, obedience to Moscow was what was demanded of those seeking to join the movement.

At its Second Congress, held in mid-1920, the Comintern imposed twenty-one conditions of admission. Members were required to categorically reject reformism, set up parallel legal and illegal operations, prepare for social strife and even civil war, conduct systematic communist propaganda in the military, establish centralized "iron discipline" within their organizations, give unconditional support to every soviet republic, and unquestioningly obey all decisions of Congresses of the Comintern and its Executive Committee. The Communist International was explicit about its bellicosity, stating in condition number 17 that it "has declared war on the entire bourgeois world."[14] Traditionally minded citizens and elites viewed such activities as frightening and treasonous (Figure 5.4).

The Bolsheviks' Transition from "German Puppets" to "Jewish Puppets"

Indeed, the Provisional Government had considered the Bolsheviks German agents. After the Bolsheviks had seized power, this view persisted, especially when they signed the Treaty of Brest-Litovsk, which ended hostilities between Soviet Russia and the Central Powers (Germany, Austria-Hungary, and their allies) on unfavorable terms on

---

13. Vatlin and Smith, "The Comintern," 188.

14. Gerald D. Feldman and Thomas G. Barnes, eds., *Breakdown and Rebirth, 1914 to the Present*, vol. 4 of *Documentary History of Modern Europe* (Lanham, MD: University Press of America, 1982), 93.

Figure 5.4: "Join the Anti-Bolshevik League," 1919. The far-right Antibolschewistische Liga was founded in December 1918 in Berlin to counter leftwing activism with propaganda, lectures, training courses, and street demonstrations.

March 3, 1918. The fact that several Bolshevik leaders and activists were Jewish gave rise to a parallel myth, according to which "Judeo-Bolsheviks" sought to dominate and harm Russia.

The Russian Empire had been home to the largest Jewish population globally, but the overall number of Jews in the Bolshevik Party was small. Before the Bolsheviks took power, socialistically minded Jews tended to join the Bund, Paolei Zion, or the Menshevik Party.[15] After the Bolsheviks seized power in October, many more joined the ruling Bolshevik party. Yet, in 1922, only 19,500, or 5.2 percent of party members, were Jewish.[16] Many other Jewish inhabitants of Soviet Russia sympathized with the socialist ideals of universal equality and brotherhood; however, this had nothing to do with their Jewishness but mostly with their experience of oppression.

In a country where until 1906, all subjects were deprived of basic political and many civil rights, the Jews were subject to additional restrictions. They could not

15. André Gerrits, *The Myth of Jewish Communism: A Historical Interpretation* (Brussels: P.I.E. Peter Lang, 2011), 122.

16. Steven G. Marks, *How Russia Shaped the Modern World: From Art to Anti-Semitism, Ballet to Bolshevism* (Princeton, NJ: Princeton University Press, 2003), 155.

reside outside of the Pale of Settlement (the empire's western provinces), could pursue higher education only within rigid quotas, and for the most part, were condemned to misery in shtetls (small Jewish towns and villages). In sum, the Jews in Russia were victims of officially promoted antisemitism, even though all senior (and most mid-level) officials opposed anti-Jewish violence for fear that it might lead to violence against non-Jewish elites.[17]

Nevertheless, anti-Jewish violence broke out repeatedly across the Pale of Settlement—especially in 1881–1884, 1903, and 1905–1906—resulting in hundreds of dead and massive destruction of property.[18] For every major outbreak of violence, thousands of small-scale attacks and insults made the Jews feel that they did not belong in Russia. Approximately two million emigrated to the United States in 1881–1921.[19] Others departed for western Europe, South America, Canada, and Palestine. Some who remained hoped the revolution would change Russia for the better. Abraham Gootnik, who resided during tsarist times in a shtetl in southern Ukraine, later conveyed this sentiment well:

> Would not the next generation reach a stage of civilization in which savagery would be extinguished? We knew of no pogroms in the Western European countries where education was available to all—none in England or in Scandinavia, and certainly not in Germany, where there was said to be no illiteracy whatever. It seemed reasonable to hope—if only we managed to survive the present onslaughts—that we might live to see the very savages around us transformed by the revolution into peaceful, tolerant, civilized neighbors.[20]

This view was both critical of the prerevolutionary order and tragically naïve but certainly not shaped by a desire to dominate the world.

The overwhelming majority of Jewish people in Russia were neither conspirators nor revolutionaries. The choice to join the revolutionary movement was no more "Jewish" than the choice not to join it. Still, in imperial Russia, there was a long tradition of blaming revolutionary activities on the Jews. Although anti-Jewish attitudes were deeply rooted in Russian culture and society, the actions of the terrorist

---

17. Jonathan W. Daly, *Autocracy Under Siege: Security Police and Opposition in Russia, 1866–1905* (DeKalb, IL: Northern Illinois University Press, 1998), 174–75; Daly, *The Watchful State: Security Police and Opposition in Russia, 1906–1917* (DeKalb, IL: Northern Illinois University Press, 2004), 20, 39.

18. John Klier and Shlomo Lambroza, eds., *Pogroms: Anti-Jewish Violence in Modern Russian History* (Cambridge: Cambridge University Press, 1992); John Klier, *Russians, Jews, and the Pogroms of 1881–1882* (Cambridge: Cambridge University Press, 2011).

19. Annelise Orleck, *The Soviet Jewish Americans* (Westport, CT: Greenwood Press, 1999), 13.

20. Abraham Gootnik, *Oh Say, Can You See: Chaos and a Dream of Peace* (Lanham, MD: University Press of America, 1987), 103–4.

organization People's Will, which assassinated numerous government officials and the tsar in 1881, marked a turning point.

Only a few of the terrorists were ethnically Jewish (and these had repudiated their religious traditions and even their Jewish identity), but commentators singled out Jews as the main culprits. The conservative newspaper *Novoe vremia* (New Times) wrote that "these Jews, being from time immemorial the representatives of the revolutionary spirit, stand now at the head of Russian nihilists."[21] (Ironically, many socialists and antisemites viewed Jews as quintessential capitalists—they were, thus, denounced for being both pro- and anti-capitalists.[22]) Such attitudes continued through the rise of mass revolutionary organizations, the Revolution of 1905, and the constitutional era inaugurated by the Fundamental Laws of 1906. But the Bolsheviks' execution of Nicholas and his family made them, not other revolutionaries, the focal point of monarchist and ultra-nationalist anger. Some monarchists perceived the massacre as stemming in part from an evil Jewish plot.

Almost immediately, these allegations gained international traction. In his reports from Ekaterinburg on the Romanov family murder that subsequently appeared in book form, the London *Times* correspondent in Russia, Robert Wilton, did not hesitate to claim that the Bolsheviks were agents of anti-Russian forces. The Germans were still the ultimate puppet masters in his version of the conspiracy: "The Germans knew what they were doing when they sent Lenin's pack of Jews into Russia. They chose them as agents of destruction." Why? "Because the Jews were not Russians and to them the destruction of Russia was all in the way of business, revolutionary or financial. The whole record of Bolshevism in Russia is indelibly impressed with the stamp of alien invasion."[23]

The largely forged Sisson papers (mentioned in Chapter 3) were used to "prove" that the Bolsheviks were Jewish agents who received money not just from the German government but also from German Jewish bankers like Max Warburg (again, Jews appeared as both pro- and anti-capitalists). The bankers protested such accusations when they began to appear in the German press and took one newspaper to court, forcing it to withdraw the allegations.[24]

Like bigoted Western commentators, Russian émigrés helped spread the "Judeo-Bolshevik" myth. In Soviet Russia, opponents of Bolshevism were persecuted,

---

21. Erich E. Haberer, *Jews and Revolution in Nineteenth-Century Russia* (Cambridge: Cambridge University Press 1995), 203.

22. Seymour Martin Lipset, ed., *Revolution and Counterrevolution: Change and Persistence in Social Structures* (New Brunswick, NJ: Transaction Books, 1988), 377.

23. George Gustav Telberg and Robert Wilton, *The Last Days of the Romanovs* (New York: George H. Doran Co., 1920), 392–93. The book comprises documentary evidence compiled by former professor of law at Saratov University George Telberg, along with Wilton's account.

24. Walter Laqueur, *Russia and Germany: A Century of Conflict* (Boston: Little, Brown, and Company, 1965), 91.

Figure 5.5: "Peace and Freedom in Sovietland," 1919.

sometimes on a massive scale, leading over a million to flee Russia. The bitterness of some who escaped turned to hatred. This emotional state, along with past prejudice, supplied fertile ground for the spread of the "Judeo-Bolshevik" myth, which was propagated in pamphlets, newspaper articles, and anti-Bolshevik posters, like the one in Figure 5.5, produced by the anti-Bolshevik "White" government in southern Russia. It features Leon Trotsky as a demonic Jewish figure with a golden five-pointed star (perhaps meant to suggest an affinity between the Bolshevik red five-pointed star and the traditional six-pointed Star of David) and Asian-looking henchmen below.

One early variation of the anti-Russian conspiracy was advanced by Nikolai Sokolov, the chief investigator of the Romanov murder. Sokolov fled Russia after the fall of the anti-Bolshevik dictator in Siberia, Aleksandr Kolchak (Chapter 6). Sokolov not only investigated the actual crime but also searched for a conspiracy behind it. He concluded that Nicholas and his family fell victim to a conspiracy that included not only Jews and the Bolsheviks but also the dead Rasputin and the clerical circles around him.[25]

Another early contributor to the "Judeo-Bolshevik" myth was General Mikhail Diterikhs, a senior military commander appointed by Kolchak to oversee the Romanov murder investigation. A book he published in 1922 explicitly tied the Bolshevik murder of the Romanovs to the *Protocols of the Elders of Zion*, the notorious forgery discussed in Chapter 2.[26] By 1922, of course, the war was over, and a defeated

---

25. John Klier and Helen Mingay, *The Quest for Anastasia: Solving the Mystery of the Lost Romanovs* (Secaucus, NJ: Carol Publishing Group, 1997), 81.

26. It has been reprinted as M. K. Diterikhs, *Ubiistvo tsarskoii sem'i i chlenov Doma Romanovykh na Urale* (Moscow: Skify, 1991).

Germany could not compete with the Jews for the title of a supreme Bolshevik puppet master in the conspiratorial imagination. Diterikhs did not mince words:

> Jews created the revolution. Jews brought Russia to ruin. Jews shed the blood of our fathers, mothers, brothers, sister, and children of city and village, the hills and dales of Mother Russia. The Jews brutally destroyed the Royal Family. The Jews are to blame for every evil befalling Russia.[27]

Diterikhs's words and his senior position in the Kolchak regime make one wonder what kind of Russia might have emerged had Kolchak triumphed in the Russian Civil War. Equally important, they remind us that rabid antisemitism was not confined to interwar Germany or, for that matter, to any one European—or even Western—country.[28]

As was discussed in Chapter 4, Sokolov's investigation failed to uncover the human remains of the executed royal family and their servants. Sokolov concluded (erroneously, as we now know) that the bodies had been burned. Human teeth, however, cannot be easily burned, and Mikhail Diterikhs had a ready explanation: the Bolsheviks detached the heads of the Romanovs and took them to Moscow.[29]

During his investigation, Sokolov discovered four indecipherable marks and an inscription on a basement wall at Ipatiev House—something earlier investigators had not seen. The inscription was written in German and said: "Belzatsar ward in selbiger Nacht / Von seinen Knechten umgebracht" (Balthazar was on the same night murdered by his own slaves). This was a slightly distorted excerpt from a poem by the Jewish poet Heinrich Heine.[30] It is possible the inscription was made by one of the executioners with a knowledge of German. Perhaps it was added after anti-Bolshevik forces took Ekaterinburg nine days after the massacre. But Diterikhs declared that the inscription was in Yiddish (a traditional central and eastern European Jewish language), not German, and that it was made by the executioners after they had committed a ritual murder.[31] (A long-standing antisemitic myth held that Jews murdered Christians as part of a religious ritual.)

A flurry of speculation followed Diterikhs's book about the meaning of the inscriptions and the fate of Nicholas's head. In 1925, a Russian officer and self-taught Egyptologist, Mikhail Skariatin, published a booklet asserting that the marks fulfilled a Jewish conspiracy. Reports about Nicholas's head appeared in the German press in

---

27. Klier and Mingay, *Quest for Anastasia*, 80.

28. William I. Brustein, *Roots of Hate: Anti-Semitism in Europe before the Holocaust* (Cambridge: Cambridge University Press, 2003).

29. Wendy Slater, "Relics, Remains, and Revisionism: Narratives of Nicholas II in Contemporary Russia," *Rethinking History* 9, no. 1 (March 2005): 53–70 (here: 61).

30. The poem was "Belsatzar" (1820); the original lines are "Belsatzar ward aber in selbiger Nacht / Von seinen Knechten umgebracht."

31. Klier and Mingay, *Quest for Anastasia*, 80.

1928. Rasputin's old nemesis, the monk Iliodor, who, as mentioned in Chapter 1, never suffered from a lack of imagination, claimed that in a Kremlin secret chamber in 1919, he had seen "Nicholas II's severed head, a deep wound over the left eye."[32]

Two more influential books built on theories advanced by Sokolov and Diterikhs. In *Nicholas II and the Jews* (1924), Lieutenant General Aleksandr Nechvolodov, who had emigrated with other anti-Bolshevik officers, took a long view, arguing that Jewish hostility to Russia was many centuries in the making. Like Diterikhs, he declared that the establishment of Soviet Russia had resulted from the plan outlined in the *Protocols*.[33] Unlike Nechvolodov, who tied his "Judeo-Bolshevik" theory to motives of power and money, Nikolai Zhevakhov stressed its religious foundations. Zhevakhov had been a senior official of the Holy Synod, the state agency that administered the Russian Orthodox Church. (He was a member of the Rasputin circle, although Rasputin himself was not antisemitic.) "Jews and intellectual supporters of the Jews" had made the Revolution, he wrote in his memoirs in 1923.[34] Drawing heavily on the *Protocols*, Zhevakhov wrote the following showy nonsense:

> Blindly fulfilling the directives of the "Invisible Government," supplying it with colossal resources, Jews of the whole world, with Lenin and Trotsky as the general staff of the new Russian government, implemented the decrees of the Jewish God, decrees known to everyone in the least familiar with the requirements of the religion of the Jews as outlined in their Talmud.[35]

The writings of Wilton, Sokolov, Diterikhs, Nechvolodov, and Zhevakhov offer important insights into the early genesis of the "Judeo-Bolshevik" myth. Its key component—a Jewish conspiracy theory—was deeply rooted in a centuries-old antisemitic tradition and gradually emerged to overshadow other conspiratorial narratives about "the alien" Bolsheviks. The myth thrived not only on bigotry and hatred but also on mythologized graphic detail: "the severed head of the tsar" or "the ritualistic inscription." It increasingly relied on the *Protocols of the Elders of Zion* as "proof" of the Bolsheviks' nefarious intent. Finally, it had enough supporters and sympathizers to spread rapidly. What gave it traction was the fear that not just Russia but other countries and perhaps the entire world were now "Judeo-Bolshevik" targets.

---

32. Slater, "Relics, Remains, and Revisionism," 62.

33. Alexandre Netchvolodov, *L'Empereur Nicolas II et les Juifs: Essais sur la révolution russe dans ses rapports avec l'activité universelle du judaïsme contemporain* (Paris: Étienne Chiron, 1924).

34. *Vospominaniia tovarishcha ober-prokurora Sv. Sinoda Kniazia N. D. Zhevakhova*, vol. 1, *Sentiabr' 1915 g.–mart 1917 g.* (Munich: Tip. R. Ol'denburg, 1923), 309–10.

35. *Vospominaniia tovarishcha ober-prokurora Sv. Sinoda Kniazia N. D. Zhevakhova*, vol. 2, *Mart 1917 g.–ianvar' 1920 g.* (Novyi Sad, Kingdom of Serbs, Croats, and Slovenes: Tip. S. Folonova, 1923), 163.

From "Ruining Russia" to "Dominating the World"

Part of the *Protocols*' alleged master plan to establish global Jewish power was to build a network of underground railways and tunnels in all major European cities and blow them up in case the conspiracy was discovered before it could be fully executed.[36] Even believers in the veracity of the *Protocols* often had trouble swallowing this preposterous idea. Yet the supposed plot seemed superficially like the Bolsheviks' actual policy of supporting worldwide communist organizations committed to global revolution.

Believers in the "Judeo-Bolshevik" conspiracy were both angry and frightened about radical changes to the prewar world. The breakup of the Russian Empire and the German defeat allowed the Poles to rebuild their state. Yet, Polish nationalists feared Bolshevik subversion and military pressure and often imagined that Polish Jews were Bolshevik agents.[37] Many Hungarian nationalists viewed the Jews as a destructive alien force, in part because Bela Kuhn, the leader of the short-lived Hungarian Soviet Republic, and some of his associates were Jewish. Many anti-Republican fighters in the Spanish Civil War (1936–1939) believed they were combating a "Jewish-Masonic-Bolshevist" conspiracy.[38] (Ironically, the number of Jews in Spain at that time was minuscule.)

What seemed like an imminent danger to nationalist conservatives in eastern and southern Europe seemed less threatening in Britain and the United States. Yet it was menacing enough to generate much interest in the *Protocols*. George Shanks, a Moscow-born British expat, published the first English-language translation in 1920, *The Jewish Peril*. A reviewer in *The Spectator* called a Royal Commission to look into whether there existed "a worldwide conspiracy under Jewish leadership."[39] An eighteen-part series in the *Morning Post* followed, asserting that a Judeo-Masonic-Bolshevik world conspiracy was fomenting anti-colonial unrest in Dublin, Cairo, and Delhi.[40] A reviewer in the London *Times* also demanded a public inquiry into the *Protocols* and worried that Britain, having escaped a *Pax Germanica*, might now fall victim to a *Pax Judaica*.[41] A number of British politicians shared this view, including Winston Churchill, who declared that Jews had been "the mainspring of every subversive movement during the nineteenth century" and asserted further that Jewish revolutionaries had "gripped the Russian people by the hair of their heads."[42]

---

36. Laqueur, *Russia and Germany*, 110.

37. Joshua D. Zimmerman, *The Polish Underground and the Jews, 1939–1945* (New York: Cambridge University Press, 2015), 367.

38. Hanebrink, *Specter Haunting Europe*, 62 (Poland), 71 (Hungary), 94 (Spain).

39. Robert Singerman, "The American Career of the *Protocols of the Elders of Zion*," *American Jewish History* 71, no. 1 (September 1981): 48–78 (here: 65).

40. Laqueur, *Russia and Germany*, 324.

41. Colin Holmes, *Anti-Semitism in British Society, 1876–1939* (London: Routledge, 2016), 148.

42. Albert. S Lindemann, *Anti-Semitism before the Holocaust* (Harlow, UK: Longman, 2000), 80.

In America, the perception of the Bolsheviks as an alien force was broadly shared by the press and the public. Bolshevik ideas and goals were poorly understood but seemed radical and appeared to be spreading. Wartime propaganda had stressed that "Americanism" and civilization itself were under threat. With the Central Powers' defeat, the threat now appeared to emanate from Soviet Russia. Bolshevism was blamed for surging postwar strikes, mounting social tensions, and anarchist attacks. Descriptions of Bolshevism evoked images of something alien and lethal. Cautiously neutral at first, by December 1919, Woodrow Wilson had radically changed his view of Bolshevism. In asking Congress to adopt an anti-sedition bill, he denounced Bolshevism as spreading "the poison of disorder, the poison of revolt, the poison of chaos" into the American population.[43] Fear of Bolshevism led to the Red Scare of late 1919–early 1920 and the arrest and deportation of hundreds of southern and eastern European leftists orchestrated by Attorney General A. Mitchell Palmer in the so-called Palmer Raids.

Yet few American critics of Bolshevism were antisemites, and the *Protocols* were less successful commercially in the United States than in Britain.[44] Harris Houghton, a mid-level military intelligence officer, circulated the notorious tract among U.S. government officials, though it seems that few took it seriously. Supreme Court justice Louis D. Brandeis, who was Jewish, received the text in November 1918 from the U.S. attorney general, Thomas Gregory, who apparently deemed it a "rank forgery."[45]

Beginning in September 1919, a Senate subcommittee of the Judiciary Committee investigated pro-German activities in the United States. When one witness testified that Bolshevism was "the result of German propaganda," the subcommittee sought and received authorization to expand its investigation to include pro-Bolshevik activities as well.[46] This was the first "congressional investigation of political activities and opinions" in U.S. history.[47] The subcommittee took the *Protocols* seriously.[48] Nevertheless, an investigation of the pamphlet commissioned by Wilson concluded that the Bolshevik seizure of power was the result of a German, not a Jewish conspiracy.[49]

One conspiracy-monger who made some inroads into American society was Boris Brasol. A former Marxist, a highly paid theater critic, and a chief district prosecuting

43. Jeffrey S. Selinger, *Embracing Dissent: Political Violence and Party Development in the United States* (Philadelphia: University of Pennsylvania Press, 2016), 164.

44. Singerman, "American Career," 65–74.

45. Melvin L. Urofsky and David W. Levy, eds., *Letters of Louis D. Brandeis: Volume IV, 1916–1921: Mr. Justice Brandeis* (Albany: State University of New York Press, 1975), 365.

46. Richard Gid Powers, *Not Without Honor: The History of American Anticommunism* (New York: Free Press, 1995), 20.

47. Regin Schmidt, *Red Scare: FBI and the Origins of Anticommunism in the United States, 1919–1943* (Copenhagen: Museum Tusculanum Press, University of Copenhagen, 2000), 136.

48. Singerman, "American Career," 52–53.

49. Singerman, "American Career," 70.

attorney in Saint Petersburg, he helped negotiate a massive loan from Britain during the war and served as Russia's sole representative to the 1916 Inter-Allied Conference in New York City. After the Revolution, Brasol worked for the U.S. Trade Board and became a confidential advisor to Brigadier General Marlborough Churchill, chief of the U.S. War Department's Military Intelligence Division.[50] The sophisticated Brasol can be taken as proof that no amount of education guarantees immunity from prejudice and bigotry.

Brasol made his mark in 1920 when he brought an English translation of the *Protocols* to the attention of Henry Ford, the head of the Ford Motor Company and one of the most successful and influential industrialists in the world. Ford believed the text furnished evidence of an international Jewish conspiracy, as noted in Chapter 2. Ford's *Dearborn Independent*, the second largest circulating newspaper in the country, printed a series of anti-Jewish articles, many linking Jews to the Russian Revolution and Bolshevism.[51]

Ford's prominence lent credibility to the series' claims, prompting many in the mainstream media to provide favorable coverage. In response, the American Jewish Committee, *Nation* magazine, and over 100 prominent non-Jewish Americans, including President Wilson, former president William Howard Taft, and president-elect Warren Harding, denounced the series. Around the same time, the London *Times* published extracts from the *Protocols* side by side with passages from Maurice Joly's *Dialogue aux enfers* (mentioned in Chapter 2), showing that "it had been plagiarized almost verbatim."[52] Undeterred, Ford continued his crusade, for which he received grassroots support, expressed in thousands of letters sent by admirers.[53]

A key figure showcased in the Ford series, as well as four volumes into which many of the original articles were gathered for publication in 1920–1922, was Leon Trotsky. Unlike Lenin, Trotsky (b. Leiba Bronstein) came from a Jewish family. (Like nearly all Jewish revolutionaries, he repudiated both the religious and the ethnic aspects of his Jewish identity.) In fall 1917, with Lenin in hiding, Trotsky took the helm of the Bolshevik-dominated Petrograd Soviet and its Military Revolutionary Committee, which seized power from the Provisional Government on October 25, 1917. In Lenin's government, Trotsky served successively as commissar of Foreign Affairs, commissar of War, and chairman of the Military Revolutionary Council. His main achievements were negotiating the Treaty of Brest-Litovsk and building the victorious Red Army from scratch. Whether in politics, diplomacy, or military affairs, Trotsky's role in shaping and steering Soviet Russia was second only to Lenin's. This made him a central figure in the mythical antisemitic imagination.

---

50. Singerman, "American Career," 54–56.

51. Max Wallace, *The American Axis: Henry Ford, Charles Lindbergh, and the Rise of the Third Reich* (New York: St. Martin's Press, 2003), 14.

52. Wallace, *American Axis*, 15.

53. Wallace, *American Axis*, 16–18.

The *Dearborn Independent* emphasized the three months Trotsky had spent in New York City, portraying him as a new tsar-in-waiting. A witness who testified to the abovementioned Congressional hearing was quoted as asserting that 265 out of 388 members of the regional government of Petrograd in December 1918 "came from the lower East Side of New York."[54] How he could have compiled such a statistic is unclear.

The paper made an even more outlandish claim in a later issue. The Bolsheviks did not intend to destroy all capitalism, only non-Jewish capitalism. It asserted: "When Lenin and Trotsky make their farewell bow and retire under the protective influence of the Jewish capitalists of the world, it will be seen that only Gentile or Russian capital has been destroyed, and that Jewish capital has been enthroned."[55] It is impossible to reconcile such a claim with the Bolsheviks' complete eradication of private business, commerce, and property and the collapse of the Russian economy: by 1920, industrial production had fallen to 20 percent of its prewar level.[56]

Such nonsense printed by the *Dearborn Independent* attracted a broad readership (its flourishing coincided with a growth phase of the Ku Klux Klan).[57] Ford himself— facing a libel suit[58]—apologized for the series in 1927, claiming to have been deceived and to have permitted the publication of the series only by inadvertence.[59] Yet, in the Depression era, anti-Jewish radio broadcasts by the Protestant minister Gerald L. K. Smith and the Catholic priest Charles Coughlin were broadly popular in the United States.[60] However, it was in Europe that a wave of antisemitic bigotry gained the most deadly momentum.

A Myth That Killed

The spread of the "Judeo-Bolshevik" myth was tied to fear that destructive revolution could soon break out across Europe. The Spartacist uprising in Berlin (January 5–12, 1918) and the Bavarian Soviet Republic centered on Munich (April 6–May 3) showed that radical socialist and communist activists were making headway in Germany. Was Germany facing the same fate as the Russian Empire?

---

54. "The All-Jewish Mark on 'Red Russia,'" in Henry Ford, *The International Jew: The World's Foremost Problem* (Dearborn, MI: Dearborn Publishing Co., 1920), 218–19.

55. "Jewish Testimony in Favor of Bolshevism," in *International Jew*, 228.

56. Alan M. Ball, *Russia's Last Capitalists: The Nepmen, 1921–1929* (Berkeley: University of California Press, 1987), 8.

57. Roland G. Fryer Jr. and Steven D. Levitt, "Hatred and Profits: Under the Hood of the Ku Klux Klan," *Quarterly Journal of Economics* 127, no. 4 (November 2012): 1883–1925.

58. Peter Schrag, *Not Fit for Our Society: Immigration and Nativism in America* (Berkeley: University of California Press, 2010), 143.

59. Singerman, "American Career," 74.

60. Schrag, *Not Fit for Our Society*, 145–47.

Antisemitic Russian émigrés portrayed the "Judeo-Bolsheviks" as a threat not only to Russia but to all developed countries and "civilization" in general. Aleksandr Nechvolodov played such a role in France, George Shanks in Britain, Boris Brasol in the United States, and, most dangerously, Alfred Rosenberg did so in Germany.

A Baltic German born in Reval (today's Tallinn, the capital of Estonia), Rosenberg studied architecture in Riga and engineering in Moscow. Like many anti-Bolshevik émigrés, Rosenberg considered the Bolsheviks agents of an international Jewish conspiracy.

When Rosenberg arrived in Munich in late 1918, the German people were demoralized. Many sought scapegoats. Earlier that year, Prince Otto Salm-Horstmar, a prominent far-right nationalist, had warned that "international Jewry" was "secretly fomenting revolution," and his words evoked a broadly positive response.[61]

The first German edition of the *Protocols* was published by Fyodor Vinberg, a Russian officer with German roots who arrived in Berlin in 1918.[62] From 1920 to 1933, thirty-three editions of the *Protocols* appeared in Germany and Austria, each selling hundreds of thousands of copies and winning vocal supporters like General Erich von Ludendorff, the main organizer of the German war effort, and a postwar proponent of conspiracy theories.[63] Hatred, anger, and fear explain why the *Protocols* gained an avid readership.

The question of the *Protocols'* authenticity was often overlooked because advocates wanted it to be true. Comments by a rabid German antisemite, Theodor Fritsch, illustrate this well. Fritsch entertained serious doubts about the *Protocols* but concluded that they were authentic because "no Aryan mind" could have conceived such ideas. He added: "Even if it were to be assumed that these documents never emanated from a Jewish hand, they still constitute a masterpiece in describing the Jewish mind and its plots."[64] The myth mattered; truth did not.

Alfred Rosenberg actively promoted the "Judeo-Bolshevik" myth. He seems to have introduced Dietrich Eckart, the editor of an antisemitic newspaper, *Auf gut Deutsch* (In Good German), to the *Protocols* and convinced him that capitalism, communism, and Zionism "were parts of the same Jewish plot to plunge the world into chaos and achieve global domination." Rosenberg and Eckart found eager disciples among "the entire German far right" for this teaching.[65]

The "Judeo-Bolshevik" myth made a profound impression on Adolf Hitler and influenced his worldview. While he had been xenophobic during his prewar years in

---

61. Jacob Katz, *Jews and Freemasons in Europe, 1723–1939*, trans. Leonard Oschry (Cambridge, MA: Harvard University Press, 1970), 177.

62. Laqueur, *Russia and Germany*, 126–27.

63. Marks, *How Russia Shaped the Modern World*, 161, 163.

64. Katz, *Jews and Freemasons*, 185.

65. Marks, *How Russia Shaped the Modern World*, 165.

Vienna, his animosity had been directed primarily at Slavs.[66] Meetings and conversations with Eckart and Rosenberg, beginning in 1919, convinced Hitler that the Russian Revolution was the product of a "Judeo-Bolshevik" conspiracy that had destroyed imperial Russia and now threatened to destroy Germany—emphasizing "the theme of the Jewish eradication of the nationalist Russian spiritual and intellectual leadership, often through horrific means."[67] Hitler seems to have arrived at his anti-communism in tandem with his antisemitism.[68] The result was a deadly mix. As he later wrote in *Mein Kampf*, "in Russian Bolshevism we must see the attempt undertaken by the Jews in the twentieth century to achieve world domination."[69] Consequently, Hitler placed Rosenberg at the helm of the National Socialist (Nazi) Party's flagship newspaper, *Völkischer Beobachter* (People's Observer).

Even before the Nazis came to power, the "Judeo-Bolshevik" myth motivated nationalist extremists to kill. When fighting to repel Red Army aggression in 1920, Polish military commanders targeted Jews as the Bolsheviks' accomplices, killing thirty-four in Pinsk, thirty-eight in Lida, and at least sixty in Vilnius. About a half of the three thousand people killed in the aftermath of the failed attempt to build a Hungarian Soviet Republic were Jews—amid incessant reporting on Bolshevik atrocities, of which the perpetrators were invariably identified as Jews.[70] In Russia itself, the "Judeo-Bolshevik" myth contributed to violent attacks against Jews suspected of supporting the Red Army in areas temporarily reconquered by anti-Bolshevik forces, especially in Ukraine. Experts reckon the death toll to have been "anywhere in the range of 50,000 to 200,000 killed or mortally wounded" in Ukraine alone in 1919 and 1920, not to mention "the countless other victims [who] were robbed, raped, or permanently disfigured."[71] Violence against Jews in the former Russian Empire precipitated a massive flow of Jewish refugees into neighboring countries, where they met with suspicion, fear, and occasional violence.[72]

In the early 1920s, several Russian émigrés in Germany joined with Nazi activists to form the *Wirtschaftliche Aufbau-Vereinigung* (Association for Economic Development), seeking to use violence to bring the extreme right to power in both Germany

---

66. Marks, *How Russia Shaped the Modern World*, 163.

67. Michael Kellogg, *The Russian Roots of Nazism: White Emigres and the Making of National Socialism, 1917–1945* (Cambridge: Cambridge University Press, 2005), 231.

68. Laqueur, *Russia and Germany*, 67.

69. Lucy S. Dawidowicz, *The War against the Jews, 1933–1945*, 10th-anniversary ed. (New York: Bantam Books, 1986), 20.

70. Hanebrink, *Specter Haunting Europe*, 58 (accomplices), 70 (Hungary). See also William W. Hagen, *Anti-Jewish Violence in Poland, 1914–1920* (Cambridge: Cambridge University Press, 2018).

71. Oleg Budnitskii, *Russian Jews Between the Reds and the Whites, 1917–1920* (Philadelphia: University of Pennsylvania Press, 2012), 1.

72. Hanebrink, *Specter Haunting Europe*, 56.

and Russia.[73] Alfred Rosenberg, Fyodor Vinberg, and Boris Brasol were members. The organization was involved in the assassination in 1922 of the foreign minister of the Weimar Republic, Walther Rathenau. A defendant in the Rathenau murder trial apparently believed him to have been "one of the 300 'Elders of Zion,' who were seeking to bring the world under the domination of the Jews."[74] Behind the assassination stood a shadowy group called the Organization Consul, which was allegedly committed to "the cultivation and dissemination of nationalist thinking; warfare against all anti-nationalists and internationalists; warfare against Jewry, Social Democracy, and Leftist-radicalism."[75]

The "Judeo-Bolshevik" myth became a staple of Nazi ideology and propaganda. According to one scholar, "from 1919 a call to eliminate both Jews and Bolsheviks from an expanded German Reich pervaded Hitler's speeches, the two volumes of *Mein Kampf*, and his recorded 'table talk.'"[76] Russian émigrés continued to play an important role in Germany even after the Nazis came to power. For example, Nikolai Markov, a right-wing Russian émigré, former Duma deputy, and chair of the anti-semitic Union of Russian People,[77] was named the "specialist" on Jews for the Nazi Weltdienst (World Service), a propaganda agency set up to promote antisemitism internationally.[78]

The antisemitic partnership between the Nazis and Russian nationalist émigrés eventually declined, as Rosenberg and a growing number of other Nazis came to view the Russians themselves as inferior. In that worldview, the Jews were part of a broader Eastern threat, including Slavs, Armenians, and Chinese. As to the Russians themselves, Rosenberg believed they were irrevocably bastardized by the Turco-Mongol Tatars, "a fatal blood mixture." Still, nothing could match Nazi hatred for the Jews, who occupied "the most prominent place in this demonology."[79] "Judeo-Bolshevism" was invoked as the Nazis deprived German Jews of their citizenship and sent them to ghettoes.

In 1936, a triumphant Hitler declared at the Nazi Party Nuremberg rally that "Bolshevism has attacked and put into question the bases of our human state and social order, our conception of culture, our foundations of belief, our moral views." He went on to specify his understanding of the Soviet regime and what he took to

---

73. Kellogg, *Russian Roots of Nazism*, 275.

74. Laqueur, *Russia and Germany*, 105.

75. Michael Newton, *Famous Assassinations in World History: An Encyclopedia*, 2 vols. (Santa Barbara, CA: ABC-CLIO, 2014), 2:461.

76. Michael Mann, *The Dark Side of Democracy: Explaining Ethnic Cleansing* (New York: Cambridge University Press, 2005), 191.

77. George Gilbert, *The Radical Right in Late Imperial Russia: Dreams of a True Fatherland?* (Abingdon, UK: Routledge, 2016), 139–40.

78. Marks, *How Russia Shaped the Modern World*, 171.

79. Laqueur, *Russia and Germany*, 88–89.

be its expansionist intentions: "The German people will remain master in their own house! And not Judeo-Bolshevik Sovietism!"[80]

In the lead-up to the signing of the Nazi-Soviet Non-Aggression Pact in August 1939, anti-Bolshevik propaganda in Nazi Germany ceased. The central government instructed propagandists and commentators that the approach to German-Soviet relations "should be warm and sympathetic."[81]

Figure 5.6: "Satan Has Taken Off His Mask!" ca. 1942. Nazi wartime poster in Ukrainian (the mask is of Stalin's face).

After the German invasion of the Soviet Union (Operation Barbarossa) began on June 22, 1941, however, official propaganda immediately returned to the "Judeo-Bolshevik" myth (Figure 5.6). Indeed, a secret document entitled "Propaganda Instructions for Operation Barbarossa" produced in early June had already asserted that "the enemies of Germany are not the nations of the Soviet Union but the Judeo-Bolshevist Soviet regime."[82] On July 21, the Nazi government issued the pamphlet *Germany Has Entered the Fight to the Finish with the Jewish-Bolshevik System of Murder*. This text represented the war as Germany's effort to destroy "a conspiracy among Jews, Democrats, Bolsheviks, and reactionaries." The main enemy was defined as "world Jewry," as represented by "Anglo-Saxon plutocracy and Bolshevik state capitalism." Bolshevism was especially dangerous, for it was "a system of Jewish criminals and their accomplices whose purpose is the exploitation and enslavement of humanity."[83]

---

80. Hanebrink, *Specter Haunting Europe*, 97.

81. Laqueur, *Russia and Germany*, 202.

82. Yitzhak Arad, *The Holocaust in the Soviet Union* (Lincoln: University of Nebraska Press; Jerusalem: Had Vashem, 2009), 67.

83. Jeffrey Herf, *The Jewish Enemy: Nazi Propaganda during World War II and the Holocaust* (Cambridge, MA: Belknap Press of Harvard University Press, 2006), 99–100.

This attitude can be traced back to Hitler himself, who had determined that the "crusade against Bolshevism" be waged as a "conflict of annihilation." This demand was embodied in a series of decrees and guidelines, especially the Commissar Order of June 6, which "for the first time demanded that the army itself commit murder" and thus participate directly in Nazi exterminationist policies.[84] According to one scholar:

> The Commissar Order constituted an ideologically motivated program of murder that pursued first and foremost a radical end in itself in accordance with the intended "annihilation of bolshevism." Since both Nazis and many [non-party] soldiers considered bolshevism a Communist tyranny dominated by Jews, and the party functionaries in the Red Army were thus commonly suspected of being of Jewish origin, the Commissar Order also relied on widespread German anti-Semitism, even if these allegations were not mentioned in the decree itself.[85]

The "Judeo-Bolshevik" myth served to justify every manner of atrocity. In a military order on September 12, 1941, Field Marshal Wilhelm Keitel asserted that "the struggle against Bolshevism demands ruthless and energetic, rigorous action above all against the Jews, the main carriers of Bolshevism."[86] Twelve days later, booby traps left by the Red Army retreating from Kyiv destroyed the German army's headquarters. German military authorities seized on this pretext to exterminate the city's Jewish population. For two days, special forces drove thousands of Jews into an immense ravine called Babi Yar and massacred them with machine-gun fire. In all, 33,771 Jews met their death. The commanding general in Kyiv, Walter von Reichenau, represented the massacre as obligatory, given the demands of the war against the "Judeo-Bolshevik" foe.[87] Many other orders issued by senior military authorities reiterated this theme, calling the German soldier "the bearer of a pitiless racial [völkisch] ideology" aimed at destroying "the Jewish subhumans" and "liberating the German people from the Asiatic Jewish threat once and for all."[88]

The vast majority of the several million Jews who perished in the Holocaust were murdered not because they were Bolsheviks but because they were Jews. Still, the "Judeo-Bolshevik" myth helped portray them as extremely dangerous enemies who had to be not only defeated but destroyed.

---

84. Felix Römer, "The Wehrmacht in the War of Ideologies: The Army and Hitler's Criminal Orders on the Eastern Front," in *Nazi Policy on the Eastern Front, 1941: Total War, Genocide, and Radicalization*, ed. Alex J. Kay, Jeff Rutherford, and David Stahel (Rochester, NY: University of Rochester Press, 2012), 74 (Hitler), 75 (decrees).

85. Römer, "Wehrmacht in the War of Ideologies," 77.

86. Ian Kershaw, *Hitler: A Biography* (New York: W.W. Norton, 2008), 672.

87. Hanebrink, *Specter Haunting Europe*, 131–32.

88. Kershaw, *Hitler*, 672.

A Myth That Refuses to Die

Unlike many other myths of the Russian Revolution, the "Judeo-Bolshevik" myth neither disappeared with time nor evaporated in light of new evidence. Rather it was dealt crushing blows on the battlefields of World War II and declined with the fortunes of Nazi Germany. One would like to argue that it died with the Nazi regime in May 1945, but this would be wishful thinking.

Recently, Paul Hanebrink has convincingly shown the persistent resilience of the "Judeo-Bolshevik" myth in the postwar era. As the Soviets consolidated their control over eastern Europe, many locals saw it as an onslaught of "Judeo-Bolshevism."[89] Ironically, at the very same time, the Soviets began to downplay the distinctive suffering of the Jewish people in the war and commenced persecuting Soviet Jews, branding them as "rootless Cosmopolitans." As Peretz Markish lamented, "Hitler wanted to destroy us physically. Stalin wants to do it spiritually." In reality, many such Jewish intellectuals, including Markish, were murdered in an anti-Jewish massacre called the Night of the Murdered Poets (August 12, 1952).[90]

The collapse of the Soviet Union in 1991 made possible a rise of ultra-nationalist groups in Russia and the former Soviet satellite states that blamed communism on the Jews. The most well-known such organization in Russia, Pamiat' (Memory), held numerous rallies and sponsored a broad range of antisemitic pamphlets on the history of the Soviet Union replete with "Judeo-Bolshevik" mythology. According to one scholar, Pamiat', in its massively popular journal of the same name, perfectly melded the two elements of the "Judeo-Bolshevik" myth. In the early 1990s, it published "several accounts about the 'Jewish execution' of the Romanov family. The execution was cast as 'ritual murder.'"[91]

In 1995, the Holy Synod of the Russian Orthodox Church declared that the Russian official investigation following the discovery of the Romanov remains had failed to answer ten important questions, including "Was the killing of the Tsar and his family a ritual murder?" and "Had the Tsar been decapitated after death?"[92] In 2015, a Russian economist-turned-amateur-historian, Oleg Platonov, published a book called *Ritual Murders*, in which he argued that the Romanov family was killed in a ritual murder carried out by the "criminal regime of the Jewish Bolsheviks."[93]

---

89. Hanebrink, *Specter Haunting Europe*, chap. 5.

90. Joshua Rubenstein and V. P. Naumov, eds., *Stalin's Secret Pogrom: The Postwar Inquisition of the Jewish Anti-Fascist Committee* (New Haven, CT: Yale University Press, 2001), 2.

91. Elissa Bemporad, "The Blood Libel and Its Wartime Permutations: Cannibalism in Soviet Lviv," in *Ritual Murder in Russia, Eastern Europe, and Beyond: New Histories of an Old Accusation*, ed. Eugene M. Avrutin, Jonathan Dekel-Chen, and Robert Weinberg (Bloomington, IN: Indiana University Press, 2017), 226.

92. Wendy Slater, *The Many Deaths of Tsar Nicholas: Relics, Remains, and the Romanovs* (London: Routledge, 2007), 30–31.

93. Oleg Platonov, *Ritual'nye ubiistva* (Moscow: Rodnaia strana, 2015), 229.

In 2017, Bishop Tikhon Shevkunov, an influential cleric and head of an Orthodox Church commission established to study the recovered remains of Aleksei and Maria Romanov, remarked that many members of the commission believed that the imperial family had fallen victim to an act of "ritual murder."[94] Natalia Poklonskaia, a State Duma deputy in a leadership position, echoed this view, calling the execution "a frightening ritual murder."[95]

An internet search will quickly reveal that the "Judeo-Bolshevik" myth continues to attract a small handful of followers who are less interested in the history of the Russian Revolution than in validating their own prejudice and hatred. It remains toxic to this day.

---

94. Alec Luhn, "Russian Orthodox Church Suggests Tsar's Death Was a Jewish 'Ritual Murder,'" *Telegraph*, November 28, 2017, https://www.telegraph.co.uk/news/2017/11/28/russian-orthodox-church-suggests-tsars-death-jewish-ritual-murder/.

95. Will Stewart and Rory Tingle, "Fury as Russia Launches Investigation into whether the Last Tsar Nicholas II Was Killed with His Family as Part of a 'Jewish Ritual Murder,' at behest of Putin's 'Confessor,'" *Mail Online*, November 28, 2017, https://www.dailymail.co.uk/news/article-5125545/Russia-investigates-tsar-killed-Jewish-ritual.html.

6. THE MYTH OF A U.S. CRUSADE IN SIBERIA TO OVERTHROW THE BOLSHEVIKS AND COLONIZE RUSSIA, 1918–1920

> Lenin's works . . . show extensively the role of American imperialism as an active organizer and inspirer of the military intervention against young Soviet Russia during the first years of her existence.[1]
>
> —*Piotr Pospelov, director of the Institute of Marxism-Leninism, speech to Soviet leaders, 1951*

In August 1918, the American Expeditionary Force (AEF) landed in Vladivostok, Russia. Unlike in northern Russia, where American personnel served under British command and secured initial approval for intervention from Bolshevik authorities, American troops in Siberia were led by U.S. general William S. Graves, sought no such approval, and acted on direct authority from President Woodrow Wilson. For decades thereafter, Soviet (and later Russian) leaders claimed that the AEF in Siberia sought to overthrow the Bolsheviks, strangle the Soviet state, and colonize Russia. This myth, while not widely known outside Russia, continues to poison U.S.-Russian relations.

In July 1919, speaking to an American journalist, Vladimir Lenin denounced the United States' "shameless, criminal, predatory invasion of Russia," which "serves only to enrich their capitalists."[2] American leftist activists charged President Wilson with "waging a private war against Soviet Russia."[3] In 1951, during the Korean War, a senior Communist Party official blasted "the hangman-like feats of American interventionists on our soil."[4] State-controlled Soviet historians presented the American intervention in Siberia as, first, an effort to strangle the fledgling Soviet state and, second, to colonize and enslave the peoples of the former Russian Empire. Each claim is false, though in different ways.

At the same time, many Americans to this day have no idea that U.S. troops operated on Russian soil. The intervention certainly occurred, and in northern Russia, American troops even took part, under British command, in anti-Bolshevik actions.

---

1. "Text of Speech by P. N. Pospelov," *Department of State Bulletin* 24, no. 606 (February 12, 1951): 257–61 (here: 257).

2. V. I. Lenin, "Answers to an American Journalist's Questions," in *Collected Works*, 4th ed., 45 vols. (Moscow: Progress Publishers, 1960–1967), 29:515–20 (here: 516).

3. Robert K. Murray, *Red Scare: A Study in National Hysteria, 1919–1920* (Minneapolis: University of Minnesota Press, 1955), 45.

4. "Speech by Pospelov," 259.

Figure 6.1: Hospital car of American Expeditionary Forces at Khabarovsk, 1918–1920.

Still, the bulk of the American troops landed in Siberia, and their goals and activities were a far cry from overthrowing the Bolsheviks or turning Russia into a colony, as shown in this chapter.

Wilson Pressured

After Nicholas II's abdication, the United States was the first country to recognize the Provisional Government. President Woodrow Wilson hailed the fall of the Russian monarchy as a manifestation of the Russian people's desire for democratic self-government. These events also meant that the Allied Powers (France, Russia, Great Britain, and others allied with them) could be viewed as an alliance of free and democratic nations fighting against the autocratic Central Powers (the German Empire, Austria-Hungary, the Ottoman Empire, and Bulgaria) in "a war to end all wars." Wilson's decision to bring the United States into the Great War resulted mostly from alarm and outrage at Germany's resumption on February 1, 1917, of indiscriminate submarine attacks against civilian ships, including American vessels, sailing to the British Isles.[5] But the fact that America would not have to join forces with the Russian tsar reinforced his belief that an Allied victory would pave the way toward a more peaceful,

---

5. Many civilian ships carried military supplies. The German high command expected the policy would provoke war with the United States but doubted it could mobilize fast enough.

democratic, and prosperous world order. In his speech urging Congress to declare war against Germany, Wilson remarked: "Does not every American feel that assurance has been added to our hope for the future peace of the world by the wonderful and heartening things that have been happening within the last few weeks in Russia?"[6]

The collapse of the Provisional Government and the Bolshevik seizure of power complicated this rosy picture. As discussed in Chapter 3, the Bolsheviks capitalized on popular resentment toward the war and against the Provisional Government. Indeed, the first legislative act of the one-party, Bolshevik-created Council of People's Commissars was the Decree on Peace. It declared the Bolshevik commitment to end the war, demanded that the other belligerent powers begin peace negotiations, and urged workers in Britain, France, and Germany to seek "liberation from all slavery and exploitation."[7] As discussed in Chapter 5, the Decree was, in reality, a call for world revolution, a revolution the Bolsheviks hoped would "liberate humanity" by destroying capitalism itself—in Bolshevik eyes, the cause of the Great War.

Secretary of State Robert Lansing urged Wilson to denounce the Bolshevik regime "as a despotic oligarchy as menacing to liberty as any absolute monarchy on earth." Yet, in his Fourteen Points speech to Congress in January 1918, Wilson attributed to the Bolsheviks "the true spirit of modern democracy" and "a largeness of view, a generosity of spirit, and a universal human sympathy, which must challenge the admiration of every friend of mankind."[8]

Within two months, however, the Bolsheviks signed a separate peace agreement with the Central Powers—the Treaty of Brest-Litovsk. (Ukraine had already signed a separate peace treaty.) For the remaining Allied Powers, this was a nightmare in the making. The United States, while formally at war, was months away from meaningful military contributions. The treaty gave Germany access to vast industrial and agricultural resources, thus thwarting British efforts to strangle the German economy through a naval blockade.

In the first half of 1918, France, Britain, Italy, and Japan pleaded with Wilson to send troops to Siberia. The justifications ranged from preventing a complete German takeover of Russia to protecting Allied supplies in the Pacific port of Vladivostok and from denying Germany access to Siberian agricultural products to seeking to reestablish the Eastern Front against the Central Powers. Lansing advocated joint military intervention in Siberia with Japan, but Wilson resisted. He believed such action could drive the Bolsheviks closer to Germany, embolden the counterrevolutionary supporters of the old regime, and inspire Japan to threaten Russia's territorial integrity. Wilson expressed this concern in crude racist terms, which were common for

---

6. Rodney P. Carlisle, *World War I* (New York: Facts on File, 2007), 347.

7. R. J. Vincent, *Nonintervention and International Order* (Princeton, NJ: Princeton University Press, 1974), 146.

8. Adam Tooze, *The Deluge: The Great War, America and the Remaking of the Global Order, 1916–1931* (New York: Viking, 2014), 121.

his time: the United States could create the impression that the Allies were using "a yellow race to destroy a white one."[9]

As the Allies feared, the peace treaty permitted Germany to transfer thousands of troops from the Eastern to the Western Front and almost immediately threaten Paris.

Meanwhile, Czech and Slovak military units in Russia sought to rejoin the fight against the Central Powers. Aware of the ethnic diversity and political fragility of the Austro-Hungarian Empire, the Russian government had organized these units into the Czechoslovak Legion to fight for national independence. The Provisional Government inher-

Figure 6.2: M. Andre Bowles, "Allies! what d'hell?" 1918. The Treaty of Brest-Litovsk sparked Allied fears that Germany was becoming the dominant military actor in Bolshevik Russia.

ited and endorsed this policy. They were an effective fighting force, yet getting past the Central Powers to join the Western Front was logistically impossible. The only option remaining was to travel around the globe to the Western Front, starting with the Trans-Siberian Railway (Map 6.1).

The Bolshevik government agreed to this plan, and in March 1918, the Legion began to board trains heading for Vladivostok.[10] On the eastward journey, in Chelyabinsk, near the Ural Mountains, on May 14, a Czechoslovak regiment encountered a group of Hungarian POWs loyal to the Austro-Hungarian Empire. A fight broke out, and the Czechoslovaks refused Bolshevik efforts to detain them.

Until then, the Czechoslovaks had not opposed the Bolsheviks. On May 25, when Commissar of War Leon Trotsky ordered that "every armed Czechoslovak found on the railway is to be shot on the spot,"[11] they seized Chelyabinsk and several other towns,

9. Ilya Slonim, *Stillborn Crusade: The Tragic Failure of Western Intervention in the Russian Civil War, 1918–1920* (New Brunswick, NJ: Transaction Publishers, 1996), 86.

10. Alexander Rabinowitch, *The Bolsheviks in Power: The First Year of Soviet Rule in Petrograd* (Bloomington, IN: Indiana University Press, 2007), 242.

11. Laura Engelstein, *Russia in Flames: War, Revolution, Civil War, 1914–1921* (New York: Oxford University Press, 2018), 395.

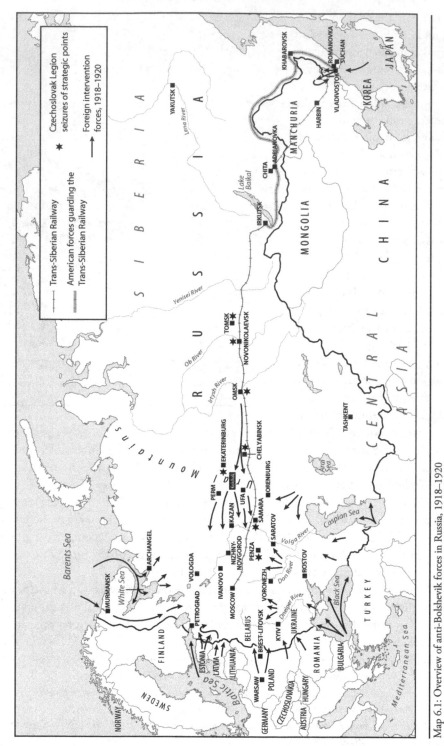

Map 6.1: Overview of anti-Bolshevik forces in Russia, 1918–1920

including Samara, on the Volga River. Six Socialist-Revolutionaries, who had been elected to the Constituent Assembly, were then in Samara founding the Committee of the Constituent Assembly (Komuch) in order to fight the Bolsheviks, reconvene the Constituent Assembly, and cancel the Brest-Litovsk peace treaty. This was exactly what the Czechoslovaks wanted: Russian allies who could help them continue their fight against the Central Powers. Thanks to Czechoslovak military support, Komuch "established its authority with astonishing speed in one province after another along the Volga."[12] Meanwhile, Czechoslovak forces seized control in Vladivostok and the eastern Siberian cities of Chita and Irkutsk before linking up with their comrades in the Ural Mountains and Volga River regions (Map 6.1).[13] This has traditionally been viewed as the commencement of the Russian Civil War, though one can argue that it began much earlier, for example when the Bolsheviks outlawed the Kadet Party in November,[14] or when they attacked newly independent Ukraine in December.[15] In any event, the Czechoslovaks' military success against the ineffectual Bolshevik forces suggested to the Czechoslovaks that they might reach the German front by pushing westward.

"Helping the Czechoslovakian allies" was yet another argument used to convince Wilson to intervene in Russia. The argument had a moral ring to it, and Wilson began to yield. On June 3, 1918, he authorized sending a small contingent of U.S. troops to the northern Russian ports of Murmansk and Arkhangelsk to serve under British command. From here, Czechoslovak troops were to be transported to the Western Front on British ships.[16] Furthermore, the Allies had vast military supplies in the Russian North that needed protection since the Treaty of Brest-Litovsk (Map 6.2) ceded extensive territory of European Russia to Germany, whose military forces were liable to advance even farther. The British also hoped that Allied military forces could inspire the local population to organize and pose a serious challenge to the Germans and the Bolsheviks.[17]

Pressure on Wilson to send troops to Siberia continued to grow. Former presidents William Howard Taft and Theodore Roosevelt urged him to intervene, as did Marshal Ferdinand Foch, the supreme commander of Allied Forces. Foch considered

---

12. Vladimir N. Brovkin, *Behind the Front Lines of the Civil War: Political Parties and Social Movements in Russia, 1918–1922* (Princeton, NJ: Princeton University Press, 1994), 18–19.

13. Robert L. Willet, *Russian Sideshow: America's Undeclared War, 1918–1920* (Washington, DC: Brassey's Inc, 2005), xxiv–xxv.

14. Adele Lindenmeyr, "The First Soviet Political Trial: Countess Sofia Panina before the Petrograd Revolutionary Tribunal," *Russian Review* 60 (October 2001): 505–25 (here: 513).

15. Andrea Graziosi, "A Century of 1917s: Ideas, Representations, and Interpretations of the October Revolution, 1917–2017," *Harvard Ukrainian Studies* 36, no. 1–2 (2019): 9–44 (here: 31).

16. Carol Willcox Melton, *Between War and Peace: Woodrow Wilson and the American Expeditionary Force in Siberia, 1918–1921* (Macon, GA: Mercer University Press, 2001), 9.

17. Liudmila Novikova, *An Anti-Bolshevik Alternative: The White Movement and the Civil War in the Russian North*, trans. Seth Bernstein (Madison, WI: University of Wisconsin Press, 2018), 53.

Map 6.2: Anti-Bolshevik forces and territories lost through Treaty of Brest-Litovsk

an expedition to Siberia "a very important factor for victory."[18] British prime minister Lloyd George agreed that it would help "the national movement in Russia" to reconstitute the Eastern Front, force Germany to withdraw troops from the West, and deny it vital Russian resources. In early July, therefore, the Allied Supreme War Council endorsed a massive and urgent allied intervention in Siberia. The Council envisioned sending one hundred thousand troops, mostly Japanese, but with units from the other Allies, including the United States, to maintain its "Allied character."[19]

Already in mid-June, Wilson had foreseen "the shadow of a plan," especially since the Czechoslovaks were "cousins of the Russians" and could perhaps count on their support. Yet he still refused to commit U.S. troops to Siberia.[20] Moreover, his top military advisors—Secretary of War Newton D. Baker and Army chief of staff, General Peyton C. March—recommended focusing on the Western Front. Wilson trusted their military analysis and, no less important, shared their condemnation of foreign interference in Russian domestic affairs. Wilson now recognized that the Bolshevik government was not democratic, and his resentment toward the Bolsheviks would grow over time. Yet he did not equate democracy with self-determination. As he stated in April 1918: "There isn't any one kind of government which we have the right to impose upon any nation. So that I am not fighting for democracy, except for the peoples that want democracy. If they want it, then I am ready to fight until they get it. If they don't want it, that is none of my business."[21]

Wilson Decides

After continuously rejecting Allied pleas for U.S. intervention in Siberia, Wilson began to change his mind. An important factor was the flow of Japanese troops into Siberia, which an American naval commander called "a commercial invasion under military convoy."[22] Two additional concerns convinced Wilson to act. Both were rooted in myths more than facts. As noted in Chapter 3, many observers considered the Bolsheviks German agents. Rumors circulated that the Bolsheviks were arming German POWs. The prospect of hundreds of thousands of battle-ready soldiers reinforcing the Central Powers alarmed Wilson. On July 4, Secretary of State Lansing alerted Wilson that the Czechoslovaks "were being attacked by released Germans and

---

18. Donald E. Davis and Eugene P. Trani, *The First Cold War: The Legacy of Woodrow Wilson in U.S.-Soviet Relations* (Columbia, MO: University of Missouri Press, 2002), 143.

19. Melton, *Between War and Peace*, 3–7.

20. Carl J. Richard, *When the United States Invaded Russia: Woodrow Wilson's Siberian Disaster* (Lanham, MD: Rowman & Littlefield, 2013), 43.

21. Tony Smith, *Why Wilson Matters: The Origin of American Liberal Internationalism and Its Crisis Today* (Princeton, NJ: Princeton University Press, 2017), 122.

22. Betty Miller Unterberger, "The Russian Revolution and Wilson's Far-Eastern Policy," *Russian Review* 16, no. 2 (April 1957): 35–46 (here: 41).

Austrians." Lansing argued that protecting and assisting the Czechoslovaks was not just a military issue but also a matter of "moral obligation."[23]

On July 6, Wilson convened his top diplomatic and military advisors to announce that he was sending seven thousand U.S. troops to Siberia to join an agreed-upon, comparable number of Japanese troops. To General March's worry that Japan would exceed that limit in pursuit of territorial aggrandizement, Wilson replied, "we will have to take that chance."[24]

The record of the meeting reveals that Wilson considered foreign military intervention incapable of reestablishing the Eastern Front but necessary for protecting the Czechoslovaks.[25] Wilson did not need a crystal ball to realize that Britain, France, and Japan would blame the United States for any eventual defeat of the Czechoslovaks. Warnings about this nightmare scenario kept coming. Admiral Austin M. Knight, commander-in-chief of the U.S. Asiatic Fleet, cabled from Vladivostok that the Czechoslovaks were suffering huge losses and could not sustain themselves for long. He added, "Germany found the means to create a new Eastern front from war prisoners and Bolsheviki, all of whom are with her." Germany was about to crush the Czechoslovaks; he warned: "We shall save Siberia in saving the CZECHS."[26] Avoiding a bad outcome for the Czechoslovaks (and for himself) appears to have been Wilson's most urgent reason to send American troops to Siberia, not toppling the Bolsheviks or colonizing Russia.

American Expectations

Wilson spent several days writing detailed instructions for the commander of the AEF in Siberia. It was no easy task. He admitted to his close foreign policy confidant, Edward M. House, that he had been "sweating blood over the question—what is right and feasible (possible) to do in Russia. It goes to pieces like quicksilver under my touch."[27]

The War Department selected for the AEF two U.S. regiments stationed in the Philippines—the 27th and 31st Infantries—and Major General William S. Graves as commander. A coded message ordered Graves to take the first train from San Francisco to Kansas City to meet with Secretary of War Baker. That train was leaving in two hours. He packed a few things and departed. Baker believed Graves had two

23. Betty Miller Unterberger, *The United States, Revolutionary Russia, and the Rise of Czechoslovakia*, new intro. (College Station: Texas A&M University Press, 2000), 236.

24. Melton, *Between War and Peace*, 23.

25. Willet, *Russian Sideshow*, xxix.

26. Melton, *Between War and Peace*, 25–26.

27. Leo J. Bacino, *Reconstructing Russia: U.S. Policy in Revolutionary Russia, 1917–1922* (Kent, OH: Kent State University Press, 1999), 76.

qualities most needed in difficult circumstances—"common sense" and "self-effacing loyalty." Secretary of State Lansing, by contrast, believed Graves lacked diplomatic tact, but Wilson sided with Baker.[28]

Graves's train arrived in Kansas City late. At the station, Secretary Baker, who was between trains, handed him a sealed envelope, saying: "This contains the policy of the United States in Russia which you are to follow. Watch your step; you will be walking on eggs loaded with dynamite. God bless you and good-bye."[29]

At his hotel, Graves read Wilson's instructions. The first half explained eloquently why the United States should *not* intervene in Russia. One could sense Wilson's frustration with months of pressure to intervene: victory on the Western Front was paramount; no part of its military force should be diverted to other goals; the Russian Far East was of little relevance to America's war effort.

Wilson's summary judgment appeared strong and unequivocal:

> It is the clear and fixed judgment of the Government of the United States . . . that military intervention [in Siberia] would add to the present sad confusion in Russia rather than cure it, injure her rather than help her, and that it would be of no advantage in the prosecution of our main design, to win the war against Germany. It cannot, therefore, take part in such intervention or sanction it in principle.[30]

Graves must have been confused, the more so as Wilson then argued that military action in Russia was admissible to help the Czechoslovaks "consolidate their forces and get into successful cooperation with their Slavic kinsmen," to guard military stockpiles, and "to render such aid as may be acceptable to Russians in the organization of their own self-defense."[31] Above all, Wilson insisted that the mission in no way

> contemplates any interference of any kind with the political sovereignty of Russia, any intervention in her internal affairs, or any impairment of her territorial integrity either now or thereafter, but that each of the associated powers has the single object of affording such aid as shall be acceptable, and only such aid as shall be acceptable, to the Russian people in their endeavor to regain control of their own affairs, their own territory, and their own destiny.[32]

Of course, Wilson was not being entirely consistent or forthright since supporting any particular group in Russia naturally involved interference in Russia's internal affairs. Wilson's instructions left key unanswered questions: "Against whom" were the

---

28. Melton, *Between War and Peace*, 46–47.

29. William S. Graves, *America's Siberian Adventure, 1918–1920* (New York: Peter Smith, 1941), 4.

30. Graves, *America's Siberian Adventure*, 7.

31. Graves, *America's Siberian Adventure*, 7–8.

32. Graves, *America's Siberian Adventure*, 9.

Czechoslovaks supposed to fight, and "against whom" was the Russian self-defense to be organized? He did not specifically mention the Bolsheviks, the Germans, or the Austro-Hungarians. Nor did Wilson distinguish between particular groups of Russians or explain what he meant by "self-government."

In summary, Wilson ordered Graves to land American troops inside Russian territory without intervening in Russia's affairs, even as the country was plunging into a civil war, in which the Czechoslovaks were playing an initially pivotal role. The American policy was built on an attempt to square a circle. No wonder Wilson had been "sweating blood."

The last paragraph of the memo was the most enigmatic. Wilson outlined plans to provide Russia with economic and humanitarian assistance by sending a commission of merchants, agricultural experts, labor advisers, Red Cross representatives, and YMCA activists, adding that the execution of this plan "will not be permitted to embarrass the military assistance rendered in the rear of the westward moving forces of the Czecho-Slovaks."[33] One can speculate that, at the time of writing his instructions to Graves, Wilson was still considering a scenario, however unlikely, in which some Czechoslovaks, especially those still in the Ural Mountains region, could rally enough popular support among the Russians to move westward and reconstitute the Eastern Front—the "shadow of a plan" he had mentioned in his letter to Lansing on June 17. If so, he seems to have abandoned this hope when he wrote to Lansing on September 5 that "the Czecho-Slovaks must (so far as our aid was to be used) be brought out eastward not got out westward."[34]

Wilson, moreover, articulated an exit strategy: the American troops must be withdrawn from the East and transferred to the Western Front if the current plans "should develop into others inconsistent with the policy to which the government of the United States feels constrained to restrict itself."[35] In other words, for example, if the Russian people or government came to view the mission as hostile to their interests.

The first American troops began to arrive in Siberia from Manila in mid-August. On September 1, 1918, General Graves arrived in Vladivostok with the remainder of the American forces, for a total of 8,388 troops in all.[36]

Siberian Realities

General Graves received no briefings on military, political, social, economic, or financial conditions in Russia. He admitted that he had pictured Siberia "as a cold, barren, and desolate country" and was pleased that the American headquarters in Vladivostok

33. Graves, *America's Siberian Adventure*, 10.

34. Unterberger, *Rise of Czechoslovakia*, 289.

35. Graves, *America's Siberian Adventure*, 8.

36. Davis and Trani, *First Cold War*, 148.

Figure 6.3: American troops marching in Vladivostok.

occupied a large building downtown with comfortable offices and accommodations for officers.[37]

Less pleasant surprises awaited him. On September 2, Graves met with Japanese general Otani Kikuzo, who declared himself commander of all Allied forces in the Russian Far East. Graves responded that he had not been ordered to recognize Kikuzo's authority, and the matter was quietly dropped.[38] The meeting also served as a reminder that Japan, not the United States, was the predominant Allied military power in Siberia: Japan's contribution of troops had ballooned to seventy-five thousand.[39] Graves's concerns about Japanese goals in Siberia gradually increased.

Graves also learned that U.S. troops were already engaged in a military operation north of Vladivostok. Serving under Japanese command, they performed rear-guard actions for active Japanese combatants seeking to clear Bolshevik forces from the Trans-Siberian Railway between Vladivostok and Khabarovsk (Map 6.3). An American intelligence official reported that "the Bolshevik strength as estimated by Otani was vastly exaggerated."[40] Graves also soon discovered that German and Austro-Hungarian

---

37. Graves, *America's Siberian Adventure*, 35 (quotation), 57 (headquarters).

38. Richard, *When the United States Invaded Russia*, 58.

39. Richard, *When the United States Invaded Russia*, 59; Jonathan Nielson, "Russia," in *The United States in the First World War: An Encyclopedia*, ed. Anne Cipriano Venzon (New York: Garland Publishing, 1995), 515.

40. Willet, *Russian Sideshow*, 173.

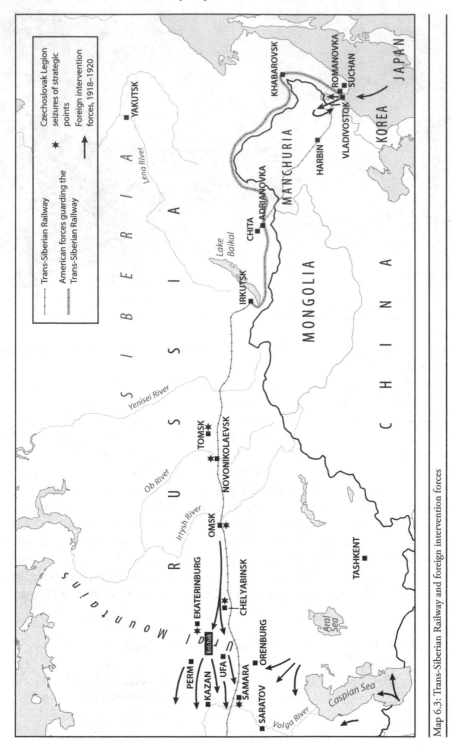

Map 6.3: Trans-Siberian Railway and foreign intervention forces

POWs in Siberia remained mostly disarmed and played little to no role in the brewing civil conflict. When U.S. forces took custody of some camps and improved the rations, prisoners flocked to them and had little incentive to flee.[41]

The Czechoslovak troops turned out to be in a less desperate situation than intelligence reports had suggested. Thousands had joined with General Mikhail Diterikhs (one of the investigators of the murder of the imperial family) and General Rudolf Gajda (a Czech military commander) and had successfully established operational control over the Trans-Siberian Railway in eastern Siberia, thanks in part to technical assistance from the U.S.-staffed Russian Railroad Service Corps. Diterikhs and Gajda then went not east but farther west. They joined the Czechoslovaks in the Ural Mountains, who were pushing westward together with other anti-Bolshevik forces, scoring victory after victory. In September, the Czechoslovaks conducted offensive operations on the European side of the Ural Mountains and gradually approached the Volga River. When Graves enthusiastically reported on these developments to Washington and inquired whether he had to start moving westward, the War Department ordered him to stay east of Lake Baikal and to concentrate on protecting Trans-Siberian Railway supply lines.[42] Throughout September, Wilson made his position clear: the Czechoslovaks needed to travel eastward to Vladivostok.[43]

Graves also discovered that "the Russians," referred to as a cohesive collective entity in Wilson's instructions, was a mythical construct. As he put it, "I could not give a Russian a shirt without being subjected to the charge of trying to help the side to which the recipient of the shirt belonged."[44] Russia had descended into a bloody mosaic of civil war. British, French, and Japanese officials in Siberia were far from neutral, actively supporting anti-Bolshevik forces and expecting Graves and the AEF to do the same.

But the more Graves learned about the anti-Bolshevik forces, the more critical he became. The various warring factions seemed to be united only by their common hatred for the Bolsheviks and desire for Allied support. On September 23, a semblance of central authority was created in the city of Ufa, west of the southern Ural Mountains. "The All-Russian Provisional Government," as it was called, was forced to flee Ufa before a Bolshevik advance and to settle in the western Siberian city of Omsk. It came to be known as the Omsk Directory, whose leaders ranged from moderate socialists to moderate nationalists.[45]

The Directory had little control over anti-Bolshevik warlords in eastern Siberia, two of whom Graves considered particularly repugnant. One was Grigorii Semenov, ataman (leader) of the Trans-Baikal Cossacks. He made Chita his stronghold, robbing,

---

41. Melton, *Between War and Peace*, 76.

42. Willet, *Russian Sideshow*, xxiv-xxv, 160, 181; Melton, *Between War and Peace*, 66.

43. Melton, *Between War and Peace*, 68–70.

44. Graves, *America's Siberian Adventure*, 79–80.

45. Engelstein, *Russia in Flames*, 422.

plundering, and killing local residents for power and profit. The Japanese provided him with military and financial support. The other was Ataman Ivan Kalmykov of the Ussuri Cossacks, who operated between Khabarovsk and Vladivostok and was also generously supported by the Japanese. Graves occasionally met with both atamans but also received a steady flow of reports of atrocities their troops committed against the local population. He reserved his harshest invective for Kalmykov, whom he considered " the worst scoundrel I ever saw or heard of."[46]

Graves realized that not all of Semenov's and Kalmykov's victims were Bolsheviks and that those who fought against the anti-Bolshevik warlords were not necessarily Bolsheviks. Such guerilla fighters called themselves "red partisans" and were often driven more by local grievances than Bolshevik ideology. The region was both intensely violent and politically complex, and anti-Bolshevik forces found it extremely difficult to mobilize grassroots support for their movement.

The Armistice and the Rise of Admiral Kolchak

On November 11, 1918, an armistice agreement ended the fighting on the Western Front. Now General Graves believed that the AEF should depart Siberia. Yet a major political event soon dragged the United States deeper into the Russian Civil War. On November 18, the Omsk Directory was overthrown in a military coup by Admiral Aleksandr Kolchak, who proclaimed himself supreme ruler of Russia.

Events in Omsk coincided with the growing awareness in the U.S. government of the radicalism and resilience of the Bolshevik regime. A flow of information from U.S. diplomatic sources convinced Secretary of State Lansing that what was at stake in Russia was more than the safety of the Czechoslovaks. On October 26, Lansing wrote that he considered Bolshevism "the most hideous and monstrous thing that the human mind had ever conceived."[47] But was the Kolchak coup really a sign that the Russians were endeavoring "to regain control of their own affairs"?[48]

Despite Allied assurances and State Department officials' praise for Kolchak, Wilson did not rush to conclusions, especially since Graves recommended a prompt troop withdrawal:

> I think some blood will be shed when troops move out but the longer we stay the greater will be the bloodshed when Allied troops do go, as in effect each day we remain here, now that the war with Germany is over, we are by our mere presence helping establish a form of autocratic government which the people of Siberia will not stand for.[49]

---

46. Graves, *America's Siberian Adventure*, 90.
47. Melton, *Between War and Peace*, 83.
48. Graves, *America's Siberian Adventure*, 9.
49. Richard, *When the United States Invaded Russia*, 66.

When Wilson left for Europe in December 1918 to participate in the Paris Peace Conference, Graves was told to stay put.

In Versailles, where the peace conference met in January–June 1919, the Allies debated whether to pursue a full-scale military intervention in Russia against the Bolsheviks, whom many now saw as an international threat. Winston Churchill, secretary of state for War and Air, was an adamant proponent of urgent action, as was French prime minister Georges Clemenceau. They were opposed by British prime minister David Lloyd George and British foreign secretary Arthur Balfour. But the strongest opposition came from Wilson himself. As he was returning to Washington, he reiterated his position in a telegram to U.S. officials in Paris: "It would be fatal to be led farther into the Russian chaos."[50]

Still, Wilson, weakened from a serious attack of influenza contracted in Paris,[51] did not order Graves to evacuate the AEF but to continue guarding the Trans-Siberian and protecting the Advisory Commission of Railway Experts, which participated in running its operations.

In June 1919, Kolchak assured the Allied Powers that he would allow a democratically elected Constituent Assembly to assume power after the defeat of the Bolsheviks. This offered Wilson a justification for providing Kolchak with financial and military assistance, something Britain and France had been doing for some time.[52]

To report to Wilson on the strength, policies, and plans of Kolchak's government, Graves and U.S. ambassador to Japan Rowland Morris traveled to Omsk in July–August 1919. The mission started well despite growing criticism of Graves in the State Department, of which Morris was probably aware. Yet Graves retained the support of General March, who insisted: "Keep a stiff upper lip. I am going to stand by you until ——freezes over."[53]

Graves and Morris witnessed the retreat of Kolchak's forces, heard accounts of their atrocities against local people, and observed firsthand the dysfunction of the Omsk government. As Morris put it, "we have not found a single individual who spoke a good word for the Kolchak regime."[54] Still, they reached opposite conclusions. Morris recommended a formal recognition of the Kolchak government; Graves demurred. Pointing to an order from the State Department dispatch, Morris turned to Graves, saying: "You will have to support Kolchak," adding, "The State Department is running this, not the War Department." Graves retorted: "The State Department is not

---

50. John W. Long, "American Intervention in Russia: The North Russian Expedition, 1918–19," *Diplomatic History* 6, no. 1 (Winter 1982): 45–67 (here: 63).

51. Alfred W. Crosby, *America's Forgotten Pandemic: The Influenza of 1918* (Cambridge and New York: Cambridge University Press, 1989), 191–93.

52. Melton, *Between War and Peace*, 152.

53. J. Robert Moskin, *American Statecraft: The Story of the U.S. Foreign Service* (New York: Thomas Dunne Books/St. Martin's Press, 2013), 316.

54. Melton, *Between War and Peace*, 187.

running me."[55] The lack of clarity from Wilson did not help. While he approved assistance to the Kolchak government, he did not change Graves's original instructions. When the Kolchak government was forced to evacuate Omsk in mid-November, "Western Siberia became a scene of total confusion and turmoil."[56]

From Peacekeeping to Counterinsurgency

Graves's insistence on what would later be called peacekeeping operations earned him accusations of Bolshevik sympathy. He tried to remain neutral. When he learned that one of his soldiers had arrested a Russian for being a Bolshevik, he chided him:

> The United States is not at war with the Bolsheviki or any other faction of Russia. You have no orders to arrest Bolsheviks or anybody else unless they disturb the peace of the community, attack the people, or the Allied soldiers.[57]

Figure 6.4: American soldiers on the Trans-Siberian Railway.

55. Richard M. Connaughton, *The Republic of the Ushakovka: Admiral Kolchak and the Allied Intervention in Siberia 1918–1920* (London: Routledge, 1990), 116–17.

56. Willet, *Russian Sideshow*, 243.

57. Members of the 31st Infantry Regiment Association, *The 31st Infantry Regiment: A History of "America's Foreign Legion" in Peace and War* (Jefferson, NC: McFarland & Co., 2018), 27.

In practice, however, American neutrality favored anti-Bolshevik forces. Any self-proclaimed Bolshevik was theoretically entitled to unimpeded passage on the Trans-Siberian Railway sectors controlled by the Americans, just like any supporter of the Kolchak government. In reality, a Bolshevik would not get very far traveling through Siberia. Thus de facto, American protection of the railroads helped the Kolchak government.

Local Bolsheviks and red partisans repeatedly attacked the rail line leading to the coal mines near the town of Suchan, a few hundred miles from the main railway (Map 6.3). In September 1918, Graves sent troops to secure access to coal supplies. Around this time, Kolchak imposed harsh military conscription measures. Resentment in Suchan intensified. Mine workers went on strike, while peasants supported and joined the pro-Bolshevik partisans. Partisan attacks on the railways multiplied. In late May, American troops defeated the insurgents.[58]

Things got worse in June when the partisans captured several American soldiers.[59] Then, two U.S. units stationed in Romanovka ("a fairly large village"), on the rail line to Suchan, suffered a devastating surprise partisan attack. At 4:45 a.m. on June 25, the insurgents opened fire at the night guards' tents. Many died instantly in their sleep; others rose and fought in their underwear. Twenty-four Americans were killed and twenty-five wounded. The survivors were surprised to recognize local villagers among the twelve dead partisans—the very people with whom they had socialized, traded, and shared meals[60]—an important insight into the fluid dynamics of insurgency warfare.

By August 1919, American, Japanese, and pro-Kolchak forces had pacified the Suchan mining district, but it was a hollow victory. The mines were no longer in operation, and red partisans still controlled many adjacent territories.[61]

For the remainder of their stay in Russia, the Americans were caught between pro- and anti-Bolshevik forces. In fall 1919, Graves was ordered to deliver one hundred thousand rifles to the Kolchak government, though he had initially refused for fear that they might be intercepted and used to commit more atrocities. Semenov's Cossacks, indeed, stopped one shipment at Chita and demanded fifteen thousand rifles. Graves gave orders not to surrender a single rifle. After a forty-hour, nerve-wracking standoff, Semenov relented, probably due to Japanese interference.[62] Indeed, Graves often resisted transferring to Kolchak Allied war equipment, for the protection of which he had been sent to Siberia. Kolchak, for his part, despised both Graves and the troops under his command, calling them "off-scourings of the American Army, Jewish immigrants, with a corresponding commanding staff," whose persistence in

---

58. Willet, *Russian Sideshow*, 218–22; Melton, *Between War and Peace*, 175–77.

59. Willet, *Russian Sideshow*, 223–34.

60. John M. House, *Wolfhounds and Polar Bears: The American Expeditionary Force in Siberia, 1918–1920* (Tuscaloosa, AL: University of Alabama Press, 2016), 132–33.

61. Willet, *Russian Sideshow*, 237.

62. Melton, *Between War and Peace*, 195.

Siberia "will lead only to a final discrediting of America and to extremely serious consequences."[63]

By late 1919–early 1920, it appeared that the only organized group that viewed American troops in Siberia with sympathy was the Czechoslovaks. They, in turn, were increasingly at odds with Kolchak and the Cossacks.

American Departure: Mission Accomplished?

In northern Russia, what had started as a mission to protect storage facilities, assist a potential Czechoslovak evacuation, and support local Russian groups, came to involve fierce anti-Bolshevik combat, especially after the Armistice. The local population resented their dependence but worried that they could not survive without Allied help.[64] By the end of summer 1919, however, the bulk of Allied troops had departed from northern Russia.

Change was also afoot in Siberia. In May, General Gajda had urged the Kolchak government "to convene a Siberian Constituent Assembly and take other measures to dissociate itself from the counterrevolutionary right."[65] Kolchak erupted in a fury, throwing an inkwell at Gajda and shouting: "You have no military education!" Gajda retorted: "You commanded three ships in the Black Sea. Does that qualify you to govern an empire?"[66] In mid-summer, Kolchak's forces abandoned Ufa and Chelyabinsk, and Gajda resigned.

Members of the Socialist-Revolutionary movement, who actively opposed the Bolsheviks throughout Siberia, coalesced around efforts to topple Kolchak and make the anti-Bolshevik government more democratic. Hoping to make peace with the Bolsheviks and create a democratic and socialist buffer state in eastern Siberia, they recruited Gajda to overthrow Kolchak. The coup attempted in mid-November 1919 failed. Then, as Bolshevik forces closed in on Omsk, Kolchak fled east. The Czechoslovaks captured him, then surrendered him to the left-wing authorities in Irkutsk in exchange for unimpeded passage east.[67] Soon after that, the Bolsheviks seized power in Irkutsk and executed Kolchak and his prime minister, the former Constitutional Democrat, Viktor Pepeliaev.[68]

---

63. Connaughton, *Republic of the Ushakovka*, 116.

64. Novikova, *An Anti-Bolshevik Alternative*, 108–10.

65. Scott B. Smith, *Captives of Revolution: The Socialist Revolutionaries and the Bolshevik Dictatorship, 1918–1923* (Pittsburgh, PA: University of Pittsburgh Press, 2011), 205.

66. Melton, *Between War and Peace*, 188.

67. Ian C. D. Moffat, *The Allied Intervention in Russia: The Diplomacy of Chaos* (Basingstoke, UK: Palgrave Macmillan, 2015), 258.

68. Kevin J. McNamara, *Dreams of a Great Small Nation: The Mutinous Army that Threatened a Revolution, Destroyed an Empire, Founded a Republic, and Remade the Map of Europe* (New York: PublicAffairs, 2016), 311–12; Moffat, *The Allied Intervention in Russia*, 260.

In these chaotic and violent conditions, Graves was finally doing what he considered to be his core mission—helping the Czechoslovaks evacuate, even while preparing for the evacuation of U.S. forces. Most of the AEF left Vladivostok in early 1920. Graves departed on April 1. As his ship steamed off, a Japanese band played the Stephen Foster tune, "Hard Times, Come Again No More."[69] American casualties in Siberia—170 killed, 52 wounded—were less than half the number suffered in northern Russia, where under British command, American forces played a more aggressive role.[70] Both figures were trivial in the context of the Russian Civil War, which saw some 2.5 million battle deaths,[71] and therefore highlight the insignificant part America played in that conflict.

Despite the limited scope of the AEF's military engagement in Siberia, its stated commitment to neutrality, and a high degree of military discipline and cohesion, the Americans committed atrocities. Robert L. Willet describes how a lieutenant in Suchan fired his semiautomatic pistol into a doorway filled with women. Lieutenant Colonel Robert L. Eichelberger witnessed the attack and later wrote: "How many were hit I do not know nor care to know." The same lieutenant then ordered the execution of a blind man.[72] The question of whether AEF soldiers always took prisoners requires further research.

A Half-Forgotten Invasion

The case of the American intervention in Siberia shows that a major historical event can give rise to powerful myths in some minds while vanishing from others. In stark contrast to their mythical reverberations in Russia, American military operations in northern and eastern Russia lodged in the periphery of American thinking about war and power.

In the interwar decades, a few U.S. diplomatic historians studied the American intervention. Some found the operations legally unjustified and diplomatically damaging, especially in the north;[73] others judged them legitimate and well-meaning.[74]

---

69. Willet, *Russian Sideshow*, 262–63.

70. Richard, *When the United States Invaded Russia*, 171.

71. Jonathan D. Smele, *Historical Dictionary of the Russian Civil Wars, 1916–1926* (London: Rowman and Littlefield, 2015), 63n4.

72. Willet, *Russian Sideshow*, 234.

73. F. L. Schuman, *American Policy toward Russia Since 1917: A Study of Diplomatic History, International Law and Public Opinion* (New York: International Publishers, 1928).

74. Leonid I. Strakhovsky, *The Origins of American Intervention in North Russia (1918)* (Princeton, NJ: Princeton University Press, 1937).

After World War II, the intervention, according to one authority, was "perhaps the favorite thesis subject of American graduate students."[75] John Albert White's thorough study, which drew upon all the relevant languages, concluded that American intervention increased popular support for the Bolsheviks and prevented a permanent incursion of Japan into Siberia.[76] As regards strictly American interests, George Kennan wrote: "never, surely, in the history of American diplomacy has so much been paid for so little."[77]

The Soviets continually pointed to the intervention. In 1959, Nikita Khrushchev, the Soviet head of state and Communist Party boss, made an official visit to the United States. During his trip, he declared:

> We remember the grim days when American soldiers went to our soil headed by their generals to help the White Guard combat the new revolution. . . . Never have any of our soldiers been on American soil, but your soldiers were on Russian soil. These are the facts.[78]

While historians and other scholars remembered these events, which figured in high school textbooks,[79] most citizens did not. According to a *New York Times* poll in 1985, only 14 percent of Americans "were aware that in 1918, the United States landed troops in northern and eastern Russia."[80]

In 1987, the American television network ABC aired a miniseries, *Amerika*, which portrayed a fictional Soviet occupation of the United States. The Soviet government complained to the network that the Soviet invasion of the United States was pure fiction, whereas the United States really had invaded Russia. "This was news to the producers of ABC News, who had never heard of the American intervention in Siberia," according to the historian Carl Richard, who received a call from ABC News. He went on to write a book about the subject.[81]

Indeed, from the 1980s onward, a number of major studies of the U.S. intervention in Russia began to appear in the West, several of them referenced in this chapter. The Cold War contributed to a fascination with the topic, as perhaps did the unsuccessful American interventions in Vietnam, Lebanon, and elsewhere.

75. Robert D. Warth, review of *The Decision to Intervene*, by George F. Kennan, *Journal of Modern History* 30, no. 4 (December 1958): 374–75 (here: 375).

76. John Albert White, *Siberian Intervention* (Princeton, NJ: Princeton University Press, 1950).

77. George F. Kennan, *The Decision to Intervene*, vol. 2 of *Soviet-American Relations, 1917–1920* (Princeton, NJ: Princeton University Press, 1958), 471.

78. Byron Farwell, *Over There: The United States in the Great War, 1917–1918* (New York: W.W. Norton, 1999), 284.

79. For example, Thomas Andrew Bailey, *The American Pageant: A History of the Republic*, 2nd ed. (Boston: D.C. Heath and Co., 1961), 746.

80. David S. Foglesong, *America's Secret War against Bolshevism: U.S. Intervention in the Russian Civil War, 1917–1920* (Chapel Hill, NC: University of North Carolina Press, 1995), 6.

81. Richard, *When the United States Invaded Russia*, ix.

The Lessons of the Intervention

Greater public awareness of the American intervention in Russia might have yielded valuable lessons about the limits of American military power. First, it could have shown the importance of reliable intelligence and the danger of making hasty assumptions about the situation on the ground. While Woodrow Wilson was appropriately cautious, many officials in the State Department rushed to conclude that the Bolsheviks were under German influence or control and exaggerated the threat of German and Austro-Hungarian POWs in Siberia.

Another important lesson had to do with the fragility of the wartime alliances. Britain and France had political goals in Russia that were increasingly at odds with the more neutral position of the United States. Meanwhile, Japan (an ally but not part of the Triple Entente) asserted its geopolitical interests in Asia despite U.S. concerns. This pattern was to play out on a grander scale after World War II, when the United States and the Soviet Union, no longer bound by the common goal of defeating the Axis powers, pursued increasingly divergent geopolitical interests in Europe and elsewhere.

There was another lesson. While in Siberia, the AEF learned how difficult peace-keeping functions could be in a fragmenting and polarizing country. They also experienced what would later be called "mission creep." The original rationale for deploying American troops evolved despite Graves's efforts to adhere to the most restrictive interpretation of Wilson's instructions. While the United States never formally recognized Kolchak and his government, it provided him with military assistance, thus becoming more deeply involved in the Russian Civil War (and even fought against Bolshevik troops in the north, albeit under British command).

As mission creep continued, the War Department and the State Department disagreed on how to assess the situation in Russia and what American involvement should be. Without an interagency body, like the National Security Council (which was created in 1947), only the president himself could resolve these disagreements. Yet Wilson had his hands full at the Paris Peace Conference and suffered from a debilitating illness. The world was becoming too complex for one person to manage.

Given the tremendous scope of human destruction perpetrated directly and indirectly by the Soviet Union, one might wonder whether the United States missed an opportunity to rid the world of communism before it became a major international force. This opinion was widespread during the First Red Scare in the United States (1919–1920) when General Graves was criticized for his restraint in Siberia. In fact, the FBI kept Graves under surveillance as a suspected Bolshevik sympathizer.[82] Retrospectively, in 1949, amid the onset of the Cold War, Winston Churchill declared that the entire "civilized world" would one day conclude that "the strangling of Bolshevism at its birth would have been an untold blessing to the human race."[83] Wilson

---

82. Melton, *Between War and Peace*, 207.

83. Deon Geldenhuys, *Foreign Political Engagement: Remaking States in the Post-Cold War World* (Houndmills, UK: Macmillan, 1998), 153.

was far more skeptical. He declared in Paris that "to try to stop a revolutionary movement with ordinary armies is like using a broom to sweep back a great sea." General Graves concurred. "There isn't a nation on earth," he asserted, "that would not resent foreigners sending troops into their country, for the purpose of putting this or that faction in charge of their Government machinery."[84] Wilson and Graves's skepticism was doubtless justified. The Kolchak government and its clients were not nearly as democratic, popular, or effective as the United States had hoped, prefiguring many other anti-communist regimes of the twentieth century.

The Americans' attempts to maintain a neutral stance were met with resentment and disappointment from the other Allies, the Kolchak government, and even the Czechoslovaks, while the red partisans and Bolsheviks viewed the Americans as outright enemies. But siding unequivocally with Kolchak would probably have alienated even more Siberians, who increasingly saw him as worse than the red partisans and Bolsheviks. Some U.S. government officials would not have cared. According to Graves, Lieutenant Colonel Benjamin McCroskey, a military intelligence officer, master of languages, and expert in East Asian cultures,[85] believed only the savagery of Semenov stood "between civilization and Bolshevism."[86] The dangers of choosing sides in a struggle between extremists was doubtless another lesson worth learning.

Soviet and Post-Soviet Myths

What became almost a non-event to most Americans was transformed in Soviet Russia into a powerful and sinister myth of conquest and subjugation. Soviet mythmaking began as soon as the AEF disembarked in Vladivostok. Bolshevik officials sometimes recognized "contradictions" among capitalists, but even more often, their propaganda declared all capitalist powers to constitute one mortal enemy. Speaking at the Extraordinary Sixth All-Russian Congress of Soviets in November 1918, Vladimir Lenin declared that the main goal of the "Anglo-Franco-American imperialists" was to strangle global Bolshevism and its "main cell," the Russian Soviet Republic.[87] Lenin's words sounded almost academic when compared to the language of an editorial in *Pravda*:

> Wilson and the Mikado[88] march hand in hand against Russian workers and peasants. The most advanced, the most capitalistically developed country, together with a semi-feudal country, where people still ride on

84. Graves, *America's Siberian Adventure*, 82.

85. Jamie Bisher, *White Terror: Cossack Warlords of the Trans-Siberian* (London: Routledge, 2005), 276.

86. Willet, *Russian Sideshow*, 260–61.

87. Vladimir Lenin, "Rech o mezhdunarodnom polozhenii 8 noiabria," in *Polnoe sobranie sochinenii*, 5th ed., 55 vols. (Moscow: Politizdat, 1958–1965), 37:164.

88. The Japanese emperor.

the backs of people,[89] are attacking the republic of labor with cannons and machine guns. An American banker holds a Japanese cannibal on a leash and sends him, supplying gunpowder and canned food, to "defend civilization" against the "Bolshevik gangs."[90]

Lumping together everyone the Bolsheviks considered implacable enemies was a fundamental characteristic of Soviet mythmaking from their first months in power.

The oversimplified Soviet view of the American intervention in Siberia thus contributed to the development of the bipolar, intensely paranoid conception of Soviet Russia as a communist fortress besieged by enemies at home and abroad.[91] The Bolsheviks rejected the principle of individual responsibility, invoking instead class as the sole criterion for judging culpability. Those who belonged to what they considered the "class of exploiters"—entrepreneurs, the property-owning middle class, and even better-off peasants (disparagingly called "kulaks")—were considered enemies and subject to arbitrary detention and even execution. In one article, Lenin both denounced the "plundering" offensive of "Anglo-French" and "Japanese-American" imperialism and called for the slaughter of Russian "kulaks" because, he argued, they "had always allied with *international capitalists.*"[92]

Indeed, anyone who challenged the Bolsheviks could be branded an agent of "international capital." This sweeping view reached a peak of absurdity when pro-socialist sailors in the Kronstadt fortress near Petrograd rebelled against Bolshevik rule in 1921, fighting for "soviets without [Bolshevik] commissars"[93] and adopting pro-Soviet slogans.[94] The Bolshevik leadership nevertheless presented the rebellion as a "French war plot against Russia."[95]

Thus, according to a 1919 Soviet pamphlet, Japanese and American "predators" enjoyed an easy victory and received "flowers, wine, and kisses, presented by the daughters and wives of the Russian bourgeoisie."[96] Again, internal and external enemies were depicted as collaborating closely. The purpose of the invaders, the pamphlet

---

89. The author is referring to the *kago*, a wheelless, human-powered means of transport common in early twentieth-century Japan.

90. "Ober-zhandarmy," *Pravda*, August 17, 1918.

91. A. Berezkin, *SShA—aktivnyi organizator i uchastnik voennoi interventsii protiv Sovetskoi Rossii (1918–1922 gg.)* (Moscow: Gospolitizdat, 1952), 32–33, 47, 49.

92. Vladimir Lenin, "Tovarishchi rabochie! Idem v poslednii, reshitel'nyi boi!" in *Polnoe sobranie sochinenii*, 37:38–41.

93. Geoffrey Swain, *The Origins of the Russian Civil War* (London: Longman, 1996), 3.

94. Smith, *Captives of Revolution*, 227.

95. Ian Bullock, *Romancing the Revolution: The Myth of Soviet Democracy and the British Left* (Edmonton, AB: AU Press, 2011), 334.

96. V. Vilenskii (Sibiriakov), *Chernaia godina sibirskoi reaktsii (interventsiia v Sibiri)* (Moscow: Izd. VTsIKS, 1919), 24–25.

claimed, was to reinstate for their "ruling classes" prerevolutionary loans canceled by the Bolsheviks and to capture Siberian markets.

This militant worldview, with some modifications, persisted for decades. It was one of the key dogmas of *History of the All-Union Communist Party (Bolsheviks): Short Course*, the bible of Stalinist historical orthodoxy. Written under Joseph Stalin's personal supervision and published in tens of millions of copies, it denounced the "Anglo-Franco-Japanese-American interventionists" as aiming to overthrow the Soviet government and restore the "bourgeois" order.[97] Again, collaboration was alleged between the Soviet Union's external and domestic enemies, such as Leon Trotsky.

To create the impression that by intervening in Siberia, the United States was actively seeking to overthrow the Bolshevik regime and strangle the Soviet state, U.S. support for the Czechoslovaks and for Kolchak was overblown, but at least it had some factual basis. U.S. consular officials and spies did abet anti-Bolshevik forces in European Russia as early as 1917.[98] Over time, the AEF in Siberia did increase support for Bolshevik adversaries despite Wilson's efforts "to square the circle" in his instructions to Graves. But allegations that the United States sought to colonize and partition Soviet Russia, while persistent, were completely false.

When the World War II alliance between the United States and the Soviet Union gave way to the Cold War, Soviet historians began to single out America as the most pernicious interventionist in Siberia. One declared that "American imperialism, the most reactionary, most frenzied imperialism, . . . took on the shameful role of hangman and strangler of Russian freedom."[99] Another argued that Japan was merely an American tool in the U.S. struggle against Soviet Russia.[100] Yet another claimed that the intervention by England and France was aggressive only thanks to support from "American capital."[101]

Like the myth of "American stranglers of the Soviet state," the myth of "American enslavers and colonizers" reached its hysterical peak in the early Cold War. In a study published during the Korean War (1950–1953), a Soviet author asserted that American intervention in Siberia, driven by "plundering imperialism," aimed at "enslavement and partition of Russia."[102] American control over the Trans-Siberian Railway,

97. *Istoriia Vsesoiuznoi kommunisticheskoi partii (bolshevikov). Kratkii kurs* (N.p.: Izd. TsK VKP(b) Pravda, 1938), 216–17.

98. Foglesong, *America's Secret War*.

99. A. I. Mel'chin, *Amerikanskaia interventsiia na Sovetskom Dal'nem Vostoke v 1918–1920 gg.* (Moscow: Voenno-morskoe izd. Voenno-morskogo ministerstva Soiuza SSR, 1951), 25.

100. A. P. Shurygin, *Kommunisticheskaia partiia—organizator razgroma inostrannoi voennoi interventsii i vnutrennei kontrrevoliutsii na Dal'nem Vostoke* (Moscow: Izdanie VIA, 1957), 120.

101. A. Berezkin, *Oktiabr'skaia revoliutsiia i SShA, 1917–1922 gg.* (Moscow: Nauka, 1967), 129 cited in I. Naumov, *Grazhdanskaia voina na Dal'nem vostoke v sovetskoi istoriografii serediny 1950-serediny 1980-kh godov* (Irkutsk: Izd. Irkutskogo universiteta, 1991), 110.

102. Berezkin, *SShA—aktivnyi organizator*, 46–47.

collaboration with Japanese forces, and promotion of commercial interests in Siberia added up in the minds of Stalinist propagandists to a master plan to colonize and partition Russia. Efforts to substantiate this allegation could border on the comical. One scholar pointed to a U.S. State Department map drafted in 1919, supposedly revealing "villainous plans of American imperialism against our motherland."[103] In fact, the original map and accompanying text sought to balance pursuits of national self-determination of newly independent former territories of imperial Russia with the goal of reconstituting a strong Russian state, encouraging "the reunion with Russia of those border regions of the south and west which have broken away and set up their own national governments, particularly the Baltic provinces and the Ukraine, if reunion can be accomplished with a federalized or a genuinely democratic Russia."[104] Thus, the alleged "plan to dismember Russia" recognized the break-up of the Russian Empire and attempted to mitigate its impact on the Russian state.

The myths of America as a would-be strangler of socialism and colonizer of Russia were an intrinsic part of the Soviet bipolar worldview, promoted by unscrupulous Soviet historians and propagandists for decades. The myths would have been a mere historical curiosity had they died along with the communist Soviet Union. The "strangler" of the fledgling Soviet state fell by the wayside, but the myth of the United States as seeking to despoil and partition Russia did not. In August 2018, in commemorating the U.S. landing in Vladivostok, the Facebook page for the Russian Embassy in Washington, DC, shared an article opening with the words: "100 years ago, U.S. troops landed in Vladivostok and began bloody American interference in Russia's bitter Civil War."[105] It accused Western powers of planning "to partition the largest state on the planet among themselves." The article also cited unnamed Soviet records concerning atrocities committed by American troops, including burying people alive and mutilating bodies. The article mentioned the attack on Americans in Romanovka as an example of grassroots resistance against invaders. The embassy hashtagged the post as #WeRemember and #NeverForget. The following year, the pro-government Russian Military Historical Society posted on its state-controlled website an article entitled: "A War with Yankees in Soviet Russia: How Americans Wanted to Get Their Own Piece of the Russian Pie."[106]

Similar articles have appeared in the Russian media. One alleged that Colonel Charles Morrow, commander of American forces in the Baikal sector, was responsible

103. Asia Kunina, *Proval amerikanskikh planov zavoevaniia mirovogo gospodstva v 1917–1920 gg.* (Moscow: Gospolitizdat, 1954), 95.

104. David Hunter Miller, *My Diary at the Conference of Paris*, 21 vols. (New York: Appeal Printing Co., 1924), 4:219.

105. Russian Embassy, "100 years ago, U.S. troops landed in Vladivostock," Facebook, August 15, 2018, https://www.facebook.com/RusEmbUSA/posts/862120330665025.

106. Sergei Antonov, "Voina s ianki v sovetskoi Rossii: kak amerikantsy khoteli poluchit' svoi kusok russkogo piroga," Istoria.rf, August 15, 2019, https://histrf.ru/biblioteka/b/voina-s-ianki-v-sovetskoi-rossii-kak-amierikantsy-khotieli-poluchit-svoi-kusok-rossiiskogho-pirogha.

for executing sixteen hundred people near the village of Adrianovka in the environs of Chita. It also cited as fact a Stalin-era allegation that "the invaders could not sleep unless they killed someone on a given day."[107] This undoubted falsification transitioned into the Russian blogosphere. One user, who calls himself "Mason Reptiloid," cited it among other uncorroborated examples of the sadistic brutality of Americans, who, as the user argued, sought to partition and colonize Russia, treating Russians "as genetic trash." Americans in this article appeared not only evil but also nearly all-powerful: "The USA brought to power Trotsky (Russia) and Kolchak (Siberia), while the Czechoslovaks (White Czechs) were punitive shock troops in the Anglo-American coalition and were personally subordinated to General Graves."[108] The same article appeared verbatim on several other platforms, making it hard to identify its original author. An amateur Russian historian fact-checked the Morrow story, tracing it to a 1922 *New York Tribune* article reporting that Morrow had accused Semenov's Cossacks of the Adrianovka atrocity.[109] (Recent Western historiography confirms that Morrow and the soldiers under his command were horrified at such atrocities.[110]) Such misrepresentations—rarely challenged in the Russian blogosphere—continue to multiply and poison U.S.-Russian relations.

Nevertheless, serious academic research on this topic has advanced in Russia in the past decade.[111] At least among professional historians in Russia and America, it seems the historical record of American intervention in Russia will no longer slip into oblivion or myths and half-truths of propaganda.

---

107. "Zverstva amerikantsev v Rossii: '...ne mogli usnut' ne ubiv kogo-nibud,'" June 2, 2012, https://topwar.ru/14988-zverstva-amerikancev-v-rossii-ne-mogli-usnut-ne-ubiv-kogo-nibud.html; Iakov Temkin and Efim Cherniak, *Razboinichii put' amerikanskikh agressorov. Istoricheskii ocherk.* (Moscow: Voennoe izd. voennogo ministerstva Soiuza SSR, 1952), 79.

108. Mason Reptiloid, "Kak SShA okkupirovali Sibir' v 1918," March 17, 2017, https://www.kramola.info/blogs/metody-genocida/kak-ssha-okkupirovali-sibir-v-1918; https://cont.ws/@water/542970; https://lsvsx.livejournal.com/781757.html.

109. Valerii Nikolaev, "Polkovnik Charl'z Kh. Morru, zhertva fal'sifikatorov istorii, lozhno obvinennyi v massovykh rasstrelakh v sele Adrianovka v 1919 godu," *Iandeks Dzen,* January 10, 2020, https://zen.yandex.ru/media/id/5ce556777ebafe00b3397ab7/polkovnik-charlz-h-morrou-jertva-falsifikatorov-istorii-lojno-obvinennyi-v-massovyh-rasstrelah-v-sele-adrianovka-v-1919-godu-5e18f663d5bbc300aee7bee2.

110. Bisher, *White Terror,* 112.

111. A. V. Dolgushev, "Prichiny i tseli amerikanskoi interventsii na severe Rossii," *Vestnik Samarskogo gosudarstvennogo universiteta,* no. 1/2(82) (2011): 104–8; V. G. Khitryi, "Partizany i amerikanskie interventy v gody grazhdanskoi voiny na Dal'nem Vostoke Rossii (1918–1920 gg.)," *Armiia i obshchestvo: Nauchno-informatsionnyi zhurnal,* no. 2 (2012): 140–46; K. A. Konev, "'Doblestnye soiuzniki' ili 'simulirovannye druz'ia': Interventsiia SShA v izobrazhenii periodicheskoi pechati Sibiri i Dal'nego Vostoka," *Vestnik Kemerovskogo gosudarstvennogo universiteta,* nos. 2–6 (2015): 275–80.

7. The Myth of an Inevitable Bolshevik Victory

> Only Bolshevism was consistent with and faithful to the essence of the
> revolutionary movement in Russia, and for this reason it prevailed.[1]
>
> —*Peter Struve*

> . . . yes, the Russian people has accomplished a revolution, it
> has risen from the dead and now is partaking in the great global
> cause—the building of new and ever freer forms of life![2]
>
> —*Maxim Gorky*

The Russian Empire before the revolution in 1917 was no longer an absolute monarchy. The powers of Tsar Nicholas II and his government were limited by numerous constitutional restraints. Passing laws required the consent of the bicameral legislature (the Duma and the State Council), and the judicial system was independent. The right to form unions and voluntary associations was guaranteed. At the same time, administrative officials retained wide powers, could arrest and even exile "suspicious people" without judicial approval, and often mistreated and disrespected ordinary people. In February/March, the monarchy fell, and the Provisional Government declared the dawn of a new era of freedom. Yet the Great War raged on, social and economic tensions persisted, and to many, the new era did not feel that new after all.

As discussed in previous chapters, by the end of 1917, Vladimir Lenin and the Bolsheviks—the most radical group of leftist revolutionaries ever to govern any country—had smashed traditional hierarchies, swept away the constitutional restraints, and created the first one-party dictatorship in history. They were committed to transforming not just Russia but the entire world according to communist principles. Nothing could remain of the previous system, the Bolsheviks declared. Independent courts, the legislatures, and guaranteed political rights were to be replaced by "revolutionary consciousness," Bolshevik party control, and institutions favoring the lower classes. Anyone resisting the Bolshevik agenda was trying to reverse the tide of history, a tide, they argued, driving inevitably to the Bolshevik triumph.

---

1. Peter Struve, *Razmyshleniia o russkoi revoliutsii* (Sofiia: Rossisko-bolgarskoe knigoizdatel'stvo, 1921), 31.
2. Maxim Gorkii, *Nesvoevremennye mysli* (Moscow: Kniga po trebovaniiu, 2016), 8.

Our reflexive perception of history as a linear course of events has fostered acceptance of this Bolshevik perspective. After all, when we look back at what happened, we see one course of successive developments. These historical facts are real, and "alternative facts" are not. But does this mean that historical outcomes are predetermined, and events could not have unfolded differently? Was the Bolshevik victory an inevitable outcome of a fixed historical trajectory?

Historians search for multiple causal factors, including chance, to explain complex historical events. Among explanations for the Bolsheviks' victory, various scholars emphasize unprecedented use of violence, popular support, brilliant organizational skills, and the use of propaganda, among others.[3] The lining up of such factors contributes to the impression that there were no plausible alternatives to Bolshevik victory.

This closing chapter seeks to address not specific errors, falsehoods, or oversimplifications in relation to facts or events of the Russian Revolution but a broader mythical mode of thinking about the revolution as a series of events that followed one fixed trajectory with an allegedly inevitable outcome. Yet how can one disprove the myth of a predetermined historical outcome without generating myths of alternative outcomes? We cannot travel back in time to supply more flour to hungry Petrograd in January 1917, prevent Lenin from boarding the German train, talk Kerensky out of launching his summer offensive, or urge Wilson to send a massive invasion force to Siberia—and then see whether the Bolsheviks could still seize power in October 1917 or keep it in 1918.

Instead of speculating about such imagined trajectories, we will discuss the life course of three real people who fought for what they believed was "their" revolution. We will often refer to them by first names since they were quite young when they first embarked on their revolutionary journeys. They stand in for thousands of political actors with a diverse range of agendas and visions. Some won to varying degrees; others lost. Taking a closer look at their aspirations and choices will help us recognize the uncertainty of revolutionary outcomes and of history itself.

A Woman Soldier's Patriotic Revolution

The main source of information for the life of Maria Bochkareva (b. Frolkova) until 1917 is her memoir, which the Russian-born American journalist Isaac Don Levine set down after one hundred hours of interviews with the functionally illiterate Maria.[4]

---

3. Vladimir Brovkin, *Behind the Frontlines of the Civil War* (Princeton, NJ: Princeton University Press, 2015), 3–7.

4. Isaac Don Levine, introduction to *Yashka, My Life as Peasant, Exile, and Soldier*, by Maria Botchkareva, as set down by Isaac Don Levine (London: Constable and Company, 1919), viii. Paul E. Richardson recently republished the book as *Maria's War: A Soldier's Autobiography* (Montpelier, VT: Russian Life, 2016).

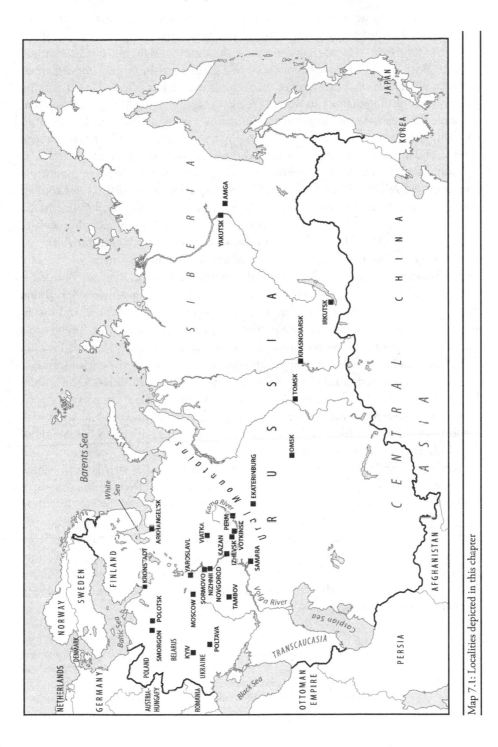

Map 7.1: Localities depicted in this chapter

Historians drawing on archival records have corroborated many parts of her story, especially as she transitioned from soldier to public activist.[5]

Before the Great War, Maria's peasant life followed a tragic but not uncommon pattern. Born in 1889 into the household of a former serf in Nizhegorod Province, three hundred miles east of Moscow, the third of four sisters, she lived on the brink of starvation until her family moved to Siberia to take advantage of a land allotment available through the state homesteading program. Having failed to make a go of it, the family moved to Tomsk, where its female members remained afflicted by hunger, disease, and the escapades of a drinking and abusive father. At eight-and-a-half, Maria was sent to work as a live-in babysitter. Suffering from abuse by her host family, she contemplated suicide. Thankfully, a female grocery-store owner offered her another live-in job as a house servant. Maria could not believe her luck. By the time Maria turned fourteen, her older sisters had left home, her mother was sick, her abusive alcoholic father worked less and less, and she became the family's main provider.

At fifteen, Maria had an affair with an officer who refused to marry her because of her peasant background. Soon after, she married a soldier, Afanasyi Bochkarev (pronounced Bochkaryov), not for romantic reasons but to escape increasingly brutal beatings from her father. Her husband turned out to be just as abusive and just as much of a drunkard, except that he also forced Maria to drink with him. Brought to a point when she nearly killed her husband with an axe, she ran away. Pleading for rides from train conductors while refusing their advances, she reached the city of Irkutsk.

The big city offered more anonymity and more work opportunities. As an asphalt layer, Maria was put in charge of other female and male workers, a supervisory position usually reserved for men. After losing her job due to sickness, she moved in with Jacob (Yasha) Buk, the son of a Jewish trader. Together, they opened a butcher shop. In 1912, Yasha, who had a criminal record as an armed robber, was arrested and sentenced to exile in the Yakutsk region of eastern Siberia, apparently because Maria, following a quarrel, reported some of his crimes to the police. Remorseful, she vainly sought his release and then decided to join him. Escorted to Yakutsk by foot and barge in a convoy of convicts, she pleaded with the governor for better exile conditions for Yasha. He agreed, but only in exchange for sexual favors. "Scoundrels! Beasts!" she shouted. "You men are all alike!"[6] The governor had his way. Yasha and Maria were allowed to stay in the city of Yakutsk for a while and to open a butcher shop there. Eventually, Maria's relationship with Yasha deteriorated to the point where he tried to kill her in a fit of jealousy.

---

5. Laurie S. Stoff, *They Fought for the Motherland: Russia's Women Soldiers in World War I and Revolution* (Lawrence, KS: University of Kansas Press, 2006), 71–89; Sergei Drokov, "Organizator zhenskogo bataliona smerti," *Voprosy istorii*, no. 7 (1993): 164–69; Sergei Drokov, ed., "Protokoly doprosov organizatora Petrogradskogo zhenskogo bataliona smerti," *Otechestvennye arkhivy*, no. 1 (1994): 50–66.

6. Botchkareva, *Yashka*, 49.

Russia's entry into the Great War changed Maria's life. Her sense of loyalty and duty—which had compelled her to follow Yasha to a remote region—drove her to try to enlist as a soldier. Her plan was to win awards for bravery and then plead with the tsar for Yasha's release.

In November 1914, Maria arrived at the headquarters of the 25th Reserve Battalion in Tomsk. She asked to see the commander. Everyone in the room laughed. When she was brought into the commander's office, he did not laugh but nevertheless objected: "It is very noble of you to have such a desire. But women are not allowed in the army. . . . They are too weak. What could you for instance do in the frontline?" "Your Excellency," insisted Maria, "God has given me strength, and I can defend my country as well as a man."[7] The commander still demurred. After further pleading and insistence, however, he proposed sending on Maria's behalf (her literary skills were too poor) a personal request to the tsar, whose intervention allowed Maria to join the battalion as a private.

Maria was ready to fight against the Germans, the enemy of her motherland, but she also had to struggle against the oppressive norms of imperial Russian society. She was mocked by her fellow soldiers and called a *baba*, a derogatory name for women of non-privileged backgrounds. "She will run like the devil at the first German shot," some said. "We will make it so hot for her that she will run before even getting to the front," added others.[8] These were not empty threats. From the very first night in the army, she had to defend herself against male soldiers who repeatedly tried to violate her body.

Then came the hell of combat. Maria was assigned to the 28th Polotsk Regiment of the 7th Infantry division. One-third of the 250 soldiers in her regiment were killed in the first wave of a fruitless attack in February 1915 in the Polotsk area four hundred miles west of Moscow. Many wounded were abandoned in no man's land. Maria could not stand hearing the screams and crawled to their rescue, dragging nearly 50 wounded men to safety.

Maria's courage enabled her to overcome sexist oppression. Her comrades took to calling her "Yashka"—a diminutive of her partner's name. Since there was no other way to rid herself of insect infestation, she even joined them in the bathhouses. She usually sat in a remote corner, but nobody mocked her anymore. It was her personal revolution and a personal victory. She was not completely alone: according to various estimates, the number of Russian women in combat in 1914–1916 ranged as high as several hundred.[9]

---

7. Botchkareva, *Yashka*, 72.

8. Botchkareva, *Yashka*, 75.

9. Melissa Stockdale, "'My Death for the Motherland Is Happiness': Women, Patriotism, and Soldiering in Russia's Great War, 1914–1917," *American Historical Review* 109, no. 1 (February 2004): 78–116 (here: 85).

By early 1917, Maria had fought countless times, faced poison-gas attacks, suffered multiple bullet and shrapnel wounds, and experienced frostbite. She received three decorations for bravery and was promoted to the rank of senior non-commissioned officer. But she also shared with her fellow soldiers a deep sense of frustration with the endless war. Dark rumors of traitors in high places were spreading, and the news of Rasputin's death in December 1916 only reinforced them. Concealed hatred toward government officials and contempt for the tsar and his entourage were common.

A soldier back from leave in Petrograd brought news of the revolution and the tsar's abdication to her regiment. Maria recalled an electrifying atmosphere. People were dancing and hugging. Soldiers and officers pledged to defend the revolution and defeat the Germans once and for all.[10] This revolutionary enthusiasm reminds us, according to Melissa Stockdale, "that class conflict and war weariness are but two strands of the revolutionary narrative and that liberationist forces unleashed by the revolution could merge as well as collide with the need to defend the country."[11]

Maria anticipated no such collision between liberation and the need to defend the country. She considered Germany the greatest threat and put faith in a long-expected, powerful, "final" offensive against the foe. Instead, however, she saw deterioration of discipline, fraternization with the enemy, a growing rift between officers and soldiers, and a constant flow of revolutionary agitators from the capital. Some urged defense of the revolution by continuing the war against Germany. Others claimed the war benefited only wealthy landlords and the bourgeoisie. After hearing one such anti-war speaker, Maria could not stay silent:

> You stupid fools! You can be turned one minute one way and the next minute the opposite way. . . . Now you have been incited to start a civil war so that the Kaiser can simply walk over Russia and get the whole country into his power. This is war! War, you understand, war! And in war there can be no compromise with the enemy. Give him an inch and he will take a mile! Come, let us get to work. Let us fulfill our duty.[12]

After she finished speaking, members of her regiment attacked her. She now realized it was time to leave the army.

But Maria did not give up her fight. In May 1917, she traveled to Petrograd and met with the Duma chairman, Mikhail Rodzianko, who already knew her from his earlier visit to the front. She urged Rodzianko to do something to halt the deterioration of the army. He agreed but explained that Bolshevik agitation and propaganda made this difficult. That was the first time Maria heard about the Bolsheviks, marking her entry into revolutionary politics. She was not about to let the Bolsheviks prevail. No longer a soldier, she became a public speaker and organizer. Meeting

10. Botchkareva, *Yashka*, 135–36.
11. Stockdale, "'My Death,'" 81.
12. Botchkareva, *Yashka*, 145.

with Petrograd soldier deputies, she urged them to take steps to restore discipline in the army. She also advocated a plan to create special women soldiers' "death battalions," not just to fight to their deaths but also to inspire male soldiers and raise their morale. Such battalions were being formed but did not include women. Other activists urged the creation of female soldier units. Maria's plan fused the two trends and generated great excitement. She gained three powerful allies—Rodzianko, Supreme Commander Aleksei Brusilov, and most importantly, Alexander Kerensky, the war minister and future prime minister, for whom defeating Germany was essential to the survival of the revolution.

The army taught Maria how to fight in the trenches. Now, to forge the first women's death battalion, she had to learn how to find the right words to debate, bring people together, and lead. At first, she feared speaking at Petrograd's Mariinskii Theater more than combat.

Maria's training of female volunteers earned praise and admiration from Emmeline Pankhurst, a British fighter for women's voting rights. Speaking to Maria's women battalion in Petrograd in June 1917, Pankhurst declared: "We all, millions of women, must fight for our rights in life, even for the right to defend one's own homeland and for the right to die for it. The creation of the Women's Battalion of Death is the greatest page written in the history of women since the time of Joan of Arc."[13]

Contrary to claims of Soviet and some Western historians, not only "bourgeois" (that is, middle-class) women volunteered for combat, but also noblewomen, students, workers, peasants, and servants.[14] According to recent research, their total number reached 5,000 to 6,500 by the time new enrollments were halted in September 1917.[15] This was a unique phenomenon that no other warring country experienced because "of the powerful conjuncture of total war, democratizing revolution, and national emergency that occurred in Russia alone."[16] Some of these women became part of the Provisional Government's last line of defense against the Bolsheviks' storming of the Winter Palace on October 25/November 7, 1917.

Maria believed only strict discipline could shield her battalion from the chaos consuming the Russian army. She did not mind that just over one-in-ten willingly accepted her training methods and remained in her battalion.[17] When her most senior commanding officer and War Minister Kerensky himself demanded that she permit her soldiers to form a governance committee whose members would make policy for the unit, a trend sweeping the Russian military, she categorically refused. Such a

---

13. Stoff, *They Fought*, 88.

14. Stockdale, "'My Death,'" 96–98; Richard Abraham, "Mariia L. Bochkareva and the Russian Amazons of 1917," in *Women and Society in Russia and the Soviet Union*, ed. Linda Edmondson (Cambridge: Cambridge University Press, 1992), 124–44 (here: 125).

15. Stockdale, "'My Death,'" 95; Stoff, *They Fought*, 53.

16. Stockdale, "'My Death,'" 111.

17. Stockdale, "'My Death,'" 95; Botchkareva, *Yashka*, 170.

policy, she insisted, would undermine her authority and the strict discipline traditionally thought necessary in military units and inevitably foster their disintegration.[18]
Scholars have, indeed, concluded that the proliferating committees "only reinforced
the chasm between officers and soldiers."[19]

Maria's battalion had its first combat experience in Kerensky's summer offensive at
Smorgon (now called Smarhon, Belarus), about five hundred miles west of Moscow.
An attack was planned for July 8, but to Maria's deep indignation, soldiers up and
down the line refused to fight, preferring wide-ranging discussion about the advis-
ability of attack. Thus functioned the soldiers' committees. In order to shame and
inspire the thousands of other soldiers to fight, Maria's women and several hundred
brave officers and male soldiers launched an assault, breaking through the German
lines. After several hours, word came that most soldiers "began to debate whether to
advance or not." Maria was flabbergasted:

> Here we were, a few hundred women, officers, men—all on the brink of
> a precipice, in imminent danger of being surrounded and wiped out of
> existence. And there, within a mile or two, were they, thousands of them,
> with the fate of our lives, the fate of this whole movement, nay, the fate,
> perhaps, of all Russia, in their hands. And they were debating![20]

According to one scholar, "All the male officers in the battle at Smorgon offered nothing but the highest acclaim" for Maria's soldiers in combat.[21] Nevertheless, Maria's
unit had to retreat chaotically. As noted in Chapter 3, Kerensky's summer offensive
failed miserably, and this episode helps show why.

From this point on, Maria and her battalion became targets of male soldiers' wrath
and aggression. All across the front, soldiers began lynching their officers. Twenty
women soldiers in Maria's battalion were brutally murdered as they tried to keep up
their military duties. The rest had to flee the front and self-disband.[22]

When the Bolsheviks seized power, Maria contacted General Lavr Kornilov, a
leader of early anti-Bolshevik resistance, but declined to join what at the time was an
officer-dominated force.[23] She believed only ordinary soldiers, especially peasants like
herself, were capable of seeing imperial Germany as Russia's most implacable enemy.
When peace talks between the Bolsheviks and the German high command broke
down, and the Germans launched another offensive (February 18, 1918), it seemed to

---

18. Botchkareva, *Yashka*, 171–80.

19. Matthew Rendle, "Forging a Revolutionary Army: The All-Russian Military Union in 1917,"
War in History 19, no. 1 (January 2012): 49–71 (here: 50).

20. Botchkareva, *Yashka*, 214.

21. Stoff, *They Fought*, 177. See also Jamie H. Cockfield, *Russia's Iron General: The Life of Aleksei A.
Brusilov, 1853–1926* (Lanham, MD: Lexington Books, 2019), 251.

22. Botchkareva, *Yashka*, 251–59.

23. Botchkareva, *Yashka*, 281–82.

Figure 7.1: Maria Bochkareva (front, second from right) with Women's Death Battalion members.

Maria that many Russian soldiers were beginning to turn away from the Bolsheviks. She refused to recognize the Treaty of Brest-Litovsk and traveled to the United States and then to Great Britain to raise funds for and awareness of the Russian patriotic cause. American and British suffragist women—Florence Harriman, Rheta Childe Dorr, and Emmeline Pankhurst—assisted her on the journey.[24]

In the United States, Maria dined with former president Theodore Roosevelt, who offered her money from his Nobel Peace Prize award to assist convalescing members of her battalion.[25] She also met with President Woodrow Wilson (on July 10). She began speaking calmly, then, as recalled by the suffragist Florence Harriman, who accompanied her,

> suddenly she began to tell the tale of the sufferings of her people and her tongue went like a runaway horse. She would hardly wait for her interpreter to put what she was saying into English. Her face worked. Suddenly threw herself on the floor and clasped her arms about the President's knees, begging him for help, for food, for troops to intervene against the

24. Botchkareva *Yashka*, 324–29; Angela Shpolberg, "'Women with the Gun': American Women Journalists and the Women's Battalion of Death," *Los Angeles Review of Books*, March 23, 2018, https://www.lareviewofbooks.org/article/women-with-the-gun-maria-bochkareva-and-the-womens-battalion-of-death/; Drokov, "Protokoly," 61–62.

25. Shpolberg, "'Women with the Gun.'"

Bolsheviki. The President sat with tears streaming down his cheeks and assured her of his sympathy.[26]

By that point, Wilson had already decided to send the American Expeditionary Force to Siberia (as discussed in Chapter 6), although not on the terms Maria would have preferred. In England, Maria met with King George V, who said he was "very happy to perceive a second Joan of Arc," before returning to Russia with the British Expeditionary Force that landed in Arkhangel'sk in August 1918.[27]

Once back in Russia, Maria tried to organize another women's battalion to fight for the country's freedom as she saw it. Just as in 1914, she ran into male prejudice. In late December 1918, the commander of anti-Bolshevik Russian forces in the North, General Vladimir Marushevskii, denounced female participation in "military duties that are not typical of their sex" as "a heavy reproach and a shameful stigma on the entire population of the Northern Region."[28] She could take solace in the fact that Germany, her bitterest enemy, no longer posed a threat to Russia, for World War I had ended the previous month. Meanwhile, she met in Siberia with Admiral Aleksandr Kolchak, who instructed her to form a women's volunteer medical unit.[29] The Kolchak government soon began to crumble, however. Maria's fight was finally over.

A Steel Worker's Democratic Revolution

To Maria Bochkareva, the greatest enemy of Russia and Russian freedom was imperial Germany. To worker and revolutionary activist Ivan Upovalov, it was the Russian monarchy, then the Bolshevik dictatorship. While little is known about Ivan's activities before 1917, we know that, like millions of other workers, soldiers, and peasants, he welcomed the collapse of the monarchy. In spring 1917 (and possibly for a number of previous years), he was a Menshevik Party activist.[30]

Like the Bolsheviks, the Mensheviks considered themselves Marxist socialists, and organizationally they originally belonged to the same Russian Social-Democratic Workers' Party. Over time, however, political differences between the Bolsheviks and the Mensheviks led to a split. The former were proponents of stricter party discipline and put more emphasis on political work than on improving the living and working conditions of Russian industrial workers. The latter presupposed a gradual path to

26. Mrs. J. Borden Harriman, *From Pinafores to Politics* (New York: Henry Holt and Company, 1923), 280–81.

27. Drokov, "Protokoly," 62, 66.

28. Sergei Drokov, "Maria Bochkareva: Kratkii biograficheskii ocherk russkogo voina," *Russkii istoricheskii sbornik* 2 (2010): 168–97 (here: 192).

29. Drokov, "Maria Bochkareva," 193.

30. Ivan Upovalov, "Kak my poteriali svobodu (vospominaniia rabochego sotsial-demokrata)," *Zaria* 7 (1922): 202–7 (here: 202–3).

socialism and emphasized labor-union work. The Bolsheviks resolutely opposed the world war, while the Mensheviks rallied to the patriotic cause. Still, in the struggle against the common archenemy, "tsarist autocracy," the Bolsheviks and the Mensheviks often remained comrades in arms.[31] This was especially true in the provinces where rank-and-file party members were little concerned with ideological squabbles among party leaders. Both the Bolsheviks and the Mensheviks believed that Russia would at some point transition to socialism, both appealed to industrial workers and enjoyed their broad support, and both considered industrial workers—the "proletariat" in Marxist parlance—to be the vanguard in future revolutionary transformation.

The Mensheviks rejected the Bolshevik seizure of power in October 1917 and considered it a deviation from Marxist dogma. According to Karl Marx, socialism was bound to supersede capitalism, but capitalism—along with its political add-ons: constitutional democracy, civil society, civil liberties, and the rule of law—had yet to develop fully in Russia. The Mensheviks, therefore, believed that the Bolsheviks had acted prematurely. Seizing political power, proclaiming "a dictatorship of the proletariat," and trying to implement socialism by force in a predominantly rural country was irresponsible in their view.

Ivan was a steel worker in Sormovo, an industrial town in Nizhnii Novgorod Province, 250 miles east of Moscow, with a long tradition of union activism. He was apparently a good speaker. In 1917, the Nizhnii Novgorod Menshevik Regional Committee sent him to a nearby explosives factory to address a worker rally celebrating May 1, the day of international worker solidarity. When he discovered that two factory managers had been physically assaulted by radical workers accusing them of misdeeds, Ivan passionately denounced vigilante justice. Such violence, he declared, contradicted the principle of liberty gained by the revolution, and any worker participating in such violence or sympathetic to it was preparing the ground for anarchism and monarchism. Despite shouts from radical workers, a majority of factory workers voted to send the case to the labor dispute commission, which cleared the managers of the charges. Ivan's arguments and approach to labor disputes won the day but made him more aware of the dangers posed by violent radicalism.[32]

As the Bolsheviks in Sormovo and nearby Nizhnii Novgorod imposed increasingly violent and oppressive methods of rule, Ivan concluded that a Bolshevik autocracy was in the making, no less brutal and violent than the tsarist regime that fell in 1917. Therefore, to Ivan and many other Russian socialists, fighting the Bolsheviks was a vital next step in the defense of revolutionary democracy. Based on his recollections, Ivan did not become a militant anti-Bolshevik overnight. The process started in December 1917 when the Bolsheviks shut down a Menshevik newspaper, *Zhizn'* (Life). The Mensheviks quickly reestablished it under a different name, *Svobodnaia*

---

31. Michael Melancon, "'Marching Together!': Left Bloc Activities in the Russian Revolutionary Movement, 1900 to February 1917," *Slavic Review* 49, no. 2 (Summer 1990): 239–52.

32. Upovalov, "Kak my poteriali svobodu," *Zaria* 7: 203–7.

zhizn' (Free Life). Only four issues appeared before it, too, was closed. The last issue carried an article critical of the Bolsheviks entitled, "Who Benefits from a Civil War?"[33] This was not an isolated incident. The Bolsheviks began suppressing opposition periodicals immediately after seizing power.

In spring 1918, the Mensheviks, together with the peasant-oriented Socialist-Revolutionaries, sought to vote the Bolsheviks out of power. True, the Bolsheviks in early January had dissolved the democratically elected Constituent Assembly, in which they obtained only about a quarter of seats. But there were still the soviets, elected councils of worker, peasant, and soldier representatives that spontaneously emerged during the February Revolution. In summer 1917, the Bolsheviks had gained a majority in several soviets, most importantly, the Petrograd Soviet of Worker and Soldier Deputies. In October, they had also won a majority in the Second All-Russian Congress of Soviets that convened amid the Bolshevik seizure of power. Despite Menshevik and Socialist-Revolutionary opposition, the Congress had sanctioned creating a Bolshevik-led government, the Council of People's Commissars, with Lenin at the helm. This had allowed the Bolsheviks to claim their regime was not a party dictatorship but a "dictatorship of the proletariat," expressing the will of the working masses through the soviets. It was, thus, "soviet power," or so the Bolsheviks claimed.

The Mensheviks and Socialist-Revolutionaries sought to regain majorities in local soviets, hoping to remove the Bolsheviks from power through peaceful electoral means.[34] The momentum seemed to be on their side, as Bolshevik promises of an imminent bright socialist future began to ring hollow, even to many workers.

This electoral strategy worked. The Mensheviks and Socialist-Revolutionaries gained majorities in many city soviets in spring 1918 while remaining predominant in many trade unions and town dumas.[35] Yet, wherever the Bolsheviks lost, they refused to give up power, persecuted their socialist opponents, and even dissolved some opposition-controlled soviets altogether, replacing them with "revolutionary committees."[36] That summer, some Socialist-Revolutionaries launched insurrections against the Bolsheviks.

Ivan was sympathetic to workers and peasants who took up arms but feared this would lead to more bloodshed. He preferred working within trade unions, cooperatives, and soviets. When he tried to deliver his proposals to a worker conference in Nizhnii Novgorod, however, he was arrested and, together with several other

---

33. Ivan Upovalov, "Kak my poteriali svobodu (vospominaniia rabochego sotsial-demokrata)," *Zaria* 2 (1923): 51–56 (here: 56).

34. Vladimir Brovkin, *The Mensheviks after October: Socialist Opposition and the Rise of the Bolshevik Dictatorship* (Ithaca, NY: Cornell University Press, 1987), 126–60.

35. Brovkin, *Mensheviks*, 160.

36. Vladimir Brovkin, "The Mensheviks' Political Comeback: The Elections to the Provincial City Soviets in Spring 1918," *Russian Review* 42, no. 1 (January 1983): 1–50.

conference members, jailed. Two weeks later, he was released due to pressure from Sormovo workers, a constituency the Bolsheviks could ill afford to alienate fully.[37]

Ivan continued to oppose the Bolsheviks with legal means. When they sought to nationalize the giant Sormovo Manufacturing Plant, Ivan declared to an assembly of eighteen thousand workers that factories should not be nationalized until the country reached a higher level of development. Ivan was persuasive: the motion to nationalize failed. It did not matter; the Sormovo Plant was nationalized anyway. Another resolution proposed by Ivan, condemning forcible grain confiscation, also passed overwhelmingly.[38] It also had no effect.

The following night, the Cheka, the Bolshevik secret police, arrested Ivan and threatened him with execution. Sormovo workers went on strike; violent clashes with Bolshevik forces followed. Possibly fearing further escalation, the Nizhnii Novgorod Cheka transferred Ivan to Perm in the Ural Mountains region. As a concession to Sormovo workers, Ivan was allowed to travel to Perm without a police escort. He departed on July 12. The closer he got to Perm, however, the more rumors he heard of forced grain confiscations. Most of his fellow steamboat passengers, who were carrying food or other items to be exchanged for food, disembarked along the way, fearing encounters with Bolshevik authorities. So did Ivan. He walked on foot to Votkinsk (500 miles east of Nizhnii Novgorod and 140 southwest of Perm), hoping to reconnect with local Mensheviks.[39]

Ivan arrived in Votkinsk on July 17, only to discover that the city soviet had been shut down by the Bolsheviks. He then traveled fifty miles farther east to Izhevsk and barely escaped arrest when he tried to approach the city soviet building, also shuttered by Bolshevik authorities. Back in Votkinsk, he found work as a steel worker at a local plant. He joined other Mensheviks in resisting Bolshevik efforts to subject trade unions to state control. Then came fresh news from Izhevsk: workers had taken up arms against the Bolsheviks. Votkinsk Bolsheviks mobilized workers to crush the rebellion in Izhevsk. Ivan spoke against what he called "mad fratricide" and was arrested.[40] Once again, he escaped execution, and once again, pressure from fellow workers forced the Bolsheviks to compromise: Ivan was released on the condition that he leave Votkinsk and travel to Perm. Once again, however, Ivan took a different path. Confident that the Bolsheviks in Votkinsk would soon fall from power, he stayed in a nearby village and helped with the harvest. Several days later, word came that the Votkinsk had also rebelled.[41]

---

37. Upovalov, "Kak my poteriali svobodu," *Zaria* 2: 53.

38. Upovalov, "Kak my poteriali svobodu," *Zaria* 2: 53–54.

39. Upovalov, "Kak my poteriali svobodu," *Zaria* 2: 54–56.

40. Ivan Upovalov, "Rabochee vosstanie protiv Sovetskoi vlasti," *Zaria* 3 (1923): 78–82 (here: 78–79).

41. Ivan Upovalov, "Rabochee vosstanie protiv Sovetskoi vlasti," *Zaria* 4 (1923): 115–20 (here: 115).

Ivan rushed back to the city, which now looked to him like an armed camp. A newly reconstituted city soviet led the rebellion, local officers provided military training, and food supplies came from sympathetic peasants. As to munitions, Votkinsk workers manufactured them on the spot. Both Votkinsk and Izhevsk were established centers of arms manufacturing, a major factor in the rebels' initial success. They took power from the Bolsheviks in early August and declared their commitment to the democratically elected Constituent Assembly dissolved by the Bolsheviks a half-year earlier. The executive committee of the restored Izhevsk Soviet proclaimed:

> The awakening has started. All over Russia, despite the total annihilation of freedom of speech and the press by their majesties, the People's Commissars, a joyful cry is sounded: "The people have awakened." Samara, Kazan', the cities of the Volga region, Izhevsk, and Siberia have rebelled: in Petrograd there are strikes. Is this not a triumphal cry? Great days have come![42]

The rebels' optimism was palpable. They numbered between thirty-five thousand and seventy-five thousand men. In addition to rifles, they boasted hundreds of machine guns and several cannons captured from the Bolsheviks.[43]

Mensheviks and Socialist-Revolutionaries played a major organizational role. The greater was their disappointment when they learned that a Menshevik-led all-Russian worker conference held in Moscow in July condemned armed struggle against the Bolsheviks. Senior Menshevik leaders apparently believed that they could still prevail over the Bolsheviks by peaceful means. (The Socialist-Revolutionaries also found it difficult to take up arms against fellow revolutionaries.[44]) Ivan felt betrayed, yet even he could not help wondering whether negotiations with the Bolsheviks might make insurrection unnecessary.[45]

The Ural regional Menshevik committee resolved to keep fighting, but the rebels ran short on munitions, and their numbers dwindled. By November, the weather turned freezing cold. The rebels fled Votkinsk and Izhevsk across the Kama River into remote, rural areas offering more safety. As soon as the Kama froze, however, the Bolsheviks followed. Many rebels fled all the way to Siberia, Ivan among them. He continued unionization work in territories under White control. Like many rebels, he considered Kolchak to be a lesser threat to the gains of the February Revolution and of the working class than the Bolsheviks.[46] In March 1919, Ivan returned to Votkinsk with troops from Kolchak's forces. As the Whites pushed forward, however, Kolchak

---

42. Stephen M. Berk, "The 'Class Tragedy' of Izhevsk: Working Class Opposition to Bolshevism in 1918," *Russian History* 2, no. 2 (1975): 176–90 (here: 183).

43. Upovalov, "Rabochee vosstanie," *Zaria* 4: 116; Berk, "'Class Tragedy,'" 187.

44. Scott B. Smith, *Captives of Revolution: The Socialist Revolutionaries and the Bolshevik Dictatorship, 1918–1923* (Pittsburgh, PA: University of Pittsburgh Press, 2011).

45. Upovalov, "Rabochee vosstanie," *Zaria* 4: 116.

46. Upovalov, "Rabochee vosstanie," *Zaria* 4: 117–19.

Figure 7.2: Rebel funeral. The banner says, "Glory to the Fallen Fighters for Freedom."

decommissioned the Izhevsk and Votkinsk worker battalions. Ivan then worked to revive independent labor unions destroyed by the Bolsheviks. About a thousand members joined, but Bolshevik repression left them weak and disorganized.[47] In June 1919, the Congress of Ural Trade Unions picked Ivan and three worker activists originally from Izhevsk, Perm, and Ekaterinburg to travel to England at the invitation of the Labour Party. The delegation sought to convince the British public that the Bolsheviks did not represent Russian workers. He remained firm in his commitment to fight against tyranny of any kind. In 1920, his adamant resolve became too much for the Menshevik leadership, which expelled him from the party, still naively hoping to democratize the Bolshevik-dominated soviets by peaceful means.[48]

A Writer's Humanitarian Revolution

Less well known in the West than Anton Chekhov or Maxim Gorky, Vladimir Korolenko was one of the most beloved Russian writers before the revolution. According

---

47. Ivan Upovalov, "Rabochee vosstanie protiv Sovetskoi vlasti," *Zaria* 5 (1923): 140–43 (here: 141–42); Ivan Upovalov, "Rabochee vosstanie protiv Sovetskoi vlasti," *Zaria* 6–7 (1923): 178–81 (here: 179).

48. Upovalov, "Rabochee vosstanie," *Zaria* 6–7: 179–81; Ivan Upovalov, "Kak my poteriali svobodu," in *Nezavisimoe rabochee dvizhenie v 1918 godu: Dokumenty i materialy*, ed. Mikhail Bernshtam (Paris: Ymca-Press, 1981), 243.

to George Herbert Perris, an English journalist, writer, literary agent, and publisher, Korolenko was, in 1905, "after Tolstoy, the most highly rated living Russian novelist."[49] Born in Ukraine in 1853 into a Ukrainian-Polish family of minor nobility, Vladimir pursued higher education first in Petersburg, then in Moscow. At Moscow's Petrovskaia Agricultural Academy, his revolutionary journey began.[50] Like many young people in the 1870s, Vladimir was captivated by populist ideals. The populists urged their supporters to go "to the people" to alleviate their suffering, help them fight injustice, and eventually rise against the tyranny of the autocratic state and hierarchical society. Populist publications were banned, but enough of them circulated illegally to inspire thousands of young people. Police authorities worked together with university administrations to arrest students involved in populist activities.

Vladimir's first arrest in 1876 and exile by administrative process (because the police doubted its case against him could stand up in court) resulted from his involvement in organizing a student protest against the academy's collaboration with police persecution of its own students.[51] Vladimir's activities after his first exile were modest—socializing with populists, sheltering them, and contemplating going to the people. But when radical populists formed People's Will (Narodnaia volia) to commit terrorist acts against government officials, beginning in 1879, the police began to cast a broader net. Vladimir was arrested, though he had no idea why. "I had long hair and wore glasses, tall boots, and a shawl," he recalled.[52] He was again exiled administratively, first to Viatka Province, five hundred miles northeast of Moscow, then to the city of Perm. When People's Will assassinated Tsar Alexander II on March 1, 1881, Vladimir denounced their methods but refused to take an oath of loyalty to Tsar Alexander III. This act of defiance earned him three more years of exile—in the remote Yakutian village of Amga four thousand miles beyond Perm, in northeastern Siberia.[53]

During his ordeals, Vladimir used his agricultural and shoemaking skills to earn a living (and gain standing within the local population). Equally important, he acquired a deeper knowledge of Russian society that helped his literary talent bloom. Unlike the populists, he no longer looked at "the people" in an idealized way. He had witnessed violence, debauchery, and abuse. But his short stories and novels (published, then forgotten in the West) focused on the world of human suffering—beggar children living in the ruins of a castle, a blind man reconciled to life through music,

49. G. H. Perris, *Russia in Revolution* (London: Chapman & Hall, 1905), 331.

50. Vladimir Korolenko, *Istoria moego sovremennika*, 4 vols. (Moscow and Berlin: Vozrozhdenie, 1922), 2:359.

51. Korolenko, *Istoria*, 2:360–63, 3:7–9.

52. Korolenko, *Istoria*, 3:141.

53. Korolenko, *Istoria*, 4:161–65; V. M. Vladislavlev, "Korolenko Vladimir Galaktionovich," in *Otechestvennaia istoriia: Istoriia Rossii s drevneishikh vremen do 1917 goda: Entsiklopediia*, 5 vols. to date (Moscow: Bol'shaia Rossiiskaia entsiklopediia, 1994–), 3:51–53 (here: 51).

a peasant lost in the frozen Siberian taiga (boreal forest), village metalworkers toiling in poverty, peasants afflicted by famine and epidemics, and more.

Politically engaged, Korolenko attacked government repression, defended victims of anti-Jewish pogroms, denounced militarism and false patriotism, decried administrative arbitrariness and mistreatment of the poor, and publicly defended Udmurt peasants (a Finnic people) in Viatka province "falsely accused of making human sacrifices" in 1892–1896,[54] among other stands, prompting Maxim Gorky to dub him Russia's "judge of conscience."[55] A series of essays denouncing capital punishment profoundly impacted readers, including Leo Tolstoy. After reading one essay, "An Everyday Occurrence," in March 1910, Tolstoy confided to his diary, "It's magnificent. I couldn't help sobbing."[56] Tolstoy then wrote to Korolenko, "No speeches in the Duma, no tracts, no dramas or novels

Figure 7.3: Vladimir Korolenko, portrait by Ilya Repin, 1910.

could have one thousandth part of the salutary influence which this article ought to have."[57]

Vladimir Korolenko enthusiastically welcomed the February Revolution. "Long live popular rule! Long live the democratic republic!" he declared in a speech to

54. Mark Conliffe, "Poltava in Revolution and Civil War: From the Diaries of Vladimir Korolenko and Aleksandr Nesvitskii," in *Russia's Home Front in War and Revolution, 1914–22*, Book 2, *The Experience of War and Revolution*, ed. Adele Lindenmeyr, Christopher Read, and Peter Waldron (Bloomington, IN: Slavica Publishers, 2016), 455–74 (here: 457).

55. M. G. Petrova, "Korolenko Vladimir Galaktionovich," in *Russkie pisateli, 1800–1917: Biograficheskii slovar'*, 6 vols. to date (Moscow: Bol'shaia Rossiiskaia entsiklopediia, 1989–), 3:78–84 (here: 82).

56. R. F. Christian, ed., *Tolstoy's Diaries*, vol. 2, *1895–1910* (London: Faber and Faber, 2015), 454.

57. Lev Tolstoy to Vladimir Korolenko, March 26–27, 1910, in R. F. Christian, ed., *Tolstoy's Letters*, vol. 2, *1880–1910* (London: Faber and Faber, 2010), 699.

ordinary citizens.[58] Yet he did not give in to triumphalism. He feared that the revolution could trigger another wave of antisemitic violence, like the pogroms of 1906–1907, which followed the Revolution of 1905. He also worried that civil strife could threaten Russia's freedom and independence.

This was a far cry from his earlier, naïve populism. Back when he was a student, Vladimir had attended a gathering of fellow students inspired by revolutionary populism. They debated whether it would be just to steal money desperately needed for a revolutionary cause. "Would you do it?" one student asked. Everyone began to assent until one student turned red and said: "Yes, I see that one should do it… But personally, I would say about myself: I couldn't."[59] Events following the February Revolution reminded Vladimir of this episode again and again. More important than actions driven by revolutionary fervor, he believed, was a moral awakening, enabling people to avoid terrible new mistakes. This explains why, after February 1917, he refused to join any of the revolutionary parties. He considered himself a socialist but above all hoped the revolution would end past injustices and make people more humane.

Korolenko called war "a great crime."[60] But, like Maria Bochkareva, he believed that Russia still needed national unity to confront the deadly German threat. The Bolsheviks were harming that cause, he thought, but he never believed they were German agents. He cautioned against anarchy and "a war of everyone against everyone." He protested illegal peasant seizures of gentry land, calling this *grabizhka* (plundering).[61] Weeks after the Bolsheviks took power, he wrote, "authority based on a false idea is doomed to perish from its own arbitrariness."[62] The Bolsheviks' greatest mistake, he said in a 1919 interview, "was an attempt to implement socialism without freedom. . . . socialism will either come together with freedom or not come at all."[63] In 1920, he explained his views to Emma Goldman, an American anarchist who visited Korolenko in Poltava, five hundred miles south of Moscow in Ukraine, where he had resided since 1900. The Bolsheviks' unbounded recourse to terror, violence, and repression, he argued in conversation with Goldman, completely undermined both revolutionary ideals and moral values. He went on,

> It has always been my conception that revolution means the highest expression of humanity and justice. The dictatorship has denuded it of both. At home the Communist State daily divests the Revolution of its

58. Vladimir Korolenko, *Padenie tsarskoi vlasti (Rech' prostym liudiam o sobytiiakh v Rossii)* (New York: Pervoe russkoe izd. v Amerike, 1918), 36.

59. Korolenko, *Istoria*, 2:348–49.

60. P. I. Negretov, ed., *V. G. Korolenko: V gody revoliutsii i grazhdanskoi voiny, 1917–1921: Biograficheskaia khronika* (Benson, VT: Chalidze Publications, 1985), 10.

61. Negretov, *Korolenko*, 34.

62. Negretov, *Korolenko*, 43.

63. Negretov, *Korolenko*, 185–86.

essence, substituting for it deeds that far exceed in arbitrariness and barbarity those of the Tsar. His *gendarmes*, for instance, had the authority to arrest me. The Communist Cheka has the power to shoot me, as well.[64]

Critical of the Bolsheviks, Korolenko did not unequivocally support their rivals. Instead, he championed something he considered more important than politics—the dignity and value of human life. In October 1918, he became honorary president of the Save the Children League, an organization with branches in several Ukrainian cities. Aware of the deepening food crisis in Petrograd and Moscow, he led an effort to evacuate thousands of starving children to Ukraine and to send trainloads of food to those who remained.[65] He also hoped to promote humanitarian awareness among hostile forces in the civil war and possibly lessen its ferocity.

Yet the tide of ferocity and violence kept rising. Korolenko used all his authority as a leading Russian writer—and honorary chairman of the Poltava branch of the "Political Red Cross," a human-rights organization—to save as many people from political repression and execution as possible.[66] In Poltava, where political control repeatedly shifted among Ukrainians, Russians, Cossacks, and Germans, as well as among actors of diverse political views, and sometimes fell to mere bandits, this stance continuously brought him anger and even death threats. He pushed back against them all to defend life and liberty, meeting as often as possible with officials at all levels of government.

Bolshevik troops entered Poltava in mid-January 1918 but retreated in late March as German troops pushed forward. Units of the Central Rada, a Ukrainian national government established in Kyiv under German occupation, accompanied them. Upon learning that Ukrainian officers had abused and humiliated their Russian and Jewish detainees at army headquarters, Korolenko wrote an article entitled "A Sin and a Shame," protesting these abuses.

In late 1918, the Germans departed, and their client government, headed by Hetman Skoropadskii, was swept away by a Ukrainian nationalist uprising led by Simon Petliura. A new government, the Directorate, took over. Soon Korolenko received disturbing news. The Directorate's counterintelligence section in Poltava was arresting and executing people without trial. He rushed to Poltava's Grand Hotel, which served as counterintelligence headquarters. He spoke passionately about the need to stop the escalating brutality. Grabbing an officer by the arm, he declared vehemently that only the side avoiding brutality could achieve true victory.[67]

---

64. Emma Goldman, *Living My Life*, 2 vols. (New York: Dover Publications, 1970), 2:821–22.

65. Negretov, *Korolenko*, 136–38.

66. Petrova, "Korolenko," 83.

67. Negretov, *Korolenko*, 149.

Korolenko referred to this time as the beginning of "our small circle whose goal is to fight brutality."[68] This group included his son-in-law Konstantin Liakhovich, a Menshevik returned from exile in France, and his sister-in-law, Praskovia Ivanovskaia, the Socialist-Revolutionary deputy chair of the Poltava Political Red Cross. They needed even more courage than Vladimir did since they lacked his protective aura of renown.

The Bolsheviks regained Poltava in mid-January 1919, and arbitrary arrests and executions escalated. To his horror, Vladimir observed that the Bolsheviks did not claim that their victims were guilty of any crimes. They were guilty because they belonged to the "exploitative classes," or the "bourgeoisie," a broad and ill-defined concept. Those who did not fall under that category could still be branded "agents of the bourgeoisie" or counterrevolutionaries" and executed on that basis. This policy had been proclaimed in September 1918 as the "Red Terror" following an assassination attempt against Lenin and remained in effect throughout the Civil War.

Korolenko's diary is replete with references to arbitrary arrests, executions, and the plentiful visitors who came asking for help. He dreaded the instances when he had to tell relatives who came to him for help that their loved ones had already been killed.[69] Equally numerous are references to his visits to the Cheka, meetings with Bolshevik officials, and appeals to Khristian Rakovskii, the head of the Bolshevik Ukrainian government.[70] He discovered that some government officials resented the Cheka and also that some Cheka agents could be reasoned with. Occasionally, he convinced the authorities to relent. Many other times, his advocacy for judicial process and restraint was met with objections like: "Now much brutality is necessary. But when we triumph. . . ."[71]

In late July 1919, the Bolsheviks fled Poltava before an anti-Bolshevik (White) offensive led by General Anton Denikin. On the eve of the Bolsheviks' departure, Korolenko wrote in his diary: "Our upcoming task is to protect the families of Bolsheviks from Denikinite excesses."[72]

Korolenko received a warm welcome when he arrived at the White counterintelligence headquarters with his son-in-law. Several officers thanked him for saving the lives of many White officers. Now they were eager for revenge, however, blaming the Bolsheviks and the Jews for all their troubles. He pleaded for restraint, citing the example of a Jewish teacher murdered by White forces and left to rot on the street. In

---

68. V. G. Korolenko to A. S. Korolenko, January 2/15, 1919, Korolenko Vladimir Galaktionovich, accessed April 6, 2022, http://korolenko.lit-info.ru/korolenko/pisma-korolenko/letter-318.htm.

69. Negretov, *Korolenko*, 329.

70. Vladimir Korolenko, *Dnevnik, 1917–1921. Pis'ma* (Moscow: Sovetskii pisatel', 2001), 146, 148, 151, 154, 156–64, 166, 174, 175, 186, 186–91, 192–96, 197–99, 208–11, 216, 225–27.

71. Negretov, *Korolenko*, 193.

72. Negretov, *Korolenko*, 198.

the end, the counterintelligence chief promised there would be no more extrajudicial executions.[73]

As under the Bolsheviks, Korolenko sought to meet with White authorities at every level of government. When he learned about former imperial officers being court marshaled and executed for serving in the Red Army, he protested that many had been conscripted and that not all who had served in the Bolshevik-controlled government deserved punishment. The Poltava counterintelligence chief countered: "You are wrong to speak of a change of government. There was no government here, just a gang of criminals."[74] Again, however, the Whites relented. After the initial wave of executions, the rest were demoted and sent to the front as privates. Among the rhetorical props he used was evidence of Bolshevik atrocities dug up by White investigators. Would victims of White executions look better when excavated? he asked.[75]

His health in decline, in part from the stress-inducing struggle to save lives and fight against both revolutionary and counterrevolutionary violence, Korolenko spent the fall at a sanitarium on a physician's recommendation. During his journey to the sanitarium, he met several officers, some serving on military courts. Following lengthy conversations, they said they now considered him their teacher. Vladimir urged them, as his students, never to issue politically motivated death sentences.[76]

He returned to Poltava in early January 1920, well-rested and in better health but horrified to learn about vicious anti-Jewish violence perpetrated by anti-Bolshevik forces in his absence. He concluded that the Whites behaved worse than the Bolsheviks, who had retaken power a month before his return and reimposed the Red Terror. Unsurprisingly, the flood of people pleading for his help did not subside.

In June 1920, Korolenko had an opportunity to try to influence a senior Bolshevik official. In May, Lenin ordered the Bolshevik head of culture and education (the commissar of Enlightenment), Anatolii Lunacharskii, to travel to Poltava to win Korolenko over to the Bolshevik cause.[77] In April 1917, Lunacharskii had told the French writer Romain Rolland that the new and free Russia would probably not even need a president but that he could think of no better candidate than Korolenko.[78] After Lunacharskii joined the Bolshevik government, however, his view of Korolenko became more critical.

On June 7, Lunacharskii visited Korolenko at his home, impressing his host as thoughtful and serious. Despite his usual avoidance of political events, Korolenko joined Lunacharskii at a Bolshevik pep rally to plead on behalf of five individuals

---

73. Negretov, *Korolenko*, 201.

74. Negretov, *Korolenko*, 204.

75. Negretov, *Korolenko*, 207.

76. Negretov, *Korolenko*, 214–15.

77. Negretov, *Korolenko*, 246.

78. Negretov, *Korolenko*, 27.

sentenced to death by the Cheka, at least two for buying and selling grain (even though a judicial investigator had found insufficient evidence to warrant charging them with criminal activity). Lunacharskii and the head of the Cheka, Ivanov, promised that they would be spared. Reassured by their words, Korolenko listened to Lunacharskii's inspiring speech about the advent of world revolution. In reality, the five had already been shot.[79]

Even as his health worsened, Korolenko continued to advocate for victims of political repression, appealing incessantly to political authorities and prominent cultural figures. Having learned that the Bolsheviks wanted him to move outside of the city "to rest" and "to improve his health," an ailing Korolenko jumped from his bed and shouted: "I am not going anywhere! Anywhere! I will be here! Here! I will be always writing to them!"[80] Many pages of his diary for 1920–1921 contain the names of people executed or sent to a concentration camp by the Poltava Cheka. His entry for September 30, 1920, noted that the provincial Cheka had printed a long list of people it had executed, including people taken as hostages (to ensure payment of monetary contributions or loyal service by family members). Korolenko then raged against the regime,

> and with these means they expect to build socialism! Blindness, blindness! And yet they are so blindly self-assured that when I spoke to Rakovskii of the need for freedom and the harm caused by atrocities [*zhestokostei*]—he smugly and jovially laughed, as if I had said something naïve.[81]

Korolenko famously wrote six letters to Lunacharskii in June–September 1920, voicing grave concerns about the Bolsheviks' vision and policies while still pleading on behalf of individual victims of government repression. Lunacharskii neither published nor responded to them (despite his promise to do so), though he did pass at least some to Lenin, who took an interest in them.[82] (They were not published in the USSR until 1988.[83]) Lenin also did not respond to Korolenko's passionate pleas to honor human dignity and his warnings of the great calamity likely to result from a pursuit of social justice without freedom.

Finales

Maria Bochkareva was arrested in the Siberian city of Tomsk by the Cheka in early 1920 and soon transferred to Krasnoiarsk.[84] After several interrogations, officers

---

79. Negretov, *Korolenko*, 246–49.

80. Negretov, *Korolenko*, 152.

81. Negretov, *Korolenko*, 278.

82. Negretov, *Korolenko*, 257–58.

83. A. Khrabrovitskii and P. Negretov, "Ot nauchnogo redaktora i sostavitelia," in *V. G. Korolenko: Letopis' zhizni i tvorchestva, 1917–1921*, ed. P. Negretov (Moscow: Kniga, 1990), 6.

84. Drokov, "Protokoly," 64.

determined that she was "an irreconcilable and most malicious enemy of the worker-peasant Republic."[85] She was executed by a Bolshevik firing squad on May 16.[86] In 2018, cognizant of the heavy male bias on its obituary pages, the *New York Times* published Maria's obituary: "Overlooked No More: Maria Bochkareva, Who Led Women into Battle in WWI."[87] She was thirty years old at the time of her death.

Ivan Upovalov's journey to England in summer 1919 as a union representative probably saved his life. His adamant commitment to fighting against the Bolsheviks and for the democratic ideals of the Russian Revolution would most likely have gotten him executed in Soviet Russia. He might also have suffered a similar fate at the hands of Kolchak and his supporters, who had staged a coup, expelled the socialists from the Omsk government, and moved toward nationalist authoritarianism. He settled in Germany and never returned to Russia.

Vladimir Korolenko saw the Bolsheviks triumph in the Civil War but never accepted their vision of a repressive authoritarian state or discounting the value of human life. He took some encouragement from the New Economic Policy, adopted by the Bolsheviks in spring 1921, which scaled back their confiscatory practices in the countryside and allowed a limited reintroduction of free markets. But he deplored the continued repression. In line with the official Menshevik policy, his son-in-law Konstantin tried to continue peaceful opposition activities. Like many other Mensheviks, he was arrested by the Cheka in early 1921. While Korolenko secured Konstantin's release, he was powerless to save his son-in-law from the typhus infection he contracted in prison, a common scourge of Russia's civil war years.[88] Utterly devastated and increasingly ill, Vladimir Korolenko nevertheless agreed to serve as honorary chairman of the All-Russian Committee of Famine Relief, organized by public activists to help fight the catastrophic famine that hit the Volga region in the wake of ruinous Bolshevik policies in the countryside.[89] Bolshevik approval did not last long. Fearful that the Committee would pose a political challenge, the Bolsheviks disbanded it and arrested many of its members. Vladimir Korolenko wrote his last letter in defense of a victim of the Cheka on December 16, 1921.[90] By that point, he was too ill to speak. He died of pneumonia in Poltava nine days later.

In 1922, the Bolsheviks celebrated the fifth anniversary of the October Revolution with parades, rallies, speeches, and musical and theatrical performances. In the decades that followed, they perpetuated a mythical view of the Russian Revolution,

---

85. Drokov, "Protokoly," 66.

86. Drokov, "Protokoly," 53.

87. Elizabeth Goodridge, "Overlooked No More: Maria Bochkareva, Who Led Women into Battle in WWI," *New York Times*, April 25, 2018, https://www.nytimes.com/2018/04/25/obituaries/overlooked-maria-bochkareva.html.

88. Negretov, *Korolenko*, 338–39.

89. Negretov, *Korolenko*, 342–43.

90. Negretov, *Korolenko*, 370.

equating it with themselves, their power, their supporters, and their policies. In that view, the February Revolution was merely a prelude to the even greater victory of "proletarian revolution" in October, supposedly carried out by industrial workers under Bolshevik leadership. "The proletarian revolution," they believed, would turn global, completing the universal transition from capitalism to socialism and communism, as predicted by Marx. Those who stood in the way were denounced as counterrevolutionaries and destroyed, either politically or physically. By 1922, the Bolsheviks had successfully defeated not only their main civil war adversaries—the White armies led by Denikin, Kolchak, and other military commanders—but also numerous nationalist movements in Ukraine, Transcaucasia, and Central Asia; worker uprisings in Yaroslavl', Votkinsk, and Izhevsk; peasant rebellions in Ukraine, Samara, Tambov, and Siberia; a sailor mutiny at the Kronstadt naval base; and resistance from religious believers to the confiscation of church valuables allegedly to feed the hungry in 1922, among many other opposition forces.

All these actors—both individual and collective—had visions of or at least hopes for how the revolutionary transformation could improve their lives: workers dreamed of controlling their shops, factories, and crafts; peasants of possessing and working as they wished the land and livestock they tended; religious believers of exercising a voice in parish governance or reforming church rites and institutions; lower-class people of dignified treatment; artists of completely free expression and state support; national and ethnic minorities of autonomy and self-determination; religious minorities of full official recognition; intellectuals of the right to contribute freely to public life; the politically conscious of participation in government; nationalists of a strong and unified Russia; and many others of altering society in a wide variety of ways. Myriad paths of change were open in Russia—"the freest of all the belligerent countries," in the words of Vladimir Lenin—in spring and summer 1917. How they might have contributed to the development of Russia can never be known; the triumphant Bolsheviks and their narrow vision of building socialism foreclosed them.

Even today, when one thinks about the Russian Revolution, the primary focus is often on the Bolsheviks and Lenin, Trotsky and Stalin, not grassroots political activists, moderate socialists, and defenders of human rights, among so many others. The inevitability of Bolshevik victory can be neither proven nor disproven because historians cannot travel back in time and conduct controlled experiments. Still, one could argue that the simplistic Bolshevik perception of the Russian Revolution was disrupted when the world revolution the Bolsheviks were eagerly expecting failed to occur. It was further disrupted when the Soviet state the Bolsheviks built in 1917–1922 with such vigor and violence collapsed and disintegrated in 1991 with far less violence and far greater speed. As we move toward the second centennial of the Russian Revolution, the field is open for an ever-expanding exploration of the many voices, aspirations, and trajectories of the Russian revolution that, whether successful or not, made it one of the defining events of modern history.

Conclusion

Some scholars interpret the Russian Revolution by means of social, economic, and political analysis. Others scrutinize the ideologies the revolutionaries and their opponents embraced. Still others underscore the importance of what people intuited, felt, and imagined about the revolution and its accompanying events. This book draws upon the widest range of scholarship in order to make sense of the revolutionary events, experiences, and myths. Rarely were the responses the revolution elicited merely rational. Passions, hopes, and fears—no less powerfully than ideological beliefs—gave meaning to people's experiences and drove revolutionary and counter-revolutionary actors to fight, kill, and die for or against what they believed was a world-changing cause.

Why did people believe particular myths? Why did they often reject evidence to the contrary—facts or arguments that could weaken their belief? One could posit a lack of in-depth knowledge of Russia and the revolutionary events that transformed it. Yet many promoters of the most outrageous myths were deeply immersed in revolutionary realities, observing and experiencing them firsthand. Their mythmaking did not result from a linear process. We are reminded by William G. Rosenberg that "Beneath all its complexity and contradiction the Russian revolution was at its core a vast social trauma."[1] In the midst of this trauma, deceptive and distorted mythical interpretations "came to the rescue": they appeared to make sense of painful realities, were reinforced by ideologies or politicized worldviews, gained significant popular traction (especially when aided by the sensationalism of modern mass media), and thus became particularly virulent and difficult to dispel. The short answer seems to be that people believed particular myths because they wanted to believe them. We could not find a single case of a prominent figure who believed that the Bolsheviks were German agents and then changed that view in light of more evidence. The same can be said about antisemites who believed the Bolsheviks were agents of a global Jewish conspiracy; believers in most of the other myths discussed in this book hardly fared better.

Moreover, consistent with recent findings in cognitive psychology,[2] we have observed that confronting individuals with such arguments and evidence only tends

---

1. William G. Rosenberg, "Interpreting Revolutionary Russia," in Edward Acton, Vladimir Yu. Cherniaev, and William G. Rosenberg, eds. *Critical Companion to the Russian Revolution, 1914–1921* (Bloomington, IN: Indiana University Press, 1997), 18.

2. Stephan Lewandowsky, Ulrich K. H. Ecker, Colleen M. Seifert, Norbert Schwarz, John Cook, "Misinformation and Its Correction: Continued Influence and Successful Debiasing," *Psychological Science in the Public Interest* 13, no. 3 (2012): 106–31 (here 113–14).

to strengthen their embrace of mythological interpretations, as every new point and counterpoint is incorporated into a myth's architecture. In the case of the Russian Revolution, the most stunning examples involved the many fruitless attempts by extended family and high-society well-wishers to revise Nicholas and Alexandra's view of Grigorii Rasputin, or the imperial couple's efforts to make their interlocutors see in Rasputin anything but a grotesque and sinister figure.

Thus, neither the origins of particular myths nor people's responses to myth-disrupting arguments and information seem to be fully rational or evidence-driven. We will leave it to philosophers and psychologists to discuss what this adds to our understanding of the scope and limits of human rationality. The British philosopher Bertrand Russell's view of human nature may be of some interest since it was shaped by the age of war and revolution. In his 1919 essay "Dreams and Facts," he wrote:

> The influence of our wishes upon our beliefs is a matter of common knowledge and observation, yet the nature of this influence is very generally misconceived. It is customary to suppose that the bulk of our beliefs are derived from some rational ground, and that desire is only an occasional disturbing force. The exact opposite of this would be nearer the truth: the great mass of beliefs by which we are supported in our daily life is merely the bodying forth of desire, corrected here and there, at isolated points, by the rude shock of fact. Man is essentially a dreamer, wakened sometimes for a moment by some peculiarly obtrusive element in the outer world, but lapsing again quickly into the happy somnolence of imagination.[3]

Have the myths of the Russian Revolution died out? Some have declined in potency because the evidence against them became too incontrovertible, as in the case of "Anastasia's" genetic analysis. Others faded with the deaths of their adherents or simply because other more recent and pertinent myths came to capture people's imagination. Still others were reinvigorated in the minds of new believers. Indeed, we have discovered that most of the myths considered in this volume never faded completely. A few easy web searches reveal that every myth discussed in this book continues to lurk in the nooks and crannies of people's imagination and their thinking about the past and the present of Russia and of the world.[4]

Russian revolutionary experiences also suggest that, while the myths people believed in seemed nearly indestructible, they could be enormously destructive. Thinking of Nicholas as a victim of a conspiracy, of Bolsheviks as German agents, or America as Russia's mortal enemy has contributed to hatred and sometimes inspired

3. Bertrand Russell, "Dreams and Facts," in *Uncertain Paths to Freedom: Russia and China, 1919–22,* ed. Beryl Haslam and Richard A. Rempel (London: Routledge, 2000), 14.

4. On such thinking in post-Soviet Russia, see Eliot Borenstein, *Plots Against Russia: Conspiracy and Fantasy after Socialism* (Ithaca, NY: Cornell University Press, 2019).

violent action. And nothing, of course, matches the violence and destructiveness of the "Judeo-Bolshevik" myth. Another hidden but frequent casualty of these myths was (and is) people's ability to tell fact from fiction, to understand the world as it really is. As we have observed throughout the book, imagined mythical worlds can provide a certain measure of comfort, security, and even steady purpose to those willing to embrace them, but they crumble or burst into fury when reality intervenes and launches its own revolution.

Suggested Reading

The following list, which includes both primary and secondary sources, is meant to guide readers to books in English likely to help them make sense of the complex topics discussed in this study. It does not include most of the works cited in the footnotes.

General

Acton, Edward, Vladimir Yu. Cherniaev, and William G. Rosenberg, eds. *Critical Companion to the Russian Revolution, 1914–1921*. Bloomington, IN: Indiana University Press, 1997.

Browder, Robert, and Alexander Kerensky, eds. *The Russian Provisional Government 1917: Documents*. 3 vols. Stanford, CA: Stanford University Press, 1961.

Daly, Jonathan, and Leonid Trofimov, eds. *Russia in War and Revolution, 1914–1922: A Documentary History*. Indianapolis: Hackett Publishing Company, 2009.

———. *The Russian Revolution and Its Global Impact: A Short History with Documents*. Indianapolis: Hackett Publishing Company, 2017.

Engelstein, Laura. *Russia in Flames: War, Revolution, Civil War, 1914–1921*. New York: Oxford University Press, 2018.

Pipes, Richard. *The Russian Revolution*. New York: Alfred A. Knopf, 1990.

Wade, Rex. *The Russian Revolution, 1917*. 3rd ed. Cambridge: Cambridge University Press, 2017.

Chapter 1

Fuhrmann, Joseph T., ed. *The Complete Wartime Correspondence of Tsar Nicholas II and the Empress Alexandra, April 1914–March 1917*. Westport, CT: Greenwood Press, 1999.

———. *Rasputin: The Untold Story*. Hoboken, NJ: John Wiley and Sons, 2013.

Massie, Robert K. *Nicholas and Alexandra*. New York: Ballantine Books, 2000.

Purishkevich, V. M., and Michael E. Shaw. *The Murder of Rasputin*. Ann Arbor, MI: Ardis, 1985.

Smith, Douglas. *Rasputin: Faith, Power, and the Twilight of the Romanovs*. New York: Farrar, Straus, and Giroux, 2016.

Wortman, Richard S. *Scenarios of Power: Myth and Ceremony in Russian Monarchy from Peter the Great to the Abdication of Nicholas II*. Princeton, NJ: Princeton University Press, 2006.

Youssoupoff, Prince Felix. *Lost Splendor: The Amazing Memoirs of the Man Who Killed Rasputin*. Translated by Ann Green and Nicholas Katkoff. New York: Helen Marx Books, 2003.

Chapter 2

Burdzhalov, E. N. *Russia's Second Revolution: The February 1917 Uprising in Petrograd.* Translated and edited by Donald J. Raleigh. Bloomington, IN: Indiana University Press, 1987.

Hasegawa, Tsuyoshi. *The February Revolution, Petrograd 1917.* Leiden: Brill, 2018.

Katkov, George. *Russia 1917: The February Revolution.* New York: Harper & Row, 1967.

Lyandres, Semion. *The Fall of Tsarism: Untold Stories of the February 1917 Revolution.* Oxford: Oxford University Press, 2013.

Chapter 3

Harding, Neil. *Lenin's Political Thought: Theory and Practice in the Democratic and Socialist Revolutions.* 2 vols. in one. Chicago: Haymarket Books, 2009.

McMeekin, Sean. *The Berlin-Baghdad Express: The Ottoman Empire and Germany's Bid for World Power.* Cambridge, MA: Belknap Press of Harvard University Press, 2012.

Merridale, Catherine. *Lenin on the Train.* New York: Metropolitan Books/Henry Holt, 2017.

Chapter 4

Klier, John, and Helen Mingay. *The Quest for Anastasia: Solving the Mystery of the Lost Romanovs.* Secaucus, NJ: Carol Publishing Group, 1997.

Kurth, Peter. *Anastasia: The Riddle of Anna Anderson.* Boston: Little Brown and Company, 1983.

Lovell, James Blair. *Anastasia: The Lost Princess.* New York: St. Martin's Press, 1995.

Rappaport, Helen. *The Romanov Sisters: The Lost Lives of the Daughters of Nicholas and Alexandra.* New York: St. Martin's Press, 2014.

Slater, Wendy. *The Many Deaths of Tsar Nicholas: Relics, Remains, and the Romanovs.* London: Routledge, 2007.

Chapter 5

Brustein, William I. *Roots of Hate: Anti-Semitism in Europe before the Holocaust.* Cambridge: Cambridge University Press, 2003.

Gerrits, André. *The Myth of Jewish Communism: A Historical Interpretation.* Brussels: P.I.E. Peter Lang, 2011.

Hanebrink, Paul. *A Specter Haunting Europe: The Myth of Judeo-Bolshevism.* Cambridge, MA: Belknap Press of Harvard University Press, 2018.

Kellogg, Michael. *The Russian Roots of Nazism: White Emigres and the Making of National Socialism, 1917–1945.* Cambridge: Cambridge University Press, 2005.

Chapter 6

Bacino, Leo J. *Reconstructing Russia: U.S. Policy in Revolutionary Russia, 1917–1922.* Kent, OH: Kent State University Press, 1999.

Foglesong, David S. *America's Secret War against Bolshevism: U.S. Intervention in the Russian Civil War, 1917–1920.* Chapel Hill, NC: University of North Carolina Press, 1995.

House, John M. *Wolfhounds and Polar Bears: The American Expeditionary Force in Siberia, 1918–1920.* Tuscaloosa, AL: University of Alabama Press, 2016.

Melton, Carol Willcox. *Between War and Peace: Woodrow Wilson and the American Expeditionary Force in Siberia, 1918–1921.* Macon, GA: Mercer University Press, 2001.

Novikova, Liudmila. *An Anti-Bolshevik Alternative: The White Movement and the Civil War in the Russian North.* Translated by Seth Bernstein. Madison, WI: University of Wisconsin Press, 2018.

Slonim, Ilya. *Stillborn Crusade: The Tragic Failure of Western Intervention in the Russian Civil War, 1918–1920.* New Brunswick, NJ: Transaction Publishers, 1996.

Willet, Robert L. *Russian Sideshow: America's Undeclared War, 1918–1920.* Washington, DC: Brassey's Inc, 2005.

Chapter 7

Brovkin, Vladimir. *The Mensheviks after October: Socialist Opposition and the Rise of the Bolshevik Dictatorship.* Ithaca, NY: Cornell University Press, 1987.

Korolenko, Vladimir G. *The History of My Contemporary.* Translated and abridged by Neil Parsons. New York: Oxford University Press, 1972.

Stoff, Laurie S. *They Fought for the Motherland: Russia's Women Soldiers in World War I and Revolution.* Lawrence, KS: University of Kansas Press, 2006.

Image Credits

1.1   Wikimedia Commons, https://en.wikipedia.org/wiki/Grigori_Rasputin#/media/File:%CE%A1%CE%B1%CF%83%CF%80%CE%BF%CF%8D%CF%84%CE%B9%CE%BD.jpg (accessed March 9, 2020).

1.2   Wikimedia Commons, https://upload.wikimedia.org/wikipedia/commons/d/dd/Rasputin_listovka.jpg (accessed March 9, 2020).

2.1   Wikimedia Commons, https://upload.wikimedia.org/wikipedia/commons/c/cc/Nikolaus_II._%28Russland%29.jpg (accessed March 13, 2020).

2.2   Yandex.Fotki, https://img-fotki.yandex.ru/get/4908/97833783.5c1/0_ce217_cb64f36d_XXXL.jpg (accessed April 8, 2020).

3.1   Wikimedia Commons, https://upload.wikimedia.org/wikipedia/commons/archive/6/6e/20130825205239%21Lenin_in_Stockholm_1917.jpg (accessed July 4, 2022)

3.2   Wikimedia Commons, https://upload.wikimedia.org/wikipedia/commons/5/59/Parvus_Alexander.jpg (accessed June 10, 2022).

3.3   Album / Alamy Stock Photo, https://www.alamy.com/lenin-vladimir-ilyich-ulyanov-2241870-2111924-russian-politician-half-image60148674.html (accessed June 10, 2022).

3.4   Wikimedia Commons, https://upload.wikimedia.org/wikipedia/ru/5/5b/Вернуть-Ленина-Вильгельму.jpg (accessed June 10, 2022).

3.5   Wikimedia Commons, https://upload.wikimedia.org/wikipedia/commons/0/03/O_tom_kak_nemtsy_bolshevika_na_Rossiyu_vypuskali.jpg (accessed June 10, 2022).

3.6   left: Pictorial Press Ltd / Alamy Stock Photo, https://www.alamy.com/stock-photo-razliv-russia-august-1917-vladimir-lenin-with-make-up-poses-for-a-80596476.html.

3.6   right: INTERFOTO / Alamy Stock Photo, https://www.alamy.com/stock-photo-lenin-vladimir-ilyich-ulyanov-2241870-2111924-russian-politician-barn-58480602.html.

4.1   Library of Congress, http://loc.gov/pictures/resource/ggbain.38336/ (accessed June 5, 2020).

4.2   Gleb Botkin, *Lost Tales: Stories for the Tsar's Children*, ed. Marina Botkin Schweitzer, foreword Greg King (New York: Villard, 1996), 37.

4.3   AP/Shutterstock, https://i.pinimg.com/originals/bc/06/70/bc06700062c4943a3cc2512e25f39c73.jpg (accessed April 6, 2022).

4.4 Wikimedia Commons, https://en.wikipedia.org/wiki/Anastasia_(1956_film)#/media/File:Anastasia322.jpg (accessed April 6, 2022).

4.5 Moviestore Collection Ltd / Alamy Stock Photo, https://www.alamy.com/stock-photo-demitri-anastasia-rasputin-poster-anastasia-1997-31086407.html (accessed June 15, 2021).

4.6 Tsentr po rassledovaniiu obstoiatel'stv gibeli chlenov semii doma Romanovykh, https://romanov-center.ru/news1/02102017/image011.jpg (accessed April 6, 2022).

5.1 Image courtesy of the U.S. Holocaust Memorial Museum, https://collections.ushmm.org/search/catalog/irn545124 (accessed December 11, 2020).

5.2 Courtesy of Rossiiskaia Gosudarstvennaia Biblioteka (RGB), https://rusneb.ru/catalog/000199_000009_005391589 (accessed April 6, 2022).

5.3 Pinterest, https://www.pinterest.ru/pin/333407178665656934/ (accessed June 10, 2022).

5.4 Wikimedia Commons, https://upload.wikimedia.org/wikipedia/commons/b/bf/Stephan_Krotowski_-Tretet_der_Antibolschewistischen_Liga_bei%2C_1919.jpg (accessed December 11, 2020).

5.5 Wikimedia Commons, https://upload.wikimedia.org/wikipedia/commons/c/cf/WhiteArmyPropagandaPosterOfTrotsky.jpg (accessed December 12, 2020).

5.6 Wikimedia Commons, https://upload.wikimedia.org/wikipedia/commons/5/58/Satan_has_taken_off_his_mask.jpg (accessed June 10, 2022).

6.1 Wikimedia Commons, https://commons.wikimedia.org/wiki/File:American_Expeditionary_Forces_Hospital_Car_No._1,_Train_No.1_at_Khabarovsk,_Russia,_1918-1919_(18155799199).jpg (accessed February 12, 2022).

6.2 Library of Congress, https://www.loc.gov/item/2016679565/ (accessed February 13, 2022).

6.3 Wikimedia Commons, https://upload.wikimedia.org/wikipedia/commons/d/df/American_troops_in_Vladivostok_1918_HD-SN-99-02013.JPEG (accessed February 14, 2022).

6.4 Pinterest, https://i.pinimg.com/originals/f6/75/7a/f6757afe18083bdae5a8f403809f6950.jpg (accessed July 4, 2022).

7.1 Color by Klimbim 0.1, https://klimbim2014.files.wordpress.com/2014/12/womens-battalion-of-death-bw.jpg (accessed June 10, 2022).

7.2 Gosudarstvennyi arkhiv Permskogo kraia, http://www.archive.perm.ru/upload/iblock/957/1.jpg (accessed April 6, 2022).

7.3 Wikimedia Commons, https://upload.wikimedia.org/wikipedia/commons/8/83/Vladimir_Korolenko.jpg (accessed April 6, 2022).

INDEX

Bold page numbers indicate an image or image caption.